CliffsNotes®

GRE® Math Review

CliffsNotes®

GRE® Math Review

by
BTPS Testing
with Bernard V. Zandy, M.S.

Contributors

Ron Podrasky, M.A.

Pitt Gilmore, B.A.

Ed Kohn, M.S.

David A. Kay, M.S.

Joy Mondragon-Gilmore, Ph.D.

Houghton Mifflin Harcourt
Boston • New York

I dedicate this book to the three most important
women in my life—Judy, Gina, and Lisa—who continue to be an
inspiration to me every day of my life.

–Ben Zandy

About the Authors

BTPS Testing has presented test-preparation
workshops at the California State Universities for
over 35 years. The faculty at BTPS Testing has
authored more than 30 national best-selling
guides for the ACT, SAT, CSET, CBEST, GRE,
GMAT, PPST, and RICA. Each year the authors
of this study guide conduct lectures to thousands
of students preparing for college-level entrance
examinations.

Bernard V. Zandy, M.S., is an Emeritus Professor
of Mathematics at Fullerton College and an
expert on math skills and strategies that are
integral to success on the GRE. He has
instructed at college and high school academic
levels for over 40 years and has conducted test-
preparation workshops at California State
Universities and Colleges for BTPS Testing for
more than 30 years.

Authors' Acknowledgments

We would like to thank Christina Stambaugh for
her careful attention to detail in editing the
manuscript, and Kelly D. Henthorne for her
assistance during the production process. We
would also like to thank Pitt Gilmore for his
support in organizing the original manuscript.

Editorial

Acquisition Editor: Greg Tubach
Project Editor: Kelly Dobbs Henthorne
Copy Editor: Christina Stambaugh
Technical Editors: David Herzog and Tom Page
Proofreader: Lynn Northrup

CliffsNotes® GRE® Math Review

Copyright © 2013 by Houghton Mifflin Harcourt
Publishing Company

All rights reserved.

Library of Congress Control Number: 2013942777
ISBN: 978-1-118-35624-1 (pbk)

Printed in the United States of America

DOC 10 9 8 7 6 5 4

4500608088

For information about permission to reproduce selections from this book, write to trade.permissions@hmhco.com
or to Permissions, Houghton Mifflin Harcourt Publishing Company, 3 Park Avenue, 19th Floor, New York,
New York 10016.

www.hmhco.com

Table of Contents

PART II: REVIEW OF EXAM AREAS

PART III: FULL-LENGTH PRACTICE TESTS

Preface

In keeping with the fine tradition of *CliffsNotes*, this guide was developed by leading experts in the field of test preparation. The instructors and authors at BTPS Testing have successfully helped thousands of graduate school candidates prepare for the GRE for more than 35 years. The material, strategies, and techniques presented in this guide have been researched, tested, and evaluated in GRE preparation classes presented at leading California universities and colleges.

During our many years of conducting GRE test-preparation classes, a common theme emerged among graduate candidates—their concern about the GRE Quantitative Reasoning section. *CliffsNotes GRE Math Review* was designed and written specifically to address these concerns. This book offers an easy-to-follow, positive, and systematic learning experience that maximizes the learning of math skills and concepts. Diagnostic tests provided in each review chapter help evaluate proficiency in each quantitative topic area. The comprehensive math review material provides valuable exam-oriented approaches, instructional tools, and practice exercises. To aid in your conceptual understanding of math, this study guide uses nontechnical language consistent with the terminology and conventions you will need to know for the GRE.

If you follow the lessons and strategies in this book and practice regularly, you will statistically increase your odds for improving your score on the Quantitative Reasoning section of the GRE.

How This Book Is Organized

- **Introduction:** A general description of the GRE, test structure, scoring, using a calculator, and general tips and strategies.
- **Part I—Quantitative Reasoning:** Chapter 1, "Introduction to Quantitative Reasoning," acquaints you with the GRE question types, basic skills you'll need, skills and concepts tested, and directions. You'll also find suggested strategies with illustrated examples.
- **Part II—Review of Exam Areas:** Review chapters focus on the abilities tested in arithmetic, algebra, geometry, data analysis, and data interpretation. Diagnostic tests, intensive math skills review, illustrated example questions, and practice questions are covered in each chapter. The review chapters are broken out by math topic areas:
  - Chapter 2: Math Fundamentals
  - Chapter 3: Arithmetic
  - Chapter 4: Algebra

- Chapter 5: Geometry
- Chapter 6: Data Analysis
- Chapter 7: Data Interpretation
- **Part III—Full-Length Practice Tests:** Chapters 8 and 9 each contain a full-length Quantitative Reasoning practice test with answers and in-depth explanations. The practice tests are followed by analysis worksheets to assist you in evaluating your progress.

How to Use This Guide

Start your preparation by identifying the test content and question types, assessing your skills, understanding strategies, and practicing what you have learned. For optimal results, take detailed notes on the pages of this book to highlight important information.

1. **Become familiar with the test.** Start your preparation by establishing basic knowledge about the test—the test format, test directions, question types, test material, and scoring outlined on the official GRE website at www.ets.org/gre, or in the Introduction of this study guide. After reading the introductory material, read Chapters 1 and 2; they are excellent math resources that you will refer to throughout your preparation:

   - Chapter 1, "Introduction to Quantitative Reasoning," explains the format of each question type: quantitative comparison, multiple-choice (select one answer), multiple-choice (select one or more answers), and numeric entry (fill-in-the-blank).
   - Chapter 2, "Math Fundamentals," provides you with important math resources: symbols, basic mathematical properties, order of operations, and math terminology.

2. **Assess your math skills.** Each chapter begins with a diagnostic test to assess your strengths and weaknesses. Take the diagnostic test at the beginning of each review chapter in Chapters 3 through 7 *before* you review the subject matter to pinpoint any areas that may require more concentration and preparation time. This will help you develop a study plan for each math topic that is unique to your individual learning style and help you focus on specific areas to further develop your skills and awareness of GRE test questions.

3. **Review.** One of the most important steps in tackling Quantitative Reasoning is to break up each section into its smaller parts by math topic. This is why we have divided each chapter into a specific

GRE-related topic. Chapters 3 through 7 present a review of subject matter material and provide supporting practice questions that are arranged by question type. Read each chapter in the recommended sequence of topics. Work through each chapter's comprehensive analysis, follow the step-by-step instructions for solving problems, and work out the example problems. Take detailed notes on the pages of the book to highlight important facts and concepts. Practice questions at the end of each review are arranged by each GRE question type and provide you with extra practice to help strengthen your understanding of each topic area.

4. **Learn strategies and techniques.** Study the general strategies outlined in the Introduction and decide which strategies work best for you. If it takes you longer to recall a strategy than to solve the problem, it's probably not a good strategy for you to adopt. The goal in offering strategies is for you to be able to work easily, quickly, and efficiently. Don't get stuck on any one question. Taking time to answer the most difficult question on the test correctly but losing valuable test time will not get you the score you deserve. Most important, remember that you must answer *every* question—even if you answer with only an educated guess.

5. **Practice, practice, practice.** Empirical research has proven that consistent practice is a key to scoring higher on standardized tests. This is why we have included two full-length Quantitative Reasoning practice tests in the final two chapters. These model practice tests include answers with thorough explanations. Be sure to practice in the test format as often as possible. To benefit from computer-based practice experience, the *CliffsNotes GRE General Test* study guide has four additional full-length practice tests (quantitative and verbal) available on a CD-ROM. To get a realistic sense of the actual test, take the online practice test using the GRE PowerPrep® II software published by ETS at www.ets.org/gre.

Finally, the last part of this book includes a checklist as a reminder of "things to do" before you take your exam.

Introduction

The focus of this study guide is specific to the Quantitative Reasoning section of the GRE. It is much more than simply a review of math. *CliffsNotes GRE Math Review* is designed specifically to review, refresh, and reintroduce math concepts and skills as you practice solving problems. It is clear, concise, easy to use, and full of insights into the types of questions you will face on your exam.

This section of the study guide will help you begin your preparation by establishing a basic knowledge of the test—the test structure, question types, test contents, scoring, and general strategies outlined in this section.

GRE Test Structure

The Graduate Record Exam—GRE General Test is a standardized exam that is commonly required as part of the graduate school admissions application process. The GRE requires that you critically identify, evaluate, and apply your general abilities in three subject areas: Analytical Writing, Verbal Reasoning, and Quantitative Reasoning.

The GRE is administered by Educational Testing Service (ETS), www.ets .org/gre, P.O. Box 6000, Princeton, NJ 08541-6000, (609) 771-7670, (866) 473-4373.

Structure of the GRE General Test

Content	Question Type	Number of Questions and Length of Test
Analytical Writing Assessment	Analyze an Issue Task Analyze an Argument Task	1 Analyze an Issue task 1 Analyze an Argument task **Time: 2 writing tasks (30 minutes per task, timed separately) = 60 minutes**
Verbal Reasoning	Reading Comprehension Text Completion Sentence Equivalence *(questions intermingled)*	2 Verbal Reasoning sections (20 questions each) Total Verbal Reasoning = 40 questions **Time: 2 verbal sections (30 minutes per section) = 60 minutes**

(continued)

Structure of the GRE General Test (*continued*)

Content	Question Type	Number of Questions and Length of Test
Quantitative Reasoning	Quantitative Comparison Multiple-Choice (one answer) Multiple-Choice (one or more answers) Numeric Entry (fill-in-the-blank) (*questions intermingled*)	2 Quantitative Reasoning sections (20 questions each) Total Quantitative Reasoning = 40 questions **Time: 2 quantitative sections (35 minutes each section) = 70 minutes**
Unscored Section and Research Section	Verbal Reasoning or Quantitative Reasoning (*unidentified and identified unscored questions*)	Varies
Total Questions		**80 Multiple-Choice Questions 2 Essay Writing Tasks**
Total Testing Time		**Approximately 3 hours and 45 minutes**

There is a 1-minute optional break between each section of the exam and following the third section, there is an optional 10-minute recess.

Note: Structure, scoring, and the order of sections is subject to change. Visit www.ets.org/gre for updated exam information.

Experimental Section

The GRE computer test has experimental unidentified questions that make up an *unscored* section of the exam. These experimental questions may appear in any order after the Analytical Writing section, but *will not count* toward your GRE score. The experimental questions are multiple-choice questions that will either be verbal or quantitative questions. Experimental questions are designed for research to test future GRE questions and can be formatted in any of the above-mentioned question types. Be sure to answer all questions on the test; don't spend valuable time trying to guess which questions are experimental.

Scoring

Scores on your GRE will be reported for three separate measures. Quantitative Reasoning and Verbal Reasoning measures are scored for multiple-choice and numeric entry questions, and the Analytical Writing measure is scored for two essays. Your score is based on three factors:

- The number of questions answered
- The number of questions answered correctly
- The difficulty of the questions answered

Scaled Scores

Measure	Type of Questions	Scaled Score
Verbal Reasoning	Multiple-choice	130–170
Quantitative Reasoning	Multiple-choice	130–170
Analytical Writing	Analyzing an Issue Essay Analyzing an Argument Essay	Score 0–6 averaged by two readers Score 0–6 averaged by two readers The two final scores on each essay are totaled and averaged and then rounded up to the nearest half-point to report one score 0–6.

Section-Level Adaptive Scoring

In the **multiple-choice sections,** quantitative and verbal questions are *section-level adaptive.* Your performance on the first section of the measure determines the level of difficulty for the second section. The computer will adjust the questions so that all questions contribute equally to the final score for that measure.

Sound confusing? Just remember questions are completely random (easy, moderate, and difficult) on the first set of 20 questions of each measure. This means that your first set of 20 questions in the quantitative section will determine the degree of difficulty in the second set of quantitative questions. Your final score is based upon the number of questions you answer correctly. Keep in mind that if you are faced with a question that requires multiple answers such as "indicate one or more answers," you must indicate *all* possible answers to receive credit for a correct response. There is no partial credit.

Each measure, quantitative or verbal, computes a *raw score* that is based upon the number of questions you answer correctly. The raw score is equated and converted into a *scaled score* from 130 to 170 for each measure, with 1-point increments. The "equating" process takes into account different test editions and disparities among different tests. The scaled score also helps to determine your percentile rank that many graduate programs use to compare your score results with other applicants. The national average score on the quantitative section is 151, but all universities do not have the same score requirements. It is highly recommended that you contact the universities you wish to attend to inquire about their school admission averages and minimum score requirements. Once you take the GRE, your score will last for five years.

There is no penalty for an incorrect answer. This means that unanswered questions do not count for or against your score. Remember that scores are only based upon the number of questions you answer correctly. Since there is no penalty for guessing, it is in your best interest to take an educated guess on each question.

Using a Calculator on the GRE

A simple four-function **on-screen calculator** (with square root) is available to help you perform computations on the Quantitative Reasoning measure. The calculator will look something like this:

- **Time-Consuming Problems**—Although the calculator will help you save time compared to handwritten calculations, you must have a basic knowledge of mathematics to be able to determine whether your calculation results make sense. The general rule of thumb is that you should only use the on-screen calculator for time-consuming computations (square roots, long division, and problems with several digits). Use your time wisely and quickly determine whether a problem appears to be easy to solve mentally. Keep in mind that if you use the on-screen calculator for every math problem, you will never be able to complete the test in the allotted time.

- **Basic Functions**—Using your keyboard and mouse, you will be able to move the image of the on-screen calculator to any location on the screen. The on-screen calculator can perform the basic functions of addition, subtraction, multiplication, division, parentheses, and square roots; it also has a memory location. The on-screen calculator has basic function keys: a *clear* [C] button to help you clear the display, as well as *memory recall* [MR], *memory clear* [MC], and *memory sum* [M+] buttons.

- **Order of Operations**—The on-screen calculator is programmed to follow the rules of order of operations. This means that you will need to be aware of the correct order of operations to key in your instructions and/or number values (parentheses, exponents/square roots, multiplication/division, and addition/subtraction).

- **Transfer Display**—After you have determined that your calculated results are the best answer choice for the numeric entry questions, you can transfer your results to your answer box with one click. Keep in mind, however, that you will need to transfer calculated results in the correct form that the question asks. For example, some numeric entry questions may require you to round off to a certain decimal place, or some may ask you to convert your answer to a percent. Be sure to adjust your on-screen calculator results before transferring your answer to your answer box.

- **Practice Before the Exam Date**—To help you become familiar with the on-screen calculator, use a calculator similar to the on-screen computerized calculator while practicing sample problems from this book. The TI-108 (Texas Instruments 108) calculator has functions that are similar to the on-screen calculator. Familiarize yourself with the best keystrokes to accomplish certain math tasks as you work through sample problems in this book.

General Tips and Strategies

This section was developed as a guide to introduce general test-taking guidelines, approaches, and strategies that are useful on the GRE, and on many other standardized exams. Although this section is limited to general tips and strategies, specific strategies related to specific subject area question types are included in chapter reviews.

The goal in offering you strategies is for you to be able to work through problems quickly, accurately, and efficiently. As you practice problems using the strategies outlined in this section, determine whether the strategies fit with your individual learning style. What may work for some people may not work for others. If it takes you longer to recall a strategy than to solve the problem, it's probably not a good strategy for you to adopt. And, remember, don't get stuck on any one question. Taking time to answer the most difficult question on the test correctly but losing valuable test time won't get you the score you deserve.

Consider the following guidelines when taking the exam:

1. **Math concepts must be learned in orderly stages.** Consider math as a language of *patterns* that is best understood through orderly stages of *precise* conceptual learning in a logical sequence of developing stages. Math concepts, topics, definitions, and applications discussed in this study guide follow models of learning that present material in orderly stages—starting with a basic foundation of arithmetic concepts and gradually increasing to learning the more advanced concepts of algebra and geometry. Each stage of learning will build upon your previous understanding of a math concept. As you learn basic concepts, you will be steadily increasing your comfort level with the question types and strengthening your ability to master more advanced questions.

Learning math is a "hands-on experience." You must practice what you have studied. Always perform calculations in the practice exercises provided in the topic review sections to assimilate what you have learned.

2. **Take advantage of computer-friendly functions.** Each question will appear individually on the computer screen or will appear as part of a data interpretation set of questions that are based on facts related to tables, graphs, or other forms of graphic information. Because the GRE is a computer-based test, you must click on the matching oval or square boxes provided to mark the correct answer choice (or in some cases you must select more than one answer choice). During the administration of the exam, you will have the computer capability to skip and/or place a checkmark next to individual questions to mark

for review as you navigate back and forth within the section. Take advantage of this computer flexibility as a test-taking strategy.

The computer will provide you with a list of "incomplete" or "unanswered" questions, and you will be able to pinpoint which questions are unsolved. At the end of each section, first answer the questions you can quickly solve, and then go back to solve the remaining questions.

You can only work on one section at a time. Do not proceed to the next section without answering all questions within your section. **DO NOT EXIT THE TEST UNTIL YOU HAVE ANSWERED ALL THE QUESTIONS.** Once you exit, you cannot return.

3. **Manage your time wisely.** The Quantitative Reasoning section of the GRE is comprised of two 20-question sections, each one with a 35-minute time limit (totaling 40 math questions in 70 minutes). When you begin the exam, make a mental note of the starting time and keep track of the time indicated on the computer screen. Never spend more than 1½ minutes on any one question. With sufficient practice, you will almost automatically know when a problem is taking you too long.

4. **Glance at *all* of the answer choices.** Do not make a hasty assumption that you know the correct answer without reading the whole question and all the possible answers. The hurried test-taker commonly selects an incorrect answer when jumping to a conclusion after reading only one or two of the answer choices.

Keep in mind that quantitative questions cover a broad range of math topics while utilizing a variety of question types. The facts and concepts are often presented in subtle variations of numerical values that often make it difficult for test-takers to narrow down the correct answer. Make sure that you glance at all of the answer choices, because sometimes subtle variations in answer choices can distract you from choosing the correct answer(s).

Note that some of the answer choices only show a "part" of the correct solution. You must look at the entire list of answer choices for the complete solution.

5. **Be on alert for questions with "EXCEPT" or "NOT."** Another common mistake is misreading a question that includes the word *except* or *not*. A negative question reverses the meaning of the question and asks for the opposite to be true in order to select the correct answer. Negative questions can initially be confusing and

challenge your thinking. It is helpful to write down brief notes to avoid misreading a question (and therefore answering it incorrectly). Simply *write down* what you must answer in the question. To help answer a negative question, treat the answer choices as *true* or *false* statements, searching for the answer that is *false*.

6. **Answer every question because there is no penalty for guessing.** To guarantee the highest number of correct answers, try to push yourself all the way through each section. In the first 20 questions, it is worth taking the time you need (within reason) to do your very best to answer the questions correctly. This is because your performance on the first section determines the level of difficulty of questions you'll see on the second section. If time is tight later in the section, it might be beneficial to guess rather than spending an inordinate amount of time on any one question.

Keep in mind that the GRE does not penalize you for wrong answers, so you should answer every question. This means that unanswered questions do not count for or against your score. Scores are based only upon the number of questions you answer correctly. Since there is *no penalty for guessing,* it is in your best interest to take an educated guess on challenging questions. You can move forward and backward within each multiple-choice section; so if you have time at the end of the section, you can always go back to recheck your answers.

7. **The elimination approach.** Try to eliminate as many of the answer choices as possible, and then make an educated guess on the remaining answer choices. To help you accomplish this, you may find it helpful to quickly write down (on the notepad provided) the numeric position of the wrong answer choices (with a diagonal line through them) to prevent you from spending too much time mulling over or reconsidering the impossible choices. For example, if you know that answer choices A, C, and D (or positions 1, 3, and 4 on the list) are incorrect, write down the letters A, C, and D with diagonal lines through them. It will just take a few seconds to use this strategy to narrow down your choices.

Remember that answer choices on the actual computer exam are not numbered or lettered, but are presented with ovals or squares.

In the following example, notice that some choices are crossed out with diagonal lines and some choices are marked with question marks, signifying that they may be possible answers. Using question marks will help signify that these choices are possible answers. Either of these methods will help you narrow down your possible answers. Remember to keep this marking system very simple, and remember to number the problem if you decide to come back to it later.

A̶.

? B.

C̶.

D̶.

? E.

Don't spend too much valuable test time deciding whether or not a question is solvable. Since you have just 1 to 1½ minutes to answer each question, you must act quickly.

PART I

QUANTITATIVE REASONING

Chapter 1

Introduction to Quantitative Reasoning

The Quantitative Reasoning section of the GRE is multifaceted, and its approach to presenting math questions is unique from other college-entrance standardized tests. The Quantitative Reasoning section consists of four question types that evaluate fundamental math skills in arithmetic, algebra, geometry, data analysis, word problems, and data interpretation. This chapter focuses on these skills, which are presented within specific *question types* that appear on the GRE: quantitative comparison, multiple-choice with one answer, multiple-choice with one or more answers, and numeric entry. These question types are designed to test your ability to *think critically* and *mathematically* to solve a variety of problems.

The importance of understanding the test content and question types cannot be overstated. Research literature has shown that score results increase significantly when test-takers learn test content, processes, and procedures prior to sitting for their exams. This is why the first chapter of this guide begins by familiarizing you with the GRE Quantitative Reasoning question types and the content topic areas *before* introducing you to GRE math concepts in subsequent chapters.

As you understand and memorize the four question-type setups, you should be able to effectively manage your approach to problems and apply strategies to become proficient with any type of problem. For example, the following graph illustrates that approximately 35 percent of all math problems are *quantitative comparison*. With this information, especially if your preparation time is limited, you may decide to practice the quantitative comparison question type more often than you would, let's say, the *multiple-choice (select one or more answers)* question type that comprises only about 7 percent of the questions.

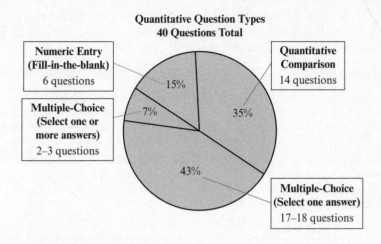

Content Style Topics versus Question Types

The following diagram identifies Quantitative Reasoning topics with possible corresponding question types. Notice that there are six different math *content style topics*, AND each topic may be matched with any one of the four different *question types*. For example, you may be given an algebra problem that is presented as a quantitative comparison question type, or you may be given an algebra problem that is presented as a multiple-choice question type (select one answer), and so on.

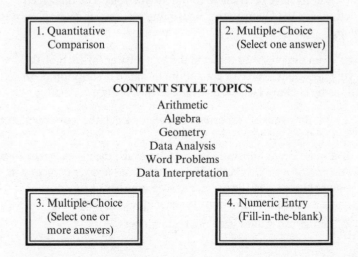

The following table summarizes the possible Quantitative Reasoning content style topics that appear in each question type. Each question type is discussed in detail later in this chapter.

		QUESTION TYPE			
		Quantitative Comparison	Multiple-Choice (one answer)	Multiple-Choice (one or more answers)	Numeric-Entry (fill-in)
Content Style Topic	Arithmetic	X	X	X	X
	Algebra	X	X	X	X
	Geometry	X	X	X	X
	Data Analysis	X	X	X	X
	Word Problems	X	X	X	X
	Data Interpretation	Possible future inclusion	X	X	X

General Quantitative Reasoning Directions

Review and memorize the test instructions *before* the day of your test to save valuable testing time. As you become more familiar with the instructions, you need to merely scan the written directions to confirm that no changes have been made to the instructions. The on-screen instructions for the Quantitative Reasoning section will be similar to the following:

Use the given directions to indicate the best answer for each of the following questions. You can get a more in-depth description of the directions by clicking Help at any time during the test.

- To use the available on-screen calculator, click the icon found at the top of the screen.
- If a question has answer choices with **ovals,** then the correct answer consists of a single choice. If a question has answer choices with **square boxes,** then the correct answer consists of one or more answer choices. Read the directions for each question carefully.
- All numerical values used are real numbers.

- Figures or diagrams are **not** necessarily drawn to scale and should not be used to estimate sizes by measurement unless they are data displays (graphs and charts) or coordinates on a pair of coordinate axes. These will always be drawn to scale.

- Lines that appear straight can be assumed to be straight.

- A symbol that appears in repeated quantities represents the same value or object for each quantity.

- On a number line, positive numbers are to the right of zero and increase to the right and negative numbers are to the left of zero and decrease to the left.

- Distances are always either zero or a positive value.

Remember that the GRE Quantitative Reasoning section is a *section-level adaptive* test. This means that the level of difficulty of the questions in the second Quantitative section is determined by how well you perform on the first Quantitative section of 20 questions.

Overview of Quantitative Comparison Question Type

Quantitative comparison questions require that you compare two quantities in two columns. After you compare Quantity A and Quantity B, you must decide which quantity is greater, if the quantities are equal, or if a comparison cannot be determined from the information given.

Skills and Concepts Tested

Quantitative comparison questions measure concepts learned in secondary mathematics classes through first-year algebra and geometry. You also will need to be familiar with statistical concepts that usually are presented as part of a second-year algebra course in high school. This type of question requires that you compare two quantities and identify their relationship. To solve this type of question correctly, you must quickly make a decision about the "relative values" of the two quantities provided. Apply your knowledge of mathematical insight, approximations, simple calculations, and common sense as you solve the problem and use the on-screen calculator as needed to help you compare values. There are no concepts tested from trigonometry, calculus, or other higher level mathematics courses.

Directions

You will be asked to compare two columns, Quantity A and Quantity B, using information centered above each quantity (if such information is provided), and select the correct statement by clicking on one of the ovals after you decide if one quantity is greater than, equal to, or cannot be determined based on the information given.

Example

x is a prime number between 4 and 10

y is a prime number between 12 and 16

Quantity A	Quantity B
$x + y$	20

Ⓐ   Quantity A is greater.

Ⓑ   Quantity B is greater.

Ⓒ   The two quantities are equal.

Ⓓ   The relationship cannot be determined from the information given.

Since x is a prime number between 4 and 10, $x = 5$ or 7.

Since y is a prime number between 12 and 16, $y = 13$.

The sum of $x + y$ can be either $5 + 13 = 18$, or $7 + 13 = 20$.

Therefore, Quantity A is either 18 or 20. Since Quantity B (20) *is* greater than Quantity A, or equal to Quantity A, the relationship cannot be determined from the information given. The correct answer is **D**.

> **REMINDER: The answer choices for questions on the actual computer version of the GRE are not labeled with letters. This study guide labels each answer choice with a letter choice, A, B, C, D, for clarity. These letter labels will not appear on the computer screen when you take the actual test.**

Suggested Strategies

1. **Memorize answer choices.** Memorize and practice using the four possible answer choices *before* your test day to save valuable testing time. The four answer choices in this question type are *always* the same. As you become more familiar with the four answer choices, on the day of the test you will only need to scan the choices to confirm that you have made the correct selection.

2. **Avoid unnecessary calculations.** Quantitative comparison questions do not require precise values to determine the correct answer. When comparing Quantity A and Quantity B, you can often determine the answer with limited or partial information so don't spend time trying to find the exact answer. For example, if Quantity A column is greater than 5, and Quantity B column is less than 5, then there is no reason to perform calculations to determine that Quantity A is greater than Quantity B. This strategy will help you become time efficient.

3. **Substitute simple numbers.** Substituting numbers for variables can often be an aid to understanding a problem; doing so can also help you to immediately recognize a simple method to solve a problem. Remember to substitute simple numbers, since you have to do the work, and remember that zero and negative numbers can sometimes be used to compare variables and may change your answer.

4. **Use choice D to immediately narrow your choices.** As you compare the two quantities, immediately determine whether choice D, "the relationship cannot be determined from the information given," can be eliminated or *considered* as a viable answer choice.

   ▪ When to eliminate choice D: There are four possible answer choices, and if Quantity A and Quantity B are given as *exact values* that can be determined, or in some arithmetic form that can be calculated to an exact value, then the last choice (D) is *not* a possible answer since the two values *can* be compared.

   ▪ When to select choice D: If you immediately determine that you are presented with quantities that show *different* relationships when substituting values for the unknowns, select choice D.

5. **Simplify your comparisons.** It is possible to perform certain arithmetic calculations on each quantity or a given relationship in order to simplify the comparisons.

   ▪ If both quantities are known to be positive, then you can square each quantity and the relationship stays the same.

   ▪ Add the same amount to each quantity or subtract the same amount from each quantity and the relationship stays the same.

   ▪ Multiply or divide each quantity by the same positive number and the relationship stays the same.

   ▪ Multiply or divide each quantity by the same negative number, but be aware that this reverses the relationship.

Sample Questions

Directions: Compare Quantity A and Quantity B, using information centered above the two quantities, if such information is given. Select one of the following four answer choices for each question:

- Ⓐ   Quantity A is greater.
- Ⓑ   Quantity B is greater.
- Ⓒ   The two quantities are equal.
- Ⓓ   The relationship cannot be determined from the information given.

Note: In each question, a symbol appearing more than once denotes the same meaning throughout the question.

	Quantity A	**Quantity B**
1.	$\dfrac{7}{11}$	$\dfrac{9}{14}$

The two fractions may be compared by cross multiplying numerators times denominators in the following order:

$$7 \times 14 \text{ and } 11 \times 9$$

Since $7 \times 14 = 98 < 11 \times 9 = 99$, the fraction $\dfrac{9}{14}$ is greater than the fraction $\dfrac{7}{11}$.

Quantity B has a greater value. The correct answer is **B.**

	Quantity A	**Quantity B**
2.	$(27)^{16}$	$(81)^{12}$

Since $27 = 3^3$, $(27)^{16} = (3^3)^{16} = 3^{48}$.

Since $81 = 3^4$, $(81)^{12} = (3^4)^{12} = 3^{48}$.

The two quantities are equal. The correct answer is **C.**

In an xy-plane, a line has the equation $5x + 4y + 20 = 0$.

	Quantity A	**Quantity B**
3.	the x-intercept of the line	the y-intercept of the line

To find the x-intercept of the line, set $y = 0$ and solve for x:

$$5x + 4(0) + 20 = 0$$
$$5x + 20 = 0$$
$$5x = -20$$
$$x = -4$$

To find the y-intercept of the line, set $x = 0$ and solve for y:

$$5(0) + 4y + 20 = 0$$
$$4y + 20 = 0$$
$$4y = -20$$
$$y = -5$$

The x-intercept value is greater than the y-intercept value. Quantity A is greater. The correct answer is **A**.

	Quantity A	**Quantity B**
4.	the radius of a circle with an area of 64π	the radius of a circle with a chord length of 10

The area A of a circle is $A = \pi r^2$. If a circle has an area of 64π,

$$\pi r^2 = 64\pi$$
$$r^2 = 64$$
$$r = 8$$

In a circle with a chord length of 10, the radius could be less than the chord, greater than the chord, or equal to the chord. Therefore, the relationship cannot be determined from the information given. The correct answer is **D**.

A set contains the integers
12 through 19 inclusively.

	Quantity A	**Quantity B**
5.	the mean of the integers	the median of the integers

The set contains the integers 12, 13, 14, 15, 16, 17, 18, and 19. The mean of the set is the sum of the numbers divided by the number of data values in the set (8). Hence, the mean is $124 \div 8 = 15\frac{1}{2}$, or 15.5. The median of the set is the middle number if there is an odd number of data values in the set, or the mean of the middle two numbers if there is an even number of data values in the set. Since there are 8 data values in the given set, the median is the mean of the two middle data values (15 and 16) of the set. The median is $(15 + 16) \div 2 = 31 \div 2 = 15\frac{1}{2}$, or 15.5. Hence, the mean and the median are equal. The correct answer is **C**.

Overview of Multiple-Choice (Select One Answer Choice) Question Type

The multiple-choice (select one answer choice) question type requires you to solve math problems and then choose the single given answer choice that best answers the question.

Skills and Concepts Tested

Multiple-choice, single-answer questions test your ability to use math insight, simple calculations, and common sense to choose the one correct answer from among a list of five answer choices. The basic skills necessary to do well on this section include concepts presented in secondary mathematics classes through first-year algebra. Questions include arithmetic, algebra, geometry, and data analysis concepts usually presented as part of a second-year algebra course in high school. Trigonometry, calculus, or other higher level mathematics are not tested on the GRE.

Directions

Solve each problem in this section by using the information given and your own mathematical calculations. Select the one correct (best) answer from the five given choices.

Suggested Strategies

1. **Only one answer.** The correct answer is always in the list provided.
2. **Look for relationships in the answer choices.** In some questions, you are asked which answer choice meets certain requirements. This usually involves examining each answer choice individually. You may notice some relationship among the answer choices that allows you to settle on the correct answer more quickly.
3. **Work from the answer choices.** Working backward from the answer choices is an accepted method to find the solution, although it usually

takes longer than reasoning to find the correct answer. If you don't immediately recognize a method or formula, or if a method will take you a great deal of time, work backward from the answer choices. This method will at least eliminate some of the choices and may help lead you to the correct answer.

4. **Approximate.** Some questions require approximation. It may be useful to look at the answer choices and see how close together or far apart they are. This will guide you in determining how close your approximation needs to be to choose the correct answer. Some questions require accurate computations; for others, estimation may be all you need to arrive at the correct answer.

5. **Substitute simple numbers.** Substituting numbers for variables can often be an aid to understanding a problem. Remember to substitute simple numbers, since you have to do the work. Sometimes you will immediately recognize a simple method to solve a problem. If this is not the case, try a reasonable approach and then check the answer choices to see which one is the most reasonable.

Sample Questions

Directions: For each question, indicate the best answer from the choices given.

1. In the sequence 3, 4, 6, 9, 13, 18, . . ., what would be the twelfth number?

   Ⓐ   58
   Ⓑ   68
   Ⓒ   69
   Ⓓ   70
   Ⓔ   81

In the sequence, the difference between the first and second number is 1. The difference between the second and third number is 2. The difference between the third and fourth number is 3, and so forth. Following the same pattern, the first eleven numbers of the sequence are 3, 4, 6, 9, 13, 18, 24, 31, 39, 48, 58, and the twelfth number is 69. The correct answer is **C.**

2. If $4a = 5b = 6c = 40$, what is the value of $15abc$?

   Ⓐ   150
   Ⓑ   600
   Ⓒ   4,000
   Ⓓ   8,000
   Ⓔ   24,000

Since $4a = 5b = 6c = 40$, $a = 10$, $b = 8$, and $c = \dfrac{40}{6} = \dfrac{20}{3}$.

Therefore, $15abc = 15(10)(8)\left(\dfrac{20}{3}\right) = 8{,}000$. The correct answer is **D**.

3. What is the area of a right triangle with a leg length of 8 and a hypotenuse length of 17?

   Ⓐ   40

   Ⓑ   60

   Ⓒ   68

   Ⓓ   120

   Ⓔ   124

The Pythagorean theorem states that in a right triangle with legs a and b and hypotenuse c,

$$c^2 = a^2 + b^2$$
$$17^2 = 8^2 + b^2$$
$$289 = 64 + b^2$$
$$225 = b^2$$
$$15 = b$$

Since the legs in a right triangle are perpendicular, one leg is the base and the other leg is the height of the triangle. The area, A, of a triangle is

$$A = \frac{1}{2}bh = \frac{1}{2}(15)(8) = 60$$

The correct answer is **B**.

4. How many four-person committees can be formed from a group of 10 people?

   Ⓐ   14

   Ⓑ   40

   Ⓒ   210

   Ⓓ   400

   Ⓔ   5,040

Since the order of the people selected for a committee does not matter, this problem is a combination of 10 items taken 4 at a time. A combination, C of n items taken r at a time, is

$$C(n,r) = \frac{n!}{r!(n-r)!}$$

$$C(10,4) = \frac{10!}{4! \cdot 6!}$$

$$= \frac{10 \cdot 9 \cdot 8 \cdot 7 \cdot 6!}{4! \cdot 6!}$$

$$= \frac{10 \cdot 9 \cdot 8 \cdot 7}{4 \cdot 3 \cdot 2 \cdot 1}$$

$$= 210$$

There could be 210 four-person committees. The correct answer is **C**.

5. If $3x - 4y = 27$ and $5x + 2y = -7$, what is the value of $y - x$?

Ⓐ 20

Ⓑ 7

Ⓒ 5

Ⓓ −5

Ⓔ −7

Multiply the second equation through by 2.

$$\begin{array}{rcl}
3x - 4y = 27 & \rightarrow & 3x - 4y = 27 \\
2(5x + 2y = -7) & \rightarrow & 10x + 4y = -14 \\
\hline
& & 13x = 13
\end{array}$$

Adding the two equations yields $13x = 13$; therefore, $x = 1$.

Substituting $x = 1$ in either of the original equations produces

$$\begin{array}{ccc}
3(1) - 4y = 27 & \text{or} & 5(1) + 2y = -7 \\
3 - 4y = 27 & & 5 + 2y = -7 \\
-4y = 24 & & 2y = -12 \\
y = -6 & & y = -6
\end{array}$$

Therefore, $x = 1$ and $y = -6$. Substitute these values into $y - x$ and solve: $-6 - 1 = -7$. The correct answer is **E**.

Overview of Multiple-Choice (Select One or More Answer Choices) Question Type

The multiple-choice (select one or more answer choices) question type requires you to solve math problems and then choose ALL the answer choices that are correct. If you do not mark all correct answer choices, you will not be given any credit; there is no partial credit.

Skills and Concepts Tested

Multiple-choice questions with one or more correct answers test your ability to use mathematical insight, approximations, simple calculations, and common sense to choose ALL the correct or possible answers from among a list of several choices. This question type tests concepts presented in secondary mathematics classes through first-year algebra and geometry. It also includes data analysis concepts usually presented as part of a second-year algebra course in high school. No concepts are tested from trigonometry, calculus, or other higher level mathematics courses.

Directions

Solve each problem in this section by using the information given and your own mathematical calculations. Select ALL of the correct choices from the list of choices given. Some questions call for one answer, while others require two or more answers.

Suggested Strategies

1. **One or more possible answers.** The correct answers are in the list provided. If your answers are not in the list, your answers are incorrect.

2. **Look for relationships in the answer choices.** In some questions, you are asked which answer choices meet certain requirements. This usually involves examining each answer choice individually. You may notice some relationship among the answer choices that allows you to settle on the correct answers more quickly.

3. **Work from the answer choices.** Working backward from the answer choices is an accepted method for solution, although it usually takes longer than reasoning to find the correct answers. If you don't immediately recognize a method or formula, or if a method will take you a great deal of time, work

backward from the answer choices. This method will at least eliminate some of the choices and may help lead you to the correct answers.

4. **Approximate.** Some questions require approximation. It may be useful to look at the answer choices and see how close together or far apart they are. This information will guide you in determining how close your approximation needs to be to choose the correct answers. Some questions require accurate computations; for others, estimation may be all you need to arrive at the correct answers.

5. **Substitute simple numbers.** Substituting numbers for variables can often be an aid to understanding a problem. Remember to substitute *simple* numbers, since you have to do the work. Sometimes you will immediately recognize a simple method to solve a problem. If this is not the case, try a reasonable approach and then check the answer choices to see which are the most reasonable.

Sample Questions

Directions: For each question, indicate ALL possible answers from the choices given.

1. Which of the following could be the units digit of 73^n, where n is a positive integer? Indicate all such digits.

   - A 1
   - B 3
   - C 5
   - D 6
   - E 7
   - F 9

The units digit, 3, in 73^n, will determine the units digit of 73^n for all positive integers n. Since $3^1 = 3$, $3^2 = 9$, $3^3 = 27$, and $3^4 = 81$, the units digits will repeat the same pattern indefinitely: $3^5 = 243$, $3^6 = 729$, $3^7 = 2,187$, $3^8 = 6,561$, and so forth. Hence, the 1, 3, 7, and 9 are the only possible units digits of 73^n. The correct answers are **A, B, E,** and **F.**

2. Which of the following could be the solution of the equation $4x^4 + 8x^3 - 60x^2 = 0$? Indicate all such solutions.

- [A] −5
- [B] −4
- [C] −3
- [D] 0
- [E] 3
- [F] 4
- [G] 5

Factoring:

$$4x^4 + 8x^3 - 60x^2 = 0$$
$$4x^2\left(x^2 + 2x - 15\right) = 0$$
$$4x^2(x+5)(x-3) = 0$$

Setting each factor equal to zero:

$$4x^2 = 0 \quad \text{or} \quad x + 5 = 0 \quad \text{or} \quad x - 3 = 0$$
$$x = 0 \quad \text{or} \quad x = -5 \quad \text{or} \quad x = 3$$

Hence the solutions are −5, 0, and 3. The correct answers are **A, D,** and **E.**

3. If a triangle has two sides with lengths of 10 and 15, which of the following could be the length of the third side? Indicate all such values.

- [A] 5
- [B] 10
- [C] 15
- [D] 20
- [E] 25
- [F] 30

The triangle inequality property states that the sum of any two sides of a triangle must be greater than the third side. If x is the third side of a triangle with sides of 10 and 15, then

$$x > 15 - 10 \quad \text{and} \quad x < 15 + 10$$
$$\text{or} \quad x > 5 \qquad \text{and} \quad x < 25$$

Therefore, the third side of the triangle could have lengths of 10, 15, and 20. The correct answers are **B, C,** and **D.**

4. Given $\sqrt{xz} = 10$, which of the following could be a value of $x + z$? Indicate all such values.

- Ⓐ 20
- Ⓑ 25
- Ⓒ 29
- Ⓓ 50
- Ⓔ 52
- Ⓕ 100
- Ⓖ 101

Since $\sqrt{xz} = 10$, $xz = 100$, and the possible values of x and z are

$$
\begin{array}{rcl}
1 \text{ and } 100 & \rightarrow & 1 + 100 = 101 \\
2 \text{ and } 50 & \rightarrow & 2 + 50 = 52 \\
4 \text{ and } 25 & \rightarrow & 4 + 25 = 29 \\
5 \text{ and } 20 & \rightarrow & 5 + 20 = 25 \\
10 \text{ and } 10 & \rightarrow & 10 + 10 = 20
\end{array}
$$

The correct answer choices are **A, B, C, E,** and **G.**

5. If a chord of a circle has a length of 24, which of the following could be the length of the radius of the circle? Indicate all such values.

- Ⓐ 5
- Ⓑ 10
- Ⓒ 12
- Ⓓ 15
- Ⓔ 20
- Ⓕ 24

Since the diameter of any circle is the longest chord of the circle, the diameter of the given circle must be greater than or equal to 24. Since the radius of a circle is equal to one-half of its diameter, the radius of the given circle must be greater than or equal to 12. The correct answer choices are **C, D, E,** and **F.**

Overview of Numeric Entry (Fill-in) Question Type

The numeric entry (fill-in) question type requires you to solve math problems with numeric answers and fill in the blank space with the correct answer based on the guidelines given in the problem.

Skills and Concepts Tested

Fill-in questions test your ability to use mathematical insight, approximations, simple calculations, and common sense to calculate a numeric response. They test concepts presented in secondary mathematics classes through first-year algebra and geometry. They also include data analysis concepts usually presented as part of a second-year algebra course in high school. There are no concepts tested from trigonometry, calculus, or other higher level mathematics courses.

Directions

Solve each problem by using the information given and your own mathematical calculations. Arrive at a numeric response based on the specifications given in the problem. Use the mouse to click in the rectangular answer area, then type in your answer. There will be one box if the answer is an integer or decimal and two boxes if the answer requires a fraction—one for the numerator and one for the denominator. Answers also may be transferred from the on-screen calculator.

Suggested Strategies

- Calculate the answer using the requirements of the problem.
- If answering a question using a decimal response, do not forget to include the decimal point, if required. For example, if the answer is "23," then answers such as "23," "23.," or "23.0" are all correct. If the answer is "5.2," then answers such as "5.2," "5.20," or "05.2" are all correct.
- If answering a question using a common fraction response, place the numerator in the upper box and the denominator in the lower box. Fractional answers do not have to be reduced. For example, if an answer is "three-fourths," then the answer could be entered as $\frac{3}{4}$, 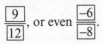 $\frac{9}{12}$, or even $\frac{-6}{-8}$.

- Information will be given in the question if an answer is required to be in reduced form.
- Rectangular answer boxes indicate that a fill-in answer is required.

Sample Questions

Directions: These types of questions require you to solve the problem and enter your answer. Single answer boxes indicate an integer or decimal answer. Two separate boxes indicate a fraction answer (numerator and denominator).

1. A line lies on the xy-plane and passes through the points $(-5, 2)$ and $(2, 4)$. What is the slope of the line? Give the answer as a fraction.

$$\boxed{} \atop \boxed{}$$

The slope, m, of a line passing through the points (x_1, y_1) and (x_2, y_2) is

$$m = \frac{y_1 - y_2}{x_1 - x_2} \quad \text{or} \quad m = \frac{y_2 - y_1}{x_2 - x_1}.$$

The slope of the line passing through the points $(-5, 2)$ and $(2, 4)$ is

$m = \dfrac{2-4}{-5-2}$ or $\dfrac{4-2}{2-(-5)} = \dfrac{2}{7}$. The correct answer is $\dfrac{2}{7}$ (or any equivalent fraction).

2. What is the greatest of four consecutive odd integers if their sum is 512?

$$\boxed{}$$

Since the four numbers are consecutive odd integers, let

$$x = \text{1st odd integer}$$
$$x + 2 = \text{2nd odd integer}$$
$$x + 4 = \text{3rd odd integer}$$
$$x + 6 = \text{4th odd integer}$$

Their sum is $(x)+(x+2)+(x+4)+(x+6)=512$

$$4x+12=512$$
$$4x=500$$
$$x=125$$
$$x+2=127$$
$$x+4=129$$
$$x+6=131$$

Therefore, 131 is the greatest of the four odd integers. The correct answer is **131**.

3. The arithmetic mean of the final exam scores of a class of m students is 74. The mean of the final exam scores of a class of n students is 89. When the scores of both classes are combined, the mean score is 82. What is the value of $\dfrac{m}{n}$?

Since the mean of the scores of m students is 74, the sum of their scores is $74m$. Likewise, since the mean of the scores of n students is 89, the sum of their scores is $89n$. Since there are $m + n$ students when the classes are combined, and their mean score is 82, the value of $\dfrac{m}{n}$ can be found as follows:

$$\frac{\text{sum of the scores}}{\text{number of scores}}=82$$
$$\frac{74m+89n}{m+n}=82$$
$$74m+89n=82(m+n)$$
$$74m+89n=82m+82n$$
$$7n=8m$$
$$\frac{7n}{8n}=\frac{8m}{8n}$$
$$\frac{7}{8}=\frac{m}{n}$$

The correct answer is $\dfrac{m}{n} = \dfrac{7}{8}$.

4. If $x \oplus y$ is defined as $x \oplus y = \dfrac{x^2 + y^2}{y}$ for all integers x and y, and $y \neq 0$,

then what is the value of $(6 \oplus 3) \oplus 5$?

$$6 \oplus 3 = \frac{6^2 + 3^2}{3} = \frac{36 + 9}{3} = \frac{45}{3} = 15 \text{ and}$$

$$(6 \oplus 3) \oplus 5 = 15 \oplus 5 = \frac{15^2 + 5^2}{5} = \frac{225 + 25}{5} = \frac{250}{5} = 50.$$

The correct answer is **50**.

5. If $5^x + 5^x + 5^x + 5^x + 5^x = 5^{10}$, what is the value of x?

Since $5^x + 5^x + 5^x + 5^x + 5^x = 5^x(1 + 1 + 1 + 1 + 1) = 5^x \cdot 5$

$$5^x \cdot 5 = 5^{10}$$

$$5^x = \frac{5^{10}}{5}$$

$$5^x = 5^9$$

Therefore, $x = 9$; the correct answer is **9**.

PART II

REVIEW OF EXAM AREAS

Chapter 2

Math Fundamentals

Overview

The fundamentals of math—including symbols, terms, sets of numbers, math properties, expanded notation, scientific notation, order of operations, and English and metric system measurements—are covered in this chapter. Bookmark this chapter as a reference for your entire preparation. These basic math references are time-saving tools that prove valuable as you review, study, and practice problems in subsequent chapters.

The following are common *math symbol* references that you will need to know for all basic math, algebra, and geometry questions.

Common Math Symbols

Symbol	Definition	Example	Written Example
$=$	is equal to	$x = 3$	x is equal to 3
$\neq$	is not equal to	$x \neq 3$	x is not equal to 3
$\approx$ or $\doteq$	is approximately equal to	$x \approx y$	x is approximately equal to y
$>$	is greater than	$x > 3$	x is greater than 3
$\geq$	is greater than or equal to	$x \geq 3$	x is greater than or equal to 3
$<$	is less than	$x < 3$	x is less than 3
$\leq$	is less than or equal to	$x \leq 3$	x is less than or equal to 3
$|x|$	the absolute value of a number x	$|3|$	the absolute value of 3
$\sqrt{}$	the square root of, or "radical"	$\sqrt{9}$	the square root of 9
$\sqrt[n]{x}$	nth root of a number x	$\sqrt[3]{64}$	3rd root of 64
$!$	factorial	$n!$	the product of the positive integers 1, 2, 3, ..., n

(continued)

Symbol	Definition	Example	Written Example
$\perp$	is perpendicular to	$a \perp b$	line a is perpendicular to line b
$\parallel$	is parallel to	$a \parallel b$	line a is parallel to line b
~	is similar to	$\triangle ABC \sim \triangle DEF$	triangle ABC is similar to triangle DEF
$\cong$	is congruent to	$\angle A \cong \angle C$	angle A is congruent to angle C

Common Terminology: Words That Signal an Operation

The following list describes the language of basic math operations.

Term	Operation	Example
Sum	The answer to an addition problem.	What is the sum of $4 + 17$?
Difference or remainder	The answer to a subtraction problem.	What is the difference between 17 and 4? What is the remainder if you subtract 4 from 17?
Product	The answer to a multiplication problem.	What is the product of 4×17?
Quotient or ratio	The answer to a division problem.	What is the quotient of $17 \div 4$? What is the ratio of 24 to 35, or $\frac{24}{35}$?

Special Sets of Numbers

In completing arithmetic and algebra problems, you will work with several groups of numbers.

Number	Definition
Natural or counting numbers	$\{1, 2, 3, 4, 5, ...\}$
Whole numbers	$\{0, 1, 2, 3, 4, ...\}$

(continued)

Number	Definition
Prime numbers	Prime numbers are all natural numbers greater than 1 that are divisible only by 1 and the number itself. For example, 17 is a prime number because it can be divided by only 17 and 1. The only even prime number is 2. Zero and 1 are *not* prime numbers. The first ten prime numbers are 2, 3, 5, 7, 11, 13, 17, 19, 23, and 29.
Composite numbers	Composite numbers are all natural numbers greater than 1 that are not prime. A composite number is divisible by more than just 1 and itself. For example, 4, 6, 8, 9 10, 12, 14, 15, … *Note: 1 is neither prime nor composite.*
Integers Even integers Odd integers	$\{…, -3, -2, -1, 0, 1, 2, 3, …\}$ The whole numbers and their opposites. All integers that are exactly divisible by 2. $\{…, -6, -4, -2, 0, 2, 4, 6, …\}$ All integers that are *not* exactly divisible by 2. $\{…, -5, -3, -1, 0, 1, 3, 5, …\}$
Rational numbers	Rational numbers are all numbers that can be expressed as a fraction of the form $\frac{a}{b}$, where a and b are integers and $b \neq 0$. Rational numbers may also be expressed as a terminating or repeating decimal. For example, $\frac{1}{4} = 0.25$, $\frac{1}{12} = 0.08333… = 0.08\overline{3}$. *All integers are rational numbers.*
Irrational numbers	Irrational numbers are all numbers that cannot be expressed in the form of a fraction $\frac{a}{b}$, where a and b are integers and $b \neq 0$. Some examples of irrational numbers are π, $\sqrt{5}$, and $\sqrt[3]{10}$.
Real numbers	The combination of all rational numbers and irrational numbers. On the GRE, you should *assume all problems use real numbers* unless otherwise explicitly stated.
Perfect squares	$\{(\pm 1)^2, (\pm 2)^2, (\pm 3)^2, (\pm 4)^2, …\} = \{1, 4, 9, 16, …\}$ The squares of the nonzero integers.
Perfect cubes	$\{(\pm 1)^3, (\pm 2)^3, (\pm 3)^3, (\pm 4)^3, …\} = \{\pm 1, \pm 8, \pm 27, \pm 64, …\}$ The cubes of the nonzero integers.

Multiplication Notation

The operation of multiplication may be represented in a number of ways. For example, the product of two numbers, a and b, may be expressed as

$a \times b$

$a \cdot b$

ab

$(a)(b)$

Basic Mathematical Properties

The "Special Sets of Numbers" section earlier in this chapter described the different types of *numbers*. As you may recall, all numbers on the GRE are *real numbers* (rational and irrational numbers) unless otherwise specified. The numerical value of every real number fits between the numerical values of two other real numbers, and the end result of adding or multiplying real numbers is always another real number.

This concept is described as a *closure property*. For example, if you add two even numbers, the answer will always be an even number ($8 + 6 = 14$). Therefore, the set of even numbers is called "closed for addition." This section helps you understand these basic properties of mathematical operations, makes it easier for you to work with real numbers, and helps you conceptually understand how sets of numbers fit together.

As you work with real numbers, it is also important to understand the *value* of numbers assigned in a place value system (decimal system). To assist you, this section provides you with examples of written numbers in the decimal system in expanded notation and points out the place value of each digit.

On the GRE, imaginary values such as $\sqrt{-1}$ are *not* considered. Values that have no value, real or imaginary, such as $\frac{8}{0}, \frac{0}{0}$, or 0^0, are *not* considered.

Exponents can be positive, negative, or zero.

For example, $5^2 = 5 \times 5 = 25$, $5^{-2} = \frac{1}{5^2} = \frac{1}{25}$, and $5^0 = 1$.

Properties of Addition

There are four mathematical properties of addition that are fundamental math building blocks: commutative, associative, identity, and inverse.

Property	Operation	Examples
Commutative property	The word "commute" means "move around or exchange." In the commutative property of addition, when you change the *order*, it does not affect the sum of two or more numbers.	$a + b = b + a$ $2 + 3 = 3 + 2$ ***Note:** The commutative property is NOT true for subtraction:* $2 - 3 \neq 3 - 2$

(continued)

Property	Operation	Examples
Associative property	The word "associate" means "grouping." In the associative property of addition, grouping does not affect the sum of three or more numbers. Notice that even though the grouping changes (parentheses move), the sums are still equal.	$(a + b) + c = a + (b + c)$ $(2 + 3) + 4 = 2 + (3 + 4)$ ***Note:*** *The associative property is NOT true for subtraction:* $(2 - 3) - 4 \neq 2 - (3 - 4)$
Identity property	The sum of 0 and any number is always the original number.	$a + 0 = 0 + a = a$ $5 + 0 = 0 + 5 = 5$
Inverse property	The sum of any number and its additive inverse (opposite) is always 0.	$a + (-a) = (-a) + a = 0$ $5 + (-5) = (-5) + 5 = 0$

Properties of Multiplication

The four mathematical properties of multiplication make it easier to solve problems: commutative, associative, identity, and inverse.

Property	Operation	Examples
Commutative property	The *order* does not affect the product of two or more numbers.	$a \cdot b = b \cdot a$ $2 \cdot 3 = 3 \cdot 2$ ***Note:*** *The commutative property is NOT true for division:* $a \div b \neq b \div a$ $2 \div 3 \neq 3 \div 2$
Associative property	Grouping does not affect the product of three or more numbers.	$(a \cdot b) \cdot c = a \cdot (b \cdot c)$ $(2 \cdot 3) \cdot 4 = 2 \cdot (3 \cdot 4)$ ***Note:*** *The commutative property is NOT true for division:* $(a \div b) \div c \neq a \div (b \div c)$ $(2 \div 3) \div 4 \neq 2 \div (3 \div 4)$
Identity property	The product of 1 and any number is always the original number.	$a \cdot 1 = 1 \cdot a = a$ $2 \cdot 1 = 1 \cdot 2 = 2$
Inverse property	The product of any non-zero number and its multiplicative inverse (reciprocal) is always 1.	$a \cdot \dfrac{1}{a} = \dfrac{1}{a} \cdot a = 1 \ (a \neq 0)$ ***Note:*** *0 is the only real number that does NOT have a reciprocal.* $2 \cdot \dfrac{1}{2} = \dfrac{1}{2} \cdot 2 = 1$

Distributive Properties

The distributive property is one of the most used properties in math and is considered a basis for understanding mental operations of math. To "distribute" means to "spread out," and this basic operation makes it easier for you to work with numbers as you separate them into component parts. In the distributive property, it is possible to take a number and separately distribute it across the sum of two or more other numbers before it is either added or subtracted to the product for the same result. The following examples show two important distributive properties: multiplication over addition and multiplication over subtraction.

Property	Operation	Examples
Multiplication over addition	This distributive property shows the process of distributing the number on the outside of the parentheses to each term on the inside.	$a \cdot (b+c) = a \cdot b + a \cdot c$ $2 \cdot (3+4) = 2 \cdot 3 + 2 \cdot 4$ and $a \cdot b + a \cdot c = a \cdot (b+c)$ $2 \cdot 3 + 2 \cdot 4 = 2 \cdot (3+4)$
Multiplication over subtraction	This distributive property shows the process of distributing multiplication over subtraction.	$a \cdot (b-c) = a \cdot b - a \cdot c$ $2 \cdot (3-4) = 2 \cdot 3 - 2 \cdot 4$ and $a \cdot b - a \cdot c = a \cdot (b-c)$ $2 \cdot 3 - 2 \cdot 4 = 2 \cdot (3-4)$

Place Value

Each digit in any real number has a place value. A general example of place value for the number 3,092,345,876.43629702 is:

Here's another example. In the number 629.453, the 6 is in the hundreds place, the 2 is in the tens place, the 9 is in the ones place, the 4 is in the tenths place, the 5 is in the hundredths place, and the 3 is in the thousandths place.

Expanded Notation

Numbers can be expressed in expanded notation to emphasize the place value for each digit. The number 629.453 can be written in expanded notation as

$$600 \ + \ 20 \ + \ 9 \ + \ 0.4 \ + \ 0.05 \ + \ 0.003$$

$$(6 \times 100) + (2 \times 10) + (9 \times 1) + \left(4 \times \frac{1}{10}\right) + \left(5 \times \frac{1}{100}\right) + \left(3 \times \frac{1}{1,000}\right)$$

Using exponents, 629.453 can be written as

$$\left(6 \times 10^2\right) + \left(2 \times 10^1\right) + \left(9 \times 10^0\right) + \left(4 \times 10^{-1}\right) + \left(5 \times 10^{-2}\right) + \left(3 \times 10^{-3}\right)$$

Scientific Notation

Any real number may be expressed in scientific notation as the product of a number between 1 and 10 multiplied by a power of 10. Some examples of numbers expressed in scientific notation are

$$345 = 3.45 \times 10^2$$
$$0.0016 = 1.6 \times 10^{-3}$$
$$15{,}394 = 1.5394 \times 10^4$$

Operations Using Real Numbers

Grouping Symbols

Parentheses ( ), brackets [ ], and braces { } frequently are needed to group numbers in mathematics. Generally, parentheses are used first, followed by brackets, and then braces. Operations inside grouping symbols must be performed before any operations outside the grouping symbols are performed.

Order of Operation Rules

When performing operations on real numbers, the following order rules must be followed:

1. Work grouping symbols from the inside out.
2. Work exponents and roots in order from left to right.
3. Work multiplication and division in order from left to right.
4. Work addition and subtraction in order from left to right.

Parentheses

Parentheses are used to group numbers or variables. Calculations inside parentheses take precedence and should be performed before any other operations.

$$50(2 + 6) = 50(8) = 400$$

If a parenthesis is preceded by a minus sign, the parentheses must be removed before calculations can be performed. To remove the parentheses, change the plus or minus sign of each term within the parentheses.

$$6 - (-3 + a - 2b + c) = 6 + 3 - a + 2b - c = 9 - a + 2b - c$$

Brackets and Braces

Brackets and braces are also used to group numbers or variables. Sometimes, instead of brackets or braces, you'll see the use of larger parentheses:

$$((3+4) \cdot 5) + 2$$

An expression using all three grouping symbols might look like this:

$$2\{1+[4(2+1)+3]\}$$

The above expression can be simplified as follows (notice that you work from the inside out):

$$
\begin{aligned}
2\{1+[4(2+1)+3]\} &= 2\{1+[4(3)+3]\} \\
&= 2\{1+[12+3]\} \\
&= 2\{1+[15]\} \\
&= 2\{16\} \\
&= 32
\end{aligned}
$$

Examples

1. $[15+3(10-6)]-8 \cdot 3 =$

$$[15+3(10-6)]-8 \cdot 3 \quad \text{(parentheses first)}$$
$$=[15+3(4)]-8 \cdot 3 \quad \text{(brackets, mult/div from left to right)}$$
$$=[15+12]-8 \cdot 3 \quad \text{(brackets, add/subtract from left to right)}$$
$$= 27-8 \cdot 3 \quad \text{(multiply)}$$
$$= 27-24 \quad \text{(subtract)}$$
$$= 3$$

2. $10 - 3 \times 6 + 10^2 + \underline{(6+1)} \times 4$ (parentheses first)

$= 10 - 3 \times 6 + \underline{10^2} + 7 \times 4$ (exponents next)

$= 10 - \underline{3 \times 6} + 100 + \underline{7 \times 4}$ (mult/div from left to right)

$= \underline{10 - 18} + 100 + 28$ (add/subtract from left to right)

$= \underline{-8 + 100} + 28$ (add/subtract from left to right)

$= 92 + 28$

$= 120$

Customary English and Metric System Measurements

Basic Metric Prefixes

milli (m) = $\dfrac{1}{1,000}$, or 0.001	deca (da) = 10
centi (c) = $\dfrac{1}{100}$, or 0.01	hecto (h) = 100
deci (d) = $\dfrac{1}{10}$, or 0.1	kilo (k) = 1,000

Length

English	Metric
12 inches (in) = 1 foot (ft)	10 millimeters (mm) = 1 centimeter (cm)
3 feet = 1 yard (yd)	10 centimeters = 1 decimeter (dm)
36 inches = 1 yard	10 decimeters = 1 meter (m)
5,280 feet = 1 mile (mi)	10 meters = 1 decameter (dam)
1,760 yards = 1 mile	10 decameters = 1 hectometer (hm)
	10 hectometers = 1 kilometer (km)
Note: The basic unit of length in the metric system is the meter (m). It is approximately 3 inches more than a yard, or approximately 39 inches.	
1 kilometer is about 0.6 mile	

Weight

English	Metric
16 ounces (oz) = 1 pound (lb)	10 milligrams (mg) = 1 centigram (cg)
2,000 pounds = 1 ton (T)	10 centigrams = 1 decigram (dg)
	10 decigrams = 1 gram (g)
	10 grams = 1 decagram (dag)
	10 decagrams = 1 hectogram (hg)
	10 hectograms = 1 kilogram (kg)

Note: The basic unit of weight in the metric system is the gram (g). 1 ounce is approximately 28 grams. A more useful measure of weight is the kilogram (kg), or 1,000 grams, which is approximately 2.2 pounds.

1,000 kilograms = 1 metric ton

Volume (capacity)

English	Metric
1 cup (C) = 8 fluid ounces (fl oz)	10 milliliters (ml or mL) = 1 centiliter (cl or cL)
2 cups = 1 pint (pt)	10 centiliters = 1 deciliter (dl or dL)
2 pints = 1 quart (qt)	10 deciliters = 1 liter (l or L)
4 quarts = 1 gallon (gal)	10 liters = 1 decaliter (dal or daL)
	10 decaliters = 1 hectoliter (hl or hL)
	10 hectoliters = 1 kiloliter (kl or kL)

Note: The basic unit of volume in the metric system is the liter (L). One liter is approximately 1 quart.

Time

60 seconds = 1 minute
60 minutes = 1 hour
24 hours = 1 day
7 days = 1 week
365 days = 1 year
12 months = 1 year
52 weeks = 1 year

Months of the Year

It is useful to know the number of days in each of the 12 months of the year.
February: 28 days (29 days in a leap year)
April, June, September, and November: 30 days
Remaining 7 months: 31 days

Converting Units of Measure – English System

Examples

1. How many inches in 9 yards?

    Since 1 yard = 36 inches, 9 yards = $9 \times 36 = 324$ inches.

2. How many miles in 7,040 yards?

    Since 1 mile = 1,760 yards, 7,040 yards = $7{,}040 \div 1{,}760 = 4$ miles.

3. How many pounds in 352 ounces?

    Since 1 pound = 16 ounces, 352 ounces = $352 \div 16 = 22$ pounds.

4. How many pints in 7 gallons?

    Since 1 gallon = 4 quarts, 7 gallons = $7 \times 4 = 28$ quarts.
    Since 1 quart = 2 pints, 28 quarts = $28 \times 2 = 56$ pints.

5. How many weeks in 343 days?

    Since 1 week = 7 days, 343 days = $343 \div 7 = 49$ weeks.

6. How many minutes in 6 days?

    Since 1 day = 24 hours, 6 days = $24 \times 6 = 144$ hours.
    Since 1 hour = 60 minutes, 144 hours = $144 \times 60 = 8{,}640$ minutes.

Converting Units of Measure – Metric System

Examples

1. 1 kilometer = 1,000 meters

2. 1 milligram = 0.001 gram

3. 1 centiliter = 0.01 liter

4. 1 meter = 100 centimeters

5. 1 liter = 10 deciliters

6. 1 gram = 0.001 kilogram

7. 1 centimeter = 10 millimeters

8. 1 decigram = 10 centigrams

9. 1 deciliter = 100 milliliters

Chapter 3

Arithmetic

Arithmetic is the foundation for *all mathematical concepts* and shares the basic properties of counting (adding, subtracting, multiplying, and dividing) for all GRE math topics. Since math concepts are best understood through orderly stages of conceptual learning, you will need to have a solid understanding of arithmetic *before* you undertake the more advanced topics of algebra, geometry, and data analysis. Some students skip this section and move directly to algebra and geometry, but it would be in your best interest to at least skim through the topic headings before you proceed to subsequent advanced chapters. By studying arithmetic first, you will be strengthening your ability to understand forgotten math concepts and will be increasing your ability to tackle more challenging problems in later chapters.

Charting Your Progress

The following chart will help you keep track of arithmetic topics to study. Use the list to check off topics as you read practice topics with sample exercises. As you evaluate your understanding of each topic area, pinpoint areas that require further study by placing a check mark next to the topic. Continue to measure your progress and refer to this list as often as necessary. Remember, studying arithmetic is a *preliminary stage* of your review; repeated review and practice are *normal* steps to build interconnected associations to math concepts.

After you have reviewed the arithmetic topics, reinforce what you have learned by working the practice questions at the end of this chapter. Answers and explanations provide further clarification. Practice exercises are arranged by question type to help you practice solving arithmetic problems that are specific to the GRE.

Arithmetic Topics You Should Know

Topic	Study Pages	Worked Examples	Further Study Required
Rounding-off numbers	pp. 57–58		
Order of operations	pp. 58–59		
Addition	p. 59		
Subtraction	p. 60		
Multiplication	p. 60		
Division	pp. 60–61		
Divisibility rules	p. 61		
Fractions	pp. 61–69		
Decimals	pp. 69–72		
Converting decimals to fractions	p. 72		
Converting fractions to decimals	p. 72		
Ratios and proportions	pp. 72–73		
Percents	pp. 73–79		
Converting percents to decimals	pp. 73–74		
Converting decimals to percents	p. 74		
Converting percents to fractions	p. 74		
Converting fractions to percents	pp. 74–75		
Square roots and cube roots	pp. 79–82		

Let's get started and see what arithmetic skills you remember. Take the arithmetic diagnostic test that follows to help you evaluate how familiar you are with the selected arithmetic topics. The diagnostic test will give you valuable insight into the topics you will need to study.

Arithmetic Diagnostic Test

25 Questions

Directions: Solve each problem in this section by using the information given and your own mathematical calculations.

1. Round 57.4283 to the nearest hundredth.

2. Round 96,372 to the nearest thousand.

3. Evaluate: $253 - 2^6 \div 4 + 20 \cdot 3^2$

4. Evaluate: $[(2^3 - 3)^2 + 5] \cdot [20 - 4 \cdot 3]$

5. Add: $\dfrac{2}{3} + \dfrac{5}{8} + \dfrac{1}{4}$

6. Subtract: $9\dfrac{1}{5} - 4\dfrac{2}{3}$

7. Multiply: $\dfrac{3}{8} \times \dfrac{4}{5} \times \dfrac{7}{24}$

8. Divide: $5\dfrac{5}{6} \div 2\dfrac{1}{3}$

9. Evaluate: $46.56 - 13.2894 + 9.5$

10. Evaluate: 8.243×5.2

11. Evaluate: $1.7375 \div 0.25$

12. Change 0.084 to a fraction.

13. Change $\dfrac{7}{8}$ to a decimal.

14. Change 36% to a fraction.

15. Find 59% of 314.

16. What percent of 240 is 150?

17. 28 is 35% of what number?

18. Find the simple interest on $15,000 borrowed for 4 years at an annual rate of 5%.

19. Find the percent increase on a product marked up from $60 to $75.

20. The value of $\sqrt{211}$ falls between what two whole numbers?

21. Simplify: $\sqrt{360}$

48

22. Express 483.65 in expanded notation.

23. Find all of the prime numbers between 20 and 40.

24. Convert 972 inches to yards.

25. Convert 17 gallons to pints.

Scoring the Diagnostic Test

The following section will assist you in scoring and analyzing your diagnostic test results. Use the answer key below to score your results on the Analysis Sheet that follows. Read through the answer explanations on pages 52–57 to clarify the solutions to the problems.

Answer Key

Rounding-Off Numbers

1. 57.43

2. 96,000

Order of Operations

3. 417

4. 240

Fractions

5. $\frac{37}{24}$, or $1\frac{13}{24}$

6. $4\frac{8}{15}$

7. $\frac{7}{80}$

8. $\frac{5}{2}$, or $2\frac{1}{2}$

Decimals

9. 42.7706

10. 42.8636

11. 6.95

Converting Decimals to Fractions

12. $\dfrac{21}{250}$

Converting Fractions to Decimals

13. 0.875

Converting Percents to Fractions

14. $\dfrac{9}{25}$

Percents

15. 185.26

16. 62.5%, or $62\dfrac{1}{2}\%$

17. 80

18. $3,000

19. 25%

Square Roots

20. 14 and 15

21. $6\sqrt{10}$

Expanded Notation

22. $(4 \times 100) + (8 \times 10) + (3 \times 1) + \left(6 \times \dfrac{1}{10}\right) + \left(5 \times \dfrac{1}{100}\right)$

Prime Numbers

23. 23, 29, 31, and 37

Measurement

24. 27 yards

25. 136 pints

Charting and Analyzing Your Diagnostic Test Results

Record your diagnostic test results in the following chart, and use these results as a guide to plan your arithmetic review goals and objectives. Mark the problems that you missed, paying particular attention to those that were missed because of a "lack of knowledge." These are the areas you will want to focus on as you study the arithmetic topics.

Arithmetic Diagnostic Test Analysis Sheet

Topic	Total Possible	Number Correct	Number Incorrect (A) Simple Mistake	(B) Misread Problem	(C) Lack of Knowledge
Rounding-off numbers	2				
Order of operations	2				
Fractions	4				
Decimals	3				
Converting decimals to fractions	1				
Converting fractions to decimals	1				
Converting percents to fractions	1				
Percents	5				
Square roots	2				
Expanded notation	1				
Prime numbers	1				
Measurement	2				
Total Possible Explanations for Incorrect Answers: Columns A, B, and C					
Total Number of Answers Correct and Incorrect	25	Add the total number of correct answers here: _____	Add columns A, B, and C: _____ Total number of incorrect answers		

Arithmetic Diagnostic Test Answers and Explanations

Rounding-Off Numbers

1. 57.43

In the number 57.4283, the 2 is in the hundredths place. Since the number immediately to the right of the hundredths place is 5 or greater, the number is rounded up to 57.43.

2. 96,000

In the number 96,372, the 6 is in the thousands place. Since the number immediately to the right of the thousands place is 4 or less, the number is rounded down to 96,000.

Order of Operations

3. 417

$$\begin{aligned}
253 - 2^6 \div 4 + 20 \cdot 3^2 &= 253 - 64 \div 4 + 20 \cdot 9 \\
&= 253 - 16 + 180 \\
&= 237 + 180 \\
&= 417
\end{aligned}$$

4. 240

$$\begin{aligned}
\left[\left(2^3 - 3\right)^2 + 5\right] \cdot [20 - 4 \cdot 3] &= \left[(8 - 3)^2 + 5\right] \cdot [20 - 12] \\
&= \left[5^2 + 5\right] \cdot [8] \\
&= [25 + 5] \cdot [8] \\
&= 30 \cdot 8 \\
&= 240
\end{aligned}$$

Fractions

5. $\dfrac{37}{24}$, or $1\dfrac{13}{24}$

$$\begin{aligned}
\frac{2}{3} + \frac{5}{8} + \frac{1}{4} &= \frac{16}{24} + \frac{15}{24} + \frac{6}{24} \\
&= \frac{37}{24}, \text{ or } 1\frac{13}{24}
\end{aligned}$$

6. $4\dfrac{8}{15}$

$$9\frac{1}{5} = 9\frac{3}{15} = 8\frac{18}{15}$$
$$-4\frac{2}{3} = 4\frac{10}{15} = 4\frac{10}{15}$$
$$\rule{4cm}{0.4pt}$$
$$4\frac{8}{15}$$

7. $\dfrac{7}{80}$

$$\frac{3}{8} \times \frac{4}{5} \times \frac{7}{24} = \frac{\overset{1}{\cancel{3}} \times \overset{1}{\cancel{4}} \times 7}{\underset{2}{\cancel{8}} \times 5 \times \underset{8}{\cancel{24}}}$$

$$= \frac{7}{80}$$

8. $\dfrac{5}{2}$, or $2\dfrac{1}{2}$

$$5\frac{5}{6} \div 2\frac{1}{3} = \frac{35}{6} \div \frac{7}{3}$$
$$= \frac{35}{6} \cdot \frac{3}{7}$$
$$= \frac{\overset{5}{\cancel{35}}}{\underset{2}{\cancel{6}}} \cdot \frac{\overset{1}{\cancel{3}}}{\underset{1}{\cancel{7}}}$$
$$= \frac{5}{2}, \text{ or } 2\frac{1}{2}$$

Decimals

9. 42.7706

$$
\begin{array}{rr}
46.5600 & 33.2706 \\
-13.2894 & +9.5000 \\
\hline
33.2706 & 42.7706 \\
\end{array}
$$

10. 42.8636

$$
\begin{array}{r}
8.243 \\
\times\ 5.2 \\
\hline
16486 \\
41215 \\
\hline
42.8636
\end{array}
$$

11. 6.95

$$
0.25.\overline{)1.73.75} \rightarrow 25\overline{)173.75}
$$

$$
\begin{array}{r}
6.95 \\
25\overline{)173.75} \\
\underline{150} \\
237 \\
\underline{225} \\
125 \\
\underline{125}
\end{array}
$$

Converting Decimals to Fractions

12. $\dfrac{21}{250}$

$$
0.084 = \frac{84}{1,000} = \frac{21}{250}
$$

Converting Fractions to Decimals

13. 0.875

$$
\frac{7}{8} \rightarrow 8\overline{)7.000}
$$

$$
\begin{array}{r}
.875 \\
8\overline{)7.000} \\
\underline{64} \\
60 \\
\underline{56} \\
40 \\
\underline{40}
\end{array}
$$

Converting Percents to Fractions

14. $\dfrac{9}{25}$

$$36\% = \frac{36}{100} = \frac{9}{25}$$

Percents

15. **185.26**

$$59\% \text{ of } 314 = (0.59)(314) = \begin{array}{r} 314 \\ \times\, 0.59 \\ \hline 2826 \\ 1570 \\ \hline 185.26 \end{array}$$

16. 62.5%, or $62\dfrac{1}{2}\%$

$$240 \cdot x = 150$$
$$x = \frac{150}{240} = \frac{5}{8} \rightarrow 8\overline{)5.000} \quad \begin{array}{r} .625 \\ \underline{48} \\ 20 \\ \underline{16} \\ 40 \\ \underline{40} \end{array}$$

$$x = 0.625$$
$$x = 62.5\%$$

17. **80**

$$(0.35) \cdot x = 28$$
$$x = \frac{28}{0.35} \rightarrow 0.35\overline{)28.00} \rightarrow 35\overline{)2800} \quad \begin{array}{r} 80 \\ \underline{280} \\ 00 \end{array}$$

18. **$3,000**

$$I = P \cdot R \cdot T$$
$$= (15,000)(0.05)(4)$$
$$= (750)(4)$$
$$I = 3,000$$

19. **25%**

$$\text{Percent Increase} = \frac{\text{Increase}}{\text{Original Amount}}$$
$$= \frac{15}{60}$$
$$= \frac{1}{4}$$
$$= 0.25$$
$$= 25\%$$

Square Roots

20. **14 and 15**

Since $14^2 = 196$ and $15^2 = 225$, the value of $\sqrt{211}$ is between 14 and 15.

21. **$6\sqrt{10}$**

$$\sqrt{360} = \sqrt{36 \cdot 10}$$
$$= \sqrt{36} \cdot \sqrt{10}$$
$$= 6\sqrt{10}$$

Expanded Notation

22. $(4 \times 100) + (8 \times 10) + (3 \times 1) + \left(6 \times \frac{1}{10}\right) + \left(5 \times \frac{1}{100}\right)$

$$483.65 = 400 + 80 + 3 + \frac{6}{10} + \frac{5}{100}$$
$$= (4 \times 100) + (8 \times 10) + (3 \times 1) + \left(6 \times \frac{1}{10}\right) + \left(5 \times \frac{1}{100}\right)$$

Prime Numbers

23. **23, 29, 31, and 37**

The only numbers between 20 and 40 whose factors are 1 and the number itself are 23, 29, 31, and 37.

Measurement

24. **27 yards**

Since 36 inches = 1 yard, 972 inches = (972 ÷ 36) yards = 27 yards.

25. **136 pints**

Since 1 gallon = 4 quarts, 17 gallons = 4 × 17 = 68 quarts.
Since 1 quart = 2 pints, 68 quarts = 2 × 68 = 136 pints.

Arithmetic Review

This part of the chapter is a comprehensive arithmetic review of topics that are important for your success on the GRE. Pace yourself as you work through each topic area, and try to focus on one concept at a time. Continue to evaluate your progress as you complete the illustrated examples that accompany each explanation. After you have completed this section, conclude your review by working the practice questions at the end of this chapter.

In addition to the information in Chapter 2, "Math Fundamentals," two other references you will find helpful are the rules for "rounding-off numbers" and "order of operations," which follow.

Rules for Rounding-Off Numbers

1. Identify the digit in the place you are rounding to.
2. Look at the digit immediately to the right of this digit.
3. If the digit to the right is 5, 6, 7, 8, or 9, then increase the indicated place digit by 1.
4. If the digit to the right is 0, 1, 2, 3, or 4, then the indicated place digit remains unchanged.
5. If the number to be rounded is a whole number, all digits to the right of the indicated place are replaced by zeros.
6. If the number to be rounded is a decimal number, all digits to the right of the indicated place are omitted.

Examples

1. 384,652 rounded to the nearest hundred is 384,700.

2. 384,652 rounded to the nearest ten thousand is 380,000.

3. 32.9847 rounded to the nearest hundredth is 32.98.

4. −42.381 rounded to the nearest tenth is −42.4.

Rules for Order of Operations

When performing math calculations on the GRE, test-takers are often confused about what to do first when faced with multiple calculations in one problem. If multiplication, division, exponents, addition, subtraction, and parentheses are all contained in one problem, the *order of operations* eliminates any confusion about which operation to perform first.

When performing operations on real numbers, the following order rules should be followed:

1. Parentheses—Grouping symbols working from the inside out
2. Exponents and roots as they occur in order from left to right
3. Multiplication and division as they occur in order from left to right
4. Addition and subtraction as they occur in order from left to right

Tip: An easy way to remember the order of operations is <u>P</u>lease <u>E</u>xcuse <u>M</u>y <u>D</u>ear <u>A</u>unt <u>S</u>ally (Parentheses, Exponents, Multiplication, Division, Addition, Subtraction).

Examples

1.
$$\left[12 + 4(9-7)^3\right] - 5 \cdot 6 \quad \text{(parentheses first)}$$
$$= \left[12 + 4(2)^3\right] - 5 \cdot 6 \quad \text{(exponents next)}$$
$$= \left[12 + 4(8)\right] - 5 \cdot 6 \quad \text{(then mult/div from left to right)}$$
$$= \left[12 + 32\right] - 30 \quad \text{(then add/subtract from left to right)}$$
$$= 44 - 30$$
$$= 14$$

2. $3\left[3^2 + 2(4+1)\right]$ (parentheses first)

$= 3\left[3^2 + 2(5)\right]$ (exponents next)

$= 3[9 + 2(5)]$ (then mult/div from left to right)

$= 3[9 + 10]$ (then add/subtract from left to right)

$= 3[19]$

$= 57$

3. $-3^2 + (-2)^3 = -1(3)^2 + (-2)^3$ $\left(\begin{array}{l}\text{the exponent 2 only applies} \\ \text{to the 3, while the exponent 3} \\ \text{applies to the entire } (-2)\end{array}\right)$

$= -1(9) + (-8)$

$= -9 + (-8)$

$= -17$

Real Number Operations

Fluency and accuracy in math begins with understanding the basic rules for real number operations, including addition, subtraction, multiplication, and division.

Addition

Steps to Adding Real Numbers

1. If the two numbers have the same sign, add their absolute values (see "Absolute Value," p. 128) and keep the same sign.
2. If the two numbers have different signs, subtract their absolute values and take the sign of the number with the largest absolute value.
3. If the two numbers are opposites, their sum is zero.

Examples

1. $(-15) + (-8) = -23$

2. $(-38) + 25 = -13$

3. $(-10) + 26 = 16$

4. $14 + (-14) = 0$

Subtraction

Steps to Subtracting Real Numbers

1. To subtract two real numbers, rewrite the subtraction as addition and take the opposite of the number being subtracted.

2. As a formula, $a - b = a +$ (the opposite of b).

Examples

1. $(-12) - 13 = (-12) + (-13) = -25$

2. $24 - (-15) = 24 + 15 = 39$

3. $(-19) - 10 = (-19) + (-10) = -29$

Multiplication

Steps to Multiplying Real Numbers

1. If the two numbers have the same sign, multiply their absolute values, and their product is positive.

2. If the two numbers have different signs, multiply their absolute values, and their product is negative.

3. If one of the numbers is zero, the product is zero.

Examples

1. $(9) \cdot (-4) = -36$

2. $(-6) \times (-10) = 60$

3. $(-3)(-4)(-2)(5) = (12)(-2)(5) = (-24)(5) = -120$

Division

Steps to Dividing Real Numbers

1. If the two numbers have the same sign, divide their absolute values, and their quotient is positive.

2. If the two numbers have different signs, divide their absolute values, and their quotient is negative.

3. If the first number is zero and the divisor is any non-zero number, the quotient is zero.

Note: The divisor cannot be zero since division by zero is undefined.

Examples

1. $80 \div (-4) = -20$

2. $(-15) \div (-3) = 5$

3. $0 \div (-6) = 0$

Divisibility Rules

The following chart outlines some basic divisibility rules. Divisibility rules are shortcuts that help you simply look at a number to quickly determine whether it can be divided with no remainder. Memorizing these rules can help you immediately evaluate and rule out incorrect answer choices.

If a number is divisible by	Divisibility Rules
2	it ends in 0, 2, 4, 6, or 8
3	the sum of its digits is divisible by 3
4	the number formed by the last two digits is divisible by 4.
5	it ends in 0 or 5
6	it is divisible by 2 and by 3 (use the rules for both).
7	N/A (no simple rule)
8	the number formed by the last three digits is divisible by 8
9	the sum of its digits is divisible by 9
10	the last digit is 0

Examples

1. 4,635 is divisible by 3, 5, and 9 but not divisible by 2, 4, 6, 7, 8, or 10.

2. 41,408 is divisible by 2, 4, and 8 but not divisible by 3, 5, 6, 7, 9, or 10.

3. 570 is divisible by 2, 3, 5, 6, and 10 but not divisible by 4, 7, 8, or 9.

Fractions

A **fraction** is the comparison of two quantities a and b by division, written as $\frac{a}{b} = a \div b$. The expression above the fraction bar is called the **numerator,** and the expression below the fraction bar is called the **denominator.** Since division by zero is undefined, the denominator cannot be zero.

Negative Fractions

Fractions that are negative may be written in any one of three ways: $-\dfrac{a}{b} = \dfrac{-a}{b} = \dfrac{a}{-b}$, although they are usually expressed with the negative sign next to the fraction bar as $-\dfrac{a}{b}$.

Proper Fractions, Improper Fractions, and Mixed Numbers

Proper Fraction—a fraction in which the numerator is less than the denominator, such as $\dfrac{3}{4}$.

Improper Fraction—a fraction in which the numerator is greater than or equal to the denominator, such as $\dfrac{17}{5}$ or $\dfrac{4}{4}$. Note that when the numerator and the denominator are equal, the fraction is equal to 1.

Mixed Number—a fraction expression that is made of a whole number and a fraction, such as $6\dfrac{2}{3}$ or $5\dfrac{1}{4}$.

Reducing/Simplifying Fractions

On the GRE, multiple-choice answer choices containing fractions are expressed in lowest terms. However, in Numeric Entry fill-in questions, fractions do not need to be reduced to lowest terms; equivalent forms of the correct answer are all correct. To express a fraction in lowest terms, divide both the numerator and denominator by the largest number that will divide them both.

Examples

1. $\dfrac{42}{48} = \dfrac{42 \div 6}{48 \div 6} = \dfrac{7}{8}$

2. $\dfrac{16}{40} = \dfrac{16 \div 8}{40 \div 8} = \dfrac{2}{5}$

Equivalent Fractions

The denominators in fractions can be expanded by multiplying both the numerator and denominator by the same number to generate an equivalent fraction.

Examples

1. $\dfrac{3}{4} = \dfrac{3 \cdot 5}{4 \cdot 5} = \dfrac{15}{20}$

2. $\dfrac{5}{8} = \dfrac{5 \cdot 10}{8 \cdot 10} = \dfrac{50}{80}$

Factors

Factors of a number are the whole numbers whose product equals the given number with no remainder.

Examples

1. The factors of 21 are 1, 3, 7, and 21 since $1 \times 21 = 21$ and $3 \times 7 = 21$.

2. The factors of 24 are 1, 2, 3, 4, 6, 8, 12, and 24 since $1 \times 24 = 24$, $2 \times 12 = 24$, $3 \times 8 = 24$, and $4 \times 6 = 24$.

Common Factors

Common factors are those factors that are the same for two or more numbers.

Example

1. Find the common factors of 6 and 8.

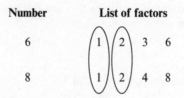

Number	List of factors
6	1 2 3 6
8	1 2 4 8

1 and 2 are common factors of 6 and 8.

> **Note: Some numbers may have many common factors.**

Greatest Common Factor (GCF)

The **greatest common factor (GCF)** is the largest factor common for two or more numbers.

Example

  1. Find the greatest common factor of 24 and 36.

Number	List of factors
24	1 2 3 4 6 8 **12** 24
36	1 2 3 4 6 9 **12** 18 36

Notice that while 1, 2, 3, 4, 6, and 12 are all common factors of 24 and 36, 12 is the greatest common factor. The GCF is 12.

Multiples

Multiples of a number are the product of that number and consecutive natural numbers.

Examples

  1. Multiples of 5 are 5, 10, 15, 20, 25, and so on.

  2. Multiples of 8 are 8, 16, 24, 32, 40, and so on.

Common Multiples

Common multiples are those multiples that are the same for two or more numbers.

Example

  1. Find the common multiples of 2 and 3.

Number	Multiples
2	2 4 6 8 10 12 14 16 18 etc.
3	3 6 9 12 15 18 etc.

The common multiples of 2 and 3 are 6, 12, 18, … Notice that common multiples go on indefinitely.

Least Common Multiple (LCM)

The **least common multiple (LCM)** is the smallest multiple common for two or more numbers.

Example

1. Find the least common multiple of 8 and 10.

Number	Multiples
8	8 16 24 32 40 48 56 etc.
10	10 20 30 40 50 60 etc.

The LCM of 8 and 10 is 40.

Note: In working with fractions, the least common denominator (LCD) of two or more fractions is the same as the LCM of the denominators.

Adding and Subtracting Fractions

When adding or subtracting fractions, the denominators must be the same. If the denominators are not the same, you must expand each fraction to the LCD of the two denominators and then add or subtract the numerators and keep the same denominator.

$$\text{Addition: } \frac{a}{c} + \frac{b}{c} = \frac{a+b}{c}$$

$$\text{Subtraction: } \frac{a}{c} - \frac{b}{c} = \frac{a-b}{c}$$

Examples

1. $\dfrac{1}{4} + \dfrac{2}{3} = \dfrac{3}{12} + \dfrac{8}{12} = \dfrac{11}{12}$

2. $\left(-\dfrac{1}{3}\right) - \dfrac{2}{5} = \left(-\dfrac{5}{15}\right) + \left(-\dfrac{6}{15}\right) = -\dfrac{11}{15}$

Adding and Subtracting Mixed Numbers

The rules for addition and subtraction also apply to mixed numbers. When adding and subtracting mixed numbers, add or subtract the whole numbers and add or subtract the fractions.

Examples

1. Addition:

$$6\frac{1}{3} = 6\frac{4}{12}$$

$$+3\frac{3}{4} = 3\frac{9}{12}$$

$$9\frac{13}{12} = 9 + \frac{13}{12} = 9 + 1\frac{1}{12} = 10\frac{1}{12}$$

2. Subtraction:

$$9\frac{3}{4} = 9\frac{6}{8}$$

$$-2\frac{5}{8} = 2\frac{5}{8}$$

$$7\frac{1}{8}$$

Tip: When you subtract mixed numbers, sometimes you may have to "borrow" from the whole number, just as you sometimes borrow from the next column when subtracting ordinary numbers.

3. Subtraction:

$$6 = \ 5\frac{5}{5} \leftarrow \Big\{ \text{borrow 1 in the form of } \frac{5}{5} \text{ from the 6}$$

$$-3\frac{1}{5} = -3\frac{1}{5}$$

$$2\frac{4}{5}$$

4. Subtraction:

$$6\frac{1}{8} - 3\frac{3}{4} = 6\frac{1}{8} - 3\frac{6}{8} = \overset{5}{\cancel{6}}\,\overset{9}{\cancel{\frac{1}{8}}} - 3\frac{6}{8} = 2\frac{3}{8}$$

Multiplying Fractions

The rules for multiplying integers also apply to multiplying fractions. Simply multiply the numerators and multiply the denominators. Reducing should be done before the multiplication if possible.

$$\frac{a}{b} \cdot \frac{c}{d} = \frac{a \cdot c}{b \cdot d}$$

When multiplying fractions, it is often possible to simplify the problem by *canceling*. To cancel, find a number that divides one numerator and one denominator. In the next example, 2 in the numerator and 12 in the denominator are both divisible by 2.

Examples

1. $\dfrac{\overset{1}{\cancel{2}}}{3} \times \dfrac{5}{\underset{6}{\cancel{12}}} = \dfrac{5}{18}$

> **Note: You can cancel only when *multiplying* fractions.**

2. $\dfrac{7}{12} \times \dfrac{8}{9} = \dfrac{7 \times \overset{2}{\cancel{8}}}{\underset{3}{\cancel{12}} \times 9} = \dfrac{14}{27}$

3. $3\dfrac{1}{3} \times \left(-5\dfrac{1}{4}\right) = \dfrac{10}{3} \times \dfrac{-21}{4} = \dfrac{\overset{5}{\cancel{10}} \times (\overset{-7}{\cancel{-21}})}{\underset{1}{\cancel{3}} \times \underset{2}{\cancel{4}}} = \dfrac{-35}{2} \text{ or } -17\dfrac{1}{2}$

Dividing Fractions

The rules for dividing integers also apply to dividing fractions. When dividing fractions, take the reciprocal (invert) of the second fraction (the one "divided by") and multiply. Simplify when possible.

$$\frac{a}{b} \div \frac{c}{d} = \frac{a}{b} \cdot \frac{d}{c} = \frac{a \cdot d}{b \cdot c}$$

Examples

1. $\dfrac{3}{14} \div \dfrac{9}{7} = \dfrac{3}{14} \cdot \dfrac{7}{9} = \dfrac{\cancel{3}^{1} \cdot \cancel{7}^{1}}{\cancel{14}_{2} \cdot \cancel{9}_{3}} = \dfrac{1}{6}$

2. $1\dfrac{1}{3} \div 4\dfrac{1}{6} = \dfrac{4}{3} \div \dfrac{25}{6} = \dfrac{4}{3} \cdot \dfrac{6}{25} = \dfrac{4 \cdot \cancel{6}^{2}}{\cancel{3}_{1} \cdot 25} = \dfrac{8}{25}$

Complex Fractions

Sometimes a division-of-fractions problem may appear in the form below. Division problems in this form are called **complex fractions.**

$$\frac{\dfrac{3}{4}}{\dfrac{7}{8}}$$

The line separating the two fractions means "divided by." This problem may be rewritten as $\dfrac{3}{4} \div \dfrac{7}{8}$. Now follow the same procedure as previously shown.

$$\frac{3}{4} \div \frac{7}{8} = \frac{3}{\cancel{4}_{1}} \times \frac{\cancel{8}^{2}}{7} = \frac{6}{7}$$

Some complex fractions require applying the order of operations.

Example

1. $\dfrac{1}{3+\dfrac{2}{1+\dfrac{1}{3}}}$

This problem can be rewritten using grouping symbols.

$\dfrac{1}{3+\dfrac{2}{1+\dfrac{1}{3}}} = 1 \div \left\{ 3 + \left[2 \div \left(1 + \dfrac{1}{3} \right) \right] \right\}$ Start with the most inside grouping.

$= 1 \div \left\{ 3 + \left[2 \div \left(\dfrac{4}{3} \right) \right] \right\}$ Do the next most inside grouping.

$= 1 \div \left\{ 3 + \left[\dfrac{\cancel{2}^{1}}{1} \times \dfrac{3}{\cancel{4}_{2}} \right] \right\}$

$= 1 \div \left\{ 3 + \left[\dfrac{3}{2} \right] \right\}$ Do the next most inside grouping.

$= 1 \div \left\{ \dfrac{9}{2} \right\}$

$= 1 \times \dfrac{2}{9}$

$= \dfrac{2}{9}$

Decimals

Each position in any decimal number has **place value.** For instance, in the number 485.03, the 4 is in the hundreds place, the 8 is in the tens place, the 5 is in the ones place, the 0 is in the tenths place, and the 3 is in the hundredths place. The following chart will help you identify place value and will help you visually identify the positions of decimal points.

millions	hundred thousands	ten thousands	thousands	hundreds	tens	ones	tenths	hundredths	thousandths	ten thousandths	hundred thousandths
							1/10	1/100	1/1,000	1/10,000	1/100,000
1,000,000	100,000	10,000	1,000	100	10	1	0.1	0.01	0.001	0.0001	0.00001
10^6	10^5	10^4	10^3	10^2	10^1	10^0	10^{-1}	10^{-2}	10^{-3}	10^{-4}	10^{-5}
				4	8	5	0	3			

Adding and Subtracting Decimals

To add or subtract decimals, line up the decimal points and add or subtract in the same manner that you would add or subtract other numbers. It is often helpful to fill in zeros to the right of the decimal point before adding or subtracting.

Examples

1.
$$632.9 + 18.34 + 0.056 = 632.900$$
$$18.340$$
$$+ \ 0.056$$
$$651.296$$

2.
$$86.7 - 17.93 = \ 86.70$$
$$-17.93$$
$$68.77$$

A whole number has an understood decimal point to its right.

3.
$$17 - 8.43 = 1\overset{6}{\cancel{7}}.\overset{\cancel{1}9}{\cancel{0}}\overset{1}{0}$$
$$- \ 8 \ . \ 4 \ 3$$
$$8 \ . \ 5 \ 7$$

Multiplying Decimals

To multiply decimals, multiply as usual and take the sum of the digits to the right of the decimal points in the original numbers to determine decimal point placement in the product. This sum indicates the number of digits to the right of the decimal point in the product. It is sometimes necessary to insert zeros immediately to the right of the decimal point in the product to have the correct number of digits.

Examples

1.

$$8.001 \leftarrow \{3 \text{ digits to the right of the decimal point}$$
$$\times \quad 2.4 \leftarrow \{1 \text{ digit to the right of the decimal point}$$
$$32004$$
$$16002$$
$$19.2024 \quad \begin{cases} \text{decimal point placed so there is the same number} \\ \text{of digits to the right of the decimal point } (1+3=4) \end{cases}$$

2.

$$24.58 \times 6.3 = 24.58 \quad (2 \text{ digits})$$
$$\times\ 6.3 \quad (1 \text{ digit})$$
$$7374$$
$$14748$$
$$154.854 \quad (3 \text{ digits})$$

Dividing Decimals

When dividing decimals, the **divisor** (the number you are dividing by) should always be a whole number. If the divisor is not a whole number, move the decimal point to the right to make the divisor a whole number and then move the decimal point the same number of places in the **dividend** (the number being divided into). Sometimes you may have to insert zeros in the dividend (the number inside the division bracket).

Examples

1. $4.872 \div 0.14 = 0.14.\overline{)4.87.2} = 14\overline{)487.2}$ with quotient 34.8

2. $48 \div 0.008 = 0.008\overline{)48.000} = 8\overline{)48,000}$ with quotient $6,000$

Converting Decimals to Fractions

When converting decimals to fractions, numbers to the left of the decimal point are whole numbers and numbers to the right of the decimal point are expressed as fractions determined by their place value.

Examples

1. $0.19 = \dfrac{19}{100}$

2. $0.084 = \dfrac{84}{1,000} = \dfrac{21}{250}$

3. $8.6 = 8\dfrac{6}{10} = 8\dfrac{3}{5}$

Converting Fractions to Decimals

To convert a fraction to a decimal, divide the numerator of the fraction by the denominator of the fraction. Zeros may be written to the right of the decimal point in the numerator without changing its value. The division will result in a decimal that either terminates (ends) or has a number or block of numbers that repeat indefinitely. To indicate a repeating decimal, a bar is used over only the number or block of numbers that repeat.

Examples

1. $\dfrac{5}{8} = 8\overline{)5.000}^{.625} = 0.625$ (terminating decimal)

2. $\dfrac{5}{12} = 12\overline{)5.00000}^{.41666} = 0.41\overline{6}$ (repeating decimal)

Ratios and Proportions

Ratios

A **ratio** is a comparison of two quantities and generally is expressed as a fraction. The ratio of a to b may be written as $\dfrac{a}{b}$, or $a{:}b$.

Examples

1. The ratio of 9 to 20 is $\dfrac{9}{20}$ or 9:20.

2. The ratio of 32 to 40 is $\dfrac{32}{40} = \dfrac{4}{5}$ or 4:5.

Proportion

A **proportion** is an equality statement between two ratios. Because $\frac{5}{10}$ and $\frac{4}{8}$ both have a value of $\frac{1}{2}$, it can be stated that $\frac{5}{10} = \frac{4}{8}$.

Cross-Products Rule

In a proportion, the cross products (multiplying across the equal sign) always produce equal answers. If $\frac{a}{b} = \frac{c}{d}$ is a true proportion, then their cross products are equal: $a \cdot d = b \cdot c$.

In the example of $\frac{5}{10} = \frac{4}{8}$, $5 \times 8 = 10 \times 4$. You can use this cross-products rule to solve proportions.

Examples

1. $\frac{32}{40} = \frac{4}{5}$ is a true proportion since $32 \cdot 5 = 40 \cdot 4$.

2. $\frac{12}{18} = \frac{3}{4}$ is not a true proportion since $12 \cdot 4 \neq 18 \cdot 3$.

Percents

A **percent** is a ratio of a number compared to 100 (hundredths). The symbol for percent is %. For example, the expression 29% is read as 29 hundredths and can be expressed either as a fraction or decimal:

$$29\% = \frac{29}{100} = 0.29$$

Converting Percents to Decimals

Steps to convert a percent to a decimal:

1. Drop the percent symbol.
2. Shift the decimal point two places to the left.
3. Add zeros if necessary.

Examples

   1. $6\% = 0.06$

   2. $37\% = 0.37$

Converting Decimals to Percents

Steps to convert a decimal to a percent:

1. Move the decimal point two places to the right.
2. Add the percent symbol.
3. Add zeros if necessary.

Examples

   1. $0.73 = 73\%$

   2. $5.2 = 520\%$

Converting Percents to Fractions

Steps to convert a percent to a fraction:

1. Drop the percent symbol.
2. Express the number as a fraction over 100 and simplify if possible.

Examples

   1. $70\% = \dfrac{70}{100} = \dfrac{7}{10}$

   2. $6\% = \dfrac{6}{100} = \dfrac{3}{50}$

Converting Fractions to Percents

Steps to convert a fraction to a percent:

1. Convert the fraction to a decimal.
2. Convert the decimal to a percent.

Examples

1. $\dfrac{4}{5} = 0.8 = 80\%$

2. $\dfrac{9}{2} = 4\dfrac{1}{2} = 4.5 = 450\%$

Fraction-Decimal-Percent Equivalents

A time-saving tip is to try to memorize some of the following equivalents before you take the GRE to eliminate unnecessary computations on the day of the exam.

$\dfrac{1}{100} = 0.01 = 1\%$

$\dfrac{1}{10} = 0.1 = 10\%$

$\dfrac{1}{5} = \dfrac{2}{10} = 0.2 = 0.20 = 20\%$

$\dfrac{3}{10} = 0.3 = 0.30 = 30\%$

$\dfrac{2}{5} = \dfrac{4}{10} = 0.4 = 0.40 = 40\%$

$\dfrac{1}{2} = \dfrac{5}{10} = 0.5 = 0.50 = 50\%$

$\dfrac{3}{5} = \dfrac{6}{10} = 0.6 = 0.60 = 60\%$

$\dfrac{7}{10} = 0.7 = 0.70 = 70\%$

$\dfrac{4}{5} = \dfrac{8}{10} = 0.8 = 0.80 = 80\%$

$\dfrac{9}{10} = 0.9 = 0.90 = 90\%$

$\dfrac{1}{4} = \dfrac{25}{100} = 0.25 = 25\%$

$\dfrac{3}{4} = \dfrac{75}{100} = 0.75 = 75\%$

$\dfrac{1}{3} = 0.33\dfrac{1}{3} = 33\dfrac{1}{3}\%$

$\dfrac{2}{3} = 0.66\dfrac{2}{3} = 66\dfrac{2}{3}\%$

$\dfrac{1}{8} = 0.125 = 0.12\dfrac{1}{2} = 12\dfrac{1}{2}\%$

$\dfrac{3}{8} = 0.375 = 0.37\dfrac{1}{2} = 37\dfrac{1}{2}\%$

$\dfrac{5}{8} = 0.625 = 0.62\dfrac{1}{2} = 62\dfrac{1}{2}\%$

$\dfrac{7}{8} = 0.875 = 0.87\dfrac{1}{2} = 87\dfrac{1}{2}\%$

$\dfrac{1}{6} = 0.16\dfrac{2}{3} = 16\dfrac{2}{3}\%$

$\dfrac{5}{6} = 0.83\dfrac{1}{3} = 83\dfrac{1}{3}\%$

$1 = 1.00 = 100\%$

$2 = 2.00 = 200\%$

$3\dfrac{1}{2} = 3.50 = 350\%$

Solving Percent Problems

Before attempting to solve a percent problem, change the percent to a fraction or decimal depending upon what seems appropriate. Keep in mind that the word "of" suggests the operation of multiplication. These are common types of problems on the GRE.

Examples

Remember that "of" means to multiply.

1. What is 15% *of* 50?

Using fractions: $15\% \text{ of } 50 = \dfrac{\overset{3}{\cancel{15}}}{\underset{\underset{2}{20}}{\cancel{100}}} \times \dfrac{\overset{5}{\cancel{50}}}{1} = \dfrac{15}{2} = 7\dfrac{1}{2}$ or 7.5

Using decimals: $15\% \text{ of } 50 = 0.15 \times 50 = 7.5$

2. What is 17% *of* 80?

To find the percent, you must eliminate the percent sign and move the decimal two places to the left (add zeros as necessary). Therefore, $17\% = 0.17$.

$0.17 \times 80 = 13.6$

3. 24 is 30% *of* what number?

$$0.30(x) = 24$$
$$x = \frac{24}{0.3}$$
$$x = 80$$

4. 24 is what percent *of* 32?

$$x(32) = 24$$
$$x = \frac{24}{32} = \frac{3}{4} = 0.75$$
$$x = 75\%$$

5. $16\frac{2}{3}\%$ *of* what is 15? ✓

Making $16\frac{2}{3}\%$ into a fraction is the best way to begin.

$$16\frac{2}{3}\% = \left(\frac{\overset{1}{\cancel{50}}}{3}\right)\left(\frac{1}{\underset{2}{\cancel{100}}}\right) = \frac{1}{6}$$

equation method	proportion method
$\left(\frac{1}{6}\right)x = 15$	$\dfrac{16\frac{2}{3}}{100} = \dfrac{15}{x}$
$x = \left(\frac{15}{1}\right)\left(\frac{6}{1}\right)$	$\dfrac{1}{6} = \dfrac{15}{x}$
$x = 90$	$x = (15)(6)$
	$x = 90$

$16\frac{2}{3}\%$ of 90 is 15. The answer is 90.

Percent Change: Finding Percent Increase or Percent Decrease

Word problems with percent changes are frequent questions on the GRE. Make sure that you are familiar with solving this type of problem. To find the percent increase/decrease, use one of the following two formulas. Note: The terms "percentage rise," "percentage fall," and "percentage change" are the same as "percent change."

Percent Change Formula 1

$$\text{percent change} = \frac{\text{increase/decrease (amount of change)}}{\text{original amount}}$$

Examples

1. Find the percent increase from 12 to 16.

   The amount of change from 12 to 16 equals 4, therefore

   $$\text{percent change} = \frac{\text{increase}}{\text{original amount}}$$
   $$= \frac{4}{12} = \frac{1}{3} = 0.33\frac{1}{3}$$
   $$= 33\frac{1}{3}\%$$

2. Find the percent decrease from 16 to 12.

   The amount of change from 16 to 12 equals 4, therefore

   $$\text{percent change} = \frac{\text{decrease}}{\text{original amount}}$$
   $$= \frac{4}{16} = \frac{1}{4} = 0.25$$
   $$= 25\%$$

Percent Change Formula 2

$$\frac{\text{amount of change}}{\text{starting amount}} \times 100\% = \text{percent change}$$

Examples

1. What is the percent decrease of Scott's salary if it went from $150 per hour to $100 per hour?

   $$\frac{\text{amount of change}}{\text{starting amount}} \times 100\% = \frac{\overset{1}{\cancel{50}}}{\underset{3}{\cancel{150}}} \times 100\%$$
   $$= \left(\frac{100}{3}\right)\%$$
   $$= 33\frac{1}{3}\% \text{ decrease}$$

2. Which is greater, the percent change from 5 to 8 or the percent change from 8 to 5?

Percent change from 5 to 8:

$$\frac{\text{amount of change}}{\text{starting amount}} \times 100\% = \frac{3}{5} \times 100\% = 60\% \text{ change}$$

Percent change from 8 to 5:

$$\frac{\text{amount of change}}{\text{starting amount}} \times 100\% = \frac{3}{8} \times 100\% = 37\frac{1}{2}\% \text{ change}$$

The percent change from 5 to 8 is greater than the percent change from 8 to 5.

Square Roots and Cube Roots

Calculating square roots can be time-consuming. One advantage in taking the GRE by computer is that you will have access to an on-screen calculator to help you easily find square root results. After calculating the square root, use your knowledge of rounding off to determine the desired place value.

Perfect Squares

A **perfect square** is a product that results from squaring a number (multiplying a number by itself). It is useful to memorize the perfect squares found by squaring the integers 1 through 15:

1, 4, 9, 16, 25, 36, 49, 64, 81, 100, 121, 144, 169, 196, and 225

Note that these are also found by squaring the integers (-1) through (-15).

Examples

1. 64 is a perfect square since $8^2 = 8 \cdot 8 = 64$.

2. 900 is a perfect square since $30^2 = 30 \cdot 30 = 900$.

Perfect Cubes

A **perfect cube** is a product that results from cubing a number (multiplying a number by itself **two** times). It is useful to memorize the perfect cubes found by cubing the integers 1 through 6:

$$1, 8, 27, 64, 125, \text{ and } 216$$

and (−1) through (−6):

$$-1, -8, -27, -64, -125, \text{ and } -216$$

Examples

1. 216 is a perfect cube since $6^3 = 6 \cdot 6 \cdot 6 = 216$.

2. −64 is a perfect cube since $(-4)^3 = (-4) \cdot (-4) \cdot (-4) = -64$.

3. 8,000 is a perfect cube since $20^3 = 20 \cdot 20 \cdot 20 = 8,000$.

Square Roots

To determine the square root of a number, you must find a number that when multiplied by itself yields the original number. The symbol for the square root is $\sqrt{}$.

Examples

1. $\sqrt{81} = 9$

2. $-\sqrt{144} = -12$

3. $\sqrt{-36}$ does not exist. Note that the square root of a negative number is not a real number.

Square Roots of Non-Perfect Squares

To find the square root of a number that is not a perfect square, it is necessary to find an approximate answer.

Example

1. Between what two consecutive integers is $\sqrt{135}$, and to which is it closer?

$\sqrt{135}$ is between $\sqrt{121}$ and $\sqrt{144}$.

$$\sqrt{121} < \sqrt{135} < \sqrt{144}, \text{ and } \sqrt{121} = 11, \sqrt{144} = 12$$
$$11 < \sqrt{135} < 12$$

Since 135 is closer to 144 than 121, $\sqrt{135}$ is closer to 12 than to 11.

Cube Roots

To determine the cube root of a number, you must find a number that when multiplied by itself two times yields the original number. The symbol for the cube root is $\sqrt[3]{\ }$.

Examples

1. $\sqrt[3]{27} = 3$

2. $\sqrt[3]{-64} = -4$

3. $\sqrt[3]{216} = 6$

Simplifying Square Roots and Cube Roots

To simplify square roots, factor the number under the square root symbol $\sqrt{\ }$ into two factors so that one of its factors is the largest perfect square that divides the number. To simplify cube roots, factor the number under the cube root symbol so that one of its factors is the largest perfect cube that divides the number.

Examples

1. $\sqrt{40} = \sqrt{4 \cdot 10} = \sqrt{4} \cdot \sqrt{10} = 2\sqrt{10}$

2. $\sqrt[3]{40} = \sqrt[3]{8 \cdot 5} = \sqrt[3]{8} \cdot \sqrt[3]{5} = 2\sqrt[3]{5}$

3. $\sqrt{700} = \sqrt{100 \cdot 7} = \sqrt{100} \cdot \sqrt{7} = 10\sqrt{7}$

4. $\sqrt[3]{750} = \sqrt[3]{125 \cdot 6} = \sqrt[3]{125} \cdot \sqrt[3]{6} = 5\sqrt[3]{6}$

Another method to simplify square roots is to completely factor the number under the $\sqrt{\ }$ into prime factors and then simplify by bringing out any factors that occur in pairs.

Example

1. Simplify $\sqrt{80}$.

$$
\begin{array}{ll}
\text{Method 1.} & \text{Method 2.} \\
\sqrt{80} = \sqrt{16 \times 5} & \sqrt{80} = \sqrt{2 \times 40} \\
\quad = \sqrt{16} \times \sqrt{5} & \quad = \sqrt{2 \times 2 \times 20} \\
\quad = 4\sqrt{5} & \quad = \sqrt{2 \times 2 \times 2 \times 10} \\
& \quad = \sqrt{2 \times 2 \times 2 \times 2 \times 5} \\
& \quad = \sqrt{2 \times 2} \times \sqrt{2 \times 2} \times \sqrt{5} \\
& \quad = 2 \times 2 \times \sqrt{5} \\
& \quad = 4\sqrt{5}
\end{array}
$$

Word Problems

Word problems can be time-consuming and challenge your thinking processes. Word problems are typical on the GRE. Make sure that you precisely identify and understand what is being asked in the problem so that it makes sense. This will help you translate the words into a math equation to solve the problem. Use scratch paper to write down notes as you organize the equation "setup" and prepare to answer the question.

Examples

1. Maria purchased a pair of jeans that sell for \$39.99. If the sales tax on the purchase was 8.5%, what was the total cost of the jeans?

$$
\begin{aligned}
\text{Sales tax} &= 8.5\% \text{ of } \$39.99 \\
&= (0.085)(\$39.99) \\
&= \$3.39915 \\
&= \$3.40 \text{ (rounded to two decimal places)}
\end{aligned}
$$

$$
\text{Total cost} = \$39.99 + \$3.40 = \$43.39
$$

2. A history class has 24 female students enrolled and 16 male students enrolled. What is the ratio of male students to the total number of students in the class?

$$\text{ratio} = \frac{\text{number of male students}}{\text{total number of students}}$$
$$= \frac{16}{24+16}$$
$$= \frac{16}{40}$$
$$= \frac{2}{5}$$

A ratio of $\frac{2}{5}$ means that there are 2 male students for every 5 students in the class.

3. Anton purchased 6 boxes of candy at a cost of $1.29 each. If he paid for the purchase with a $20 bill, how much change should he receive?

The cost of the 6 boxes of candy is $6 \times \$1.29 = \$7.74$

If he paid for the purchase with a $20 bill, the change would be

$$
\begin{array}{r}
\$20.00 \\
-\ 7.74 \\
\hline
\$12.26
\end{array}
$$

4. Nathan borrowed $20,000 for an auto loan at an annual interest rate of 4%. What is the total amount Nathan will pay for the loan if he takes 5 years for the loan repayment?

The simple interest I on a loan with a principle P, an annual interest rate R, and the time in years T to repay the loan is

$$I = P \cdot R \cdot T$$
$$= (\$20,000)(0.04)(5)$$
$$= (800)(5)$$
$$= \$4,000$$

The total amount A that Nathan will pay for the loan is

$$A = P + I$$
$$= \$20,000 + \$4,000$$
$$A = \$24,000$$

Arithmetic Practice Questions

Now that you have reviewed arithmetic topics and concepts, you can practice on your own. Questions appear in four categories by question type: quantitative comparison, multiple-choice (select one answer), multiple-choice (select one or more answers), and numeric entry (fill-in). These practice questions are grouped by question type to give you a chance to practice solving problems in the same format as the GRE. The answers and explanations that follow the questions will include strategies to help you understand how to solve the problems.

General Directions: For each question, indicate the best answer from the choices given.

- All numbers used are real numbers.
- All figures are assumed to lie in a plane unless otherwise indicated.
- Geometric figures, such as lines, circles, triangles, and quadrilaterals, are not necessarily drawn to scale. That is, you should **not** assume that quantities such as lengths and angle measurements are as they appear in the figure. You should assume, however, that lines shown as straight are actually straight, points on a line are in the order shown, and more generally, all geometric objects are in the relative position shown. For questions with geometric figures, you should base your answer on geometric reasoning, not on estimating or comparing quantities by sight or by measurement.
- Coordinate systems, such as xy-planes and number lines, are drawn to scale; therefore, you can read, estimate, or compare quantities in such figures by sight or by measurement.
- Graphical data presentations, such as bar graphs, pie graphs, and line graphs, are drawn to scale; therefore, you can read, estimate, or compare data values by sight or by measurement.

Answer choices in this study guide have lettered choices A, B, C, D, E, etc., for clarity, but letters will not appear on the actual exam. On the actual computer version of the exam, you will be required to click on ovals or squares to select your answer.

HELPFUL HINT

○ oval—answer will be a single choice.

☐ square box—answer will be one or more choices.

Quantitative Comparison

Directions: For questions 1 to 15, compare Quantity A and Quantity B, using additional information centered above the two quantities if such information is given. Select one of the following four answer choices for each question:

Ⓐ Quantity A is greater.

Ⓑ Quantity B is greater.

Ⓒ The two quantities are equal.

Ⓓ The relationship cannot be determined from the information given.

	Quantity A	**Quantity B**
1.	84% of 73	73% of 84

	Quantity A	**Quantity B**
2.	$\dfrac{13}{15}$	$\dfrac{22}{25}$

	Quantity A	**Quantity B**
3.	$\sqrt{98}$	$8\sqrt{2}$

	Quantity A	**Quantity B**
4.	13 pounds	200 ounces

	Quantity A	**Quantity B**
5.	$8^2 + 9^2$	$(8+9)^2$

Quantity A

6. the number of prime numbers between 60 and 70

Quantity B

the number of prime numbers between 70 and 80

7.

Quantity A	Quantity B
$(97 \cdot 83) \cdot 124$	$97 \cdot (83 \cdot 124)$

8.

Quantity A	Quantity B
the percent increase from 80 to 100	the percent decrease from 100 to 80

9.

Quantity A	Quantity B
the product of any two different prime numbers	10

10.

Quantity A	Quantity B
$\dfrac{1}{3} \times \dfrac{1}{4} \times \dfrac{1}{5}$	$0.3 \times 0.25 \times 0.2$

11.

Quantity A	Quantity B
the number of multiples of 6 between 1 and 50	the number of whole number factors of 24

12.

Quantity A	Quantity B
the number of days in 23 weeks	the number of hours in 7 days

13.

Quantity A	Quantity B
the remainder when 7,890 is divided by 6	the remainder when 7,890 is divided by 15

14.

Quantity A	Quantity B
$\dfrac{1}{5} + \dfrac{1}{6} + \dfrac{1}{7} + \dfrac{1}{8}$	$\dfrac{1}{6} + \dfrac{1}{7} + \dfrac{1}{8} + \dfrac{1}{9}$

15.

Quantity A	Quantity B
the least common multiple of 8 and 10	the least common multiple of 8 and 12

Multiple-Choice (Select One Answer)

Directions: Questions 16 to 30 require you to select one answer choice.

16. Which of the following numbers would lie between $\frac{1}{8}$ and $\frac{1}{9}$ on a real number line?

- Ⓐ 0.11
- Ⓑ 0.12
- Ⓒ 0.13
- Ⓓ 0.18
- Ⓔ 0.19

17. Which of the following is not a prime number?

- Ⓐ 53
- Ⓑ 61
- Ⓒ 79
- Ⓓ 87
- Ⓔ 97

18. How many numbers between 1 and 100 are multiples of both 6 and 8?

- Ⓐ 4
- Ⓑ 6
- Ⓒ 8
- Ⓓ 10
- Ⓔ 14

19. Which of the following lies between $\frac{1}{5}$ and $\frac{1}{6}$ on a real number line?

- Ⓐ $\frac{1}{30}$

- Ⓑ $\frac{1}{11}$

- Ⓒ $\frac{11}{60}$

- Ⓓ $\frac{7}{30}$

- Ⓔ $\frac{11}{30}$

20. Jorge bought a shirt for $29.99 plus 8% sales tax. How much did he pay for the shirt?

   Ⓐ $32.00

   Ⓑ $32.38

   Ⓒ $32.39

   Ⓓ $33.00

   Ⓔ $37.99

21. What is the reciprocal of $7\frac{2}{3}$?

   Ⓐ $\dfrac{3}{23}$

   Ⓑ $\dfrac{3}{17}$

   Ⓒ $\dfrac{3}{14}$

   Ⓓ $\dfrac{23}{3}$

   Ⓔ $7\dfrac{3}{2}$

22. Which of the following is the closest approximation of $\sqrt{91}$?

   Ⓐ   9.1

   Ⓑ   9.3

   Ⓒ   9.5

   Ⓓ   9.7

   Ⓔ   9.9

23. Which of the following numbers is divisible by 15?

   Ⓐ   715

   Ⓑ   730

   Ⓒ   815

   Ⓓ   905

   Ⓔ   915

24. Evaluate: $19 + 4 \cdot 2^2 - 10 \div 5$

   Ⓐ   5

   Ⓑ $16\dfrac{2}{5}$

   Ⓒ   33

   Ⓓ   81

   Ⓔ   90

25. Evaluate: $(-1)^4 \cdot (-2)^3 \cdot (-3)^2$

    Ⓐ −288

    Ⓑ −72

    Ⓒ −36

    Ⓓ 72

    Ⓔ 288

26. Simplify: $\sqrt{252}$

    Ⓐ 126

    Ⓑ $36\sqrt{7}$

    Ⓒ 16

    Ⓓ $6\sqrt{7}$

    Ⓔ $5\sqrt{2}$

27. Find the percent decrease from 75 to 60.

    Ⓐ 15

    Ⓑ 20

    Ⓒ 25

    Ⓓ 80

    Ⓔ 125

28. Evaluate: $0.0576 \div 1.2$

    Ⓐ 0.0048

    Ⓑ 0.048

    Ⓒ 0.48

    Ⓓ 4.8

    Ⓔ 48

29. Which of the following decimals is equivalent to $\dfrac{5}{16}$?

    Ⓐ 0.3125

    Ⓑ $0.\overline{3}$

    Ⓒ 0.516

    Ⓓ 3.125

    Ⓔ 3.2

30. A student answered 28 questions correctly on a test and received a score of 80%. How many questions were on the test?

 Ⓐ 25

 Ⓑ 35

 Ⓒ 36

 Ⓓ 52

 Ⓔ 108

Multiple-Choice (Select One or More Answers)

Directions: Questions 31 to 45 require you to select one or more answer choices.

31. Which of the following are prime numbers?

 A 39

 B 51

 C 61

 D 73

 E 87

32. In 2012, Toby spent between 25% and 30% of his $75,000 salary on housing. Which of the following could have been the amount that Toby spent on housing?

 A $17,000

 B $18,000

 C $19,000

 D $20,000

 E $21,000

 F $22,000

33. A test has a total of 33 questions. Which of the following could be the number of questions answered correctly to score at least 75% on the test?

 A 20

 B 21

 C 22

 D 23

 E 24

 F 25

 G 26

34. Which of the following fractions lie between $\frac{3}{5}$ and $\frac{3}{4}$ on the real number line?

    Ⓐ   0.6

    Ⓑ   0.65

    Ⓒ   0.7

    Ⓓ   0.75

    Ⓔ   0.8

    Ⓕ   0.85

    Ⓖ   0.9

35. Which of the following numbers are divisible by 6?

    Ⓐ   66

    Ⓑ   76

    Ⓒ   86

    Ⓓ   96

    Ⓔ   106

    Ⓕ   126

36. Which of the following numbers would be in the sequence 2, 3, 5, 8, 12, 17, …?

    Ⓐ   22

    Ⓑ   23

    Ⓒ   29

    Ⓓ   30

    Ⓔ   40

    Ⓕ   57

    Ⓖ   80

37. Which of the following fractions are equivalent to $\frac{3}{8}$?

    Ⓐ $\frac{6}{16}$ Ⓔ $\frac{13}{18}$

    Ⓑ $\frac{8}{13}$ Ⓕ $\frac{24}{64}$

    Ⓒ $\frac{15}{40}$ Ⓖ $\frac{9}{64}$

    Ⓓ $\frac{30}{80}$

38. Which of the following numbers are multiples of 8 and perfect squares?

   Ⓐ 8
   Ⓑ 16
   Ⓒ 40
   Ⓓ 64
   Ⓔ 100
   Ⓕ 144

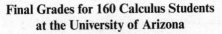

**Final Grades for 160 Calculus Students
at the University of Arizona**

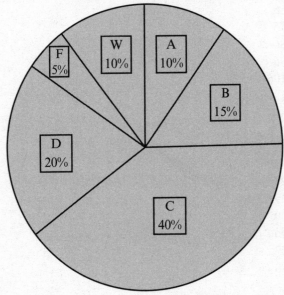

39. In the preceding graph, which grades were achieved by more than 20 calculus students at the college?

   Ⓐ A
   Ⓑ B
   Ⓒ C
   Ⓓ D
   Ⓔ F
   Ⓕ W

40. If the product of two positive integers is odd, which of the following could be one of the integers?

- Ⓐ 5
- Ⓑ 8
- Ⓒ 10
- Ⓓ 11
- Ⓔ 12
- Ⓕ 19

41. If the sum of two integers is negative, which of the following could be one of the integers?

- Ⓐ −8
- Ⓑ −1
- Ⓒ 0
- Ⓓ 1
- Ⓔ 3
- Ⓕ 6

42. If a product costs $47, which of the following sales tax rates would keep the total cost less than $50?

- Ⓐ 5.0%
- Ⓑ 5.5%
- Ⓒ 6.0%
- Ⓓ 6.5%
- Ⓔ 7.0%
- Ⓕ 7.5%

43. Which of the following decimals lie between 0.53 and 0.842 on the real number line?

- Ⓐ 0.394
- Ⓑ 0.4
- Ⓒ 0.5314
- Ⓓ 0.71
- Ⓔ 0.85
- Ⓕ 0.9

44. Which of the following fractions are greater than 7?

A $\dfrac{39}{5}$

B $\dfrac{75}{11}$

C $\dfrac{65}{9}$

D $\dfrac{20}{3}$

E $\dfrac{90}{15}$

F $\dfrac{55}{8}$

45. Which of the following fractions are equivalent to 0.75?

A $\dfrac{30}{40}$

B $\dfrac{12}{16}$

C $\dfrac{15}{20}$

D $\dfrac{3}{4}$

E $\dfrac{48}{60}$

F $\dfrac{21}{28}$

Numeric Entry (Fill-in)

Directions: Questions 46 to 60 require you to solve the problem and write your answer in a box or boxes.

- Write out your answer choice with numerals.
- Your answer may be an integer, a decimal, or a fraction, and it may be negative.
- If a question asks for a fraction, there will be two boxes—one for the numerator and one for the denominator.
- Equivalent forms of the correct answer, such as 4.5 and 4.50, are all correct. Fractions do not need to be reduced to lowest terms.
- Write out the exact answer unless the question asks you to round your answer.

46. If $\dfrac{7}{8} = \dfrac{\boxed{}}{72}$, what must the numerator of the second fraction be?

$$\boxed{}$$

47. What is the number of inches in 15 yards?

$$\boxed{}$$

48. $4^3 \cdot 3^4 = \boxed{}$

$$\boxed{}$$

49. $9 + 3 \cdot 5 - 10 \div 2 = \boxed{}$

$$\boxed{}$$

50. What percent of 8 is 11, rounded to the nearest tenth of one percent?

$$\boxed{}\%$$

51. $\sqrt{81} \times \sqrt[3]{64} \times \sqrt[3]{8} = \boxed{}$

$\boxed{}$

52. What is the first prime number greater than 80?

$\boxed{}$

53. How many hours are there in 5 weeks 3 days?

$\boxed{}$

54. What is the quotient of $6.25 \div 0.52$ to the nearest hundredth?

$\boxed{}$

55. What is the fraction expression, in simplest form, for the decimal 0.064?

56. What is 17% of 135?

$\boxed{}$

57. How many gallons are there in 140 pints?

$\boxed{}$

58. What is the closest whole number on the real number line to $\sqrt{159}$?

$\boxed{}$

59. What is 658,143 rounded to the nearest ten thousand?

> [ ]

60. What is the decimal value of 0.05^2?

> [ ]

Charting and Analyzing Your Practice Results

The first step in analyzing the practice exercises is to use the following chart to identify your strengths and areas that need further clarification. The answers and explanations following this chart will help you solve the practice problems, but you should look for trends in the types of errors (repeated errors). Look especially for low scores in *specific* topic areas. These are the areas that you may need to review again and again until the solutions become automatic.

Mark the problems that you missed and notice the topic and question type. Ask yourself, are you missing question(s) due to lack of knowledge of the topic/concept, or are you missing questions due to lack of knowledge of the question type?

Analysis/Tally Sheet

Topic	Total Possible	Number Correct	(A) Simple Mistake	(B) Misread Problem	(C) Lack of Knowledge
Rounding-off numbers Question 59	1				
Order of operations Questions 24, 49	2				
Adding, subtracting, multiplying, and dividing Questions 7, 13, 23, 35, 36, 40, 41	7				
Fractions Questions 2, 14, 19, 21, 37, 44, 46	7				

(continued)

Analysis/Tally Sheet (*continued*)

Topic	Total Possible	Number Correct	Number Incorrect (A) Simple Mistake	(B) Misread Problem	(C) Lack of Knowledge
Decimals Questions 28, 43, 54, 60	4				
Factors Questions 11, 15, 18	3				
Percents Questions 1, 8, 20, 27, 30, 32, 33, 39, 42, 50, 56	11				
Square roots and cube roots Questions 3, 22, 26, 38, 51, 58	6				
Exponents Questions 5, 25, 48	3				
Converting decimals, fractions, and percents Questions 10, 16, 29, 34, 45, 55	6				
Prime numbers Questions 6, 9, 17, 31, 52	5				
Measurement Questions 4, 12, 47, 53, 57	5				
Total Possible Explanations for Incorrect Answers: Columns A, B, and C					
Total Number of Answers Correct and Incorrect	60	Add the total number of correct answers here: ____	Add columns A, B, and C: _____ Total number of incorrect answers		

Answers and Explanations

Quantitative Comparison

1. **C.**

84% of $73 = 0.84 \times 73 = 61.32$

73% of $84 = 0.73 \times 84 = 61.32$

Hence, the two quantities are equal.

2. **B.** The least common denominator of the two fractions is 75, with $\frac{13}{15} = \frac{65}{75}$ and $\frac{22}{25} = \frac{66}{75}$. Hence, Quantity B has the greater value.

3. **B.** Simplifying, $\sqrt{98} = \sqrt{49 \cdot 2} = 7\sqrt{2}$. Therefore, Quantity B has the greater value.

4. **A.** Since 1 pound = 16 ounces, 13 pounds = $13 \times 16 = 208$ ounces. Hence, Quantity A has the greater value.

5. **B.** Since $8^2 + 9^2 = 64 + 81 = 145$ and $(8 + 9)^2 = (17)^2 = 289$, Quantity B has the greater value.

6. **B.** There are two prime numbers between 60 and 70 (61 and 67), and there are three prime numbers between 70 and 80 (71, 73, and 79). Therefore, Quantity B has the greater value.

7. **C.** The only difference in the two expressions is the grouping of the factors. Since the Associative Property of Multiplication states that a product is not affected by a change in grouping of its factors, the two quantities are equal.

8. **A.** The percent increase from 80 to 100 is

$$\frac{100 - 80}{80} = \frac{20}{80} = \frac{1}{4} = 0.25 = 25\%$$

The percent decrease from 100 to 80 is

$$\frac{100 - 80}{100} = \frac{20}{100} = \frac{1}{5} = 0.2 = 20\%$$

Hence, Quantity A has the greater value.

9. **D.** The product of two prime numbers such as $2 \times 3 = 6$ is less than 10, while the product of two prime numbers such as $5 \times 7 = 35$ is greater than 10. Therefore, the relationship cannot be determined from the given information.

10. **A.** Two of the factors, $\frac{1}{4} = 0.25$ and $\frac{1}{5} = 0.2$, are equal. However, since $\frac{1}{3} = 0.\overline{33}$ is greater than 0.3, Quantity A has the greater value.

11. **C.** There are eight multiples of 6 between 1 and 50 (6, 12, 18, 24, 30, 36, 42, and 48). There are also eight whole number factors of 24 (1, 2, 3, 4, 6, 8, 12, and 24). Hence, the two quantities are equal.

12. **B.** Since 1 week = 7 days, 23 weeks = $23 \times 7 = 161$ days.

Since 1 day = 24 hours, 7 days = $7 \times 24 = 168$ hours.

Therefore, Quantity B has the greater value.

13. **C.** Since $7,890 \div 6 = 1,315$ and $7,890 \div 15 = 526$, the remainder is zero for each quotient. Hence, the two quantities are equal.

14. **A.** Three of the addends, $\frac{1}{6}$, $\frac{1}{7}$, and $\frac{1}{8}$ are the same in the two sums. However, since $\frac{1}{5}$ is greater than $\frac{1}{9}$, Quantity A has the greater value.

15. **A.** Since $8 = 2 \cdot 2 \cdot 2$ and $10 = 2 \cdot 5$, the least common multiple of 8 and 10 is $2 \cdot 2 \cdot 2 \cdot 5 = 40$.

Since $8 = 2 \cdot 2 \cdot 2$ and $12 = 2 \cdot 2 \cdot 3$, the least common multiple of 8 and 12 is $2 \cdot 2 \cdot 2 \cdot 3 = 24$.

Therefore, Quantity A has the greater value.

Multiple-Choice (Select One Answer)

16. **B.** Since $\frac{1}{8} = 0.125$ and $\frac{1}{9} = 0.\overline{11}$ and 0.12 is between $0.\overline{11}$ and 0.125, 0.12 is between $\frac{1}{8}$ and $\frac{1}{9}$ on a real number line.

17. **D.** Since $87 = 3 \cdot 29$, it is not a prime number. Each of the other four numbers is prime since each is divisible by only 1 and the number itself.

18. **A.** The only numbers between 1 and 100 that are multiples of 6 and 8 are 24, 48, 72, and 96.

19. **C.** $\frac{1}{5} = \frac{6}{30} = \frac{12}{60}$ and $\frac{1}{6} = \frac{5}{30} = \frac{10}{60}$

Both $\frac{1}{30} = \frac{2}{60}$ and $\frac{1}{11}$ are less than $\frac{1}{5}$ and $\frac{1}{6}$, and both $\frac{7}{30} = \frac{14}{60}$ and $\frac{11}{30} = \frac{22}{60}$ are greater than $\frac{1}{5}$ and $\frac{1}{6}$. That leaves $\frac{11}{60}$, which lies between $\frac{10}{60} = \frac{1}{6}$ and $\frac{12}{60} = \frac{1}{5}$ on a real number line.

20. **C.** A tax of 8% on a purchase of \$29.99 is $0.08 \times \$29.99 = \$2.3992$. Rounding to the nearest hundredth yields a tax of \$2.40. Therefore, Jorge paid \$29.99 + \$2.40 = \$32.39 for the shirt.

21. **A.** Since $7\frac{2}{3} = \frac{(7 \times 3) + 2}{3} = \frac{23}{3}$, the reciprocal of $7\frac{2}{3}$ is $\frac{3}{23}$.

22. **C.** Note that 91 is approximately halfway between 81 and 100. Since $\sqrt{81} = 9$ and $\sqrt{100} = 10$, $\sqrt{91}$ is approximately halfway between $\sqrt{81}$ and $\sqrt{100}$, or approximately 9.5.

23. **E.** Any number divisible by 15 must be divisible by both 3 and 5. Since the sum of the digits of the number 915 is $9 + 1 + 5 = 15$ (which is divisible by 3), the number 915 is divisible by 3. Also, since the number 915 has a last digit of 5, it is divisible by 5. Hence, 915 is divisible by 15. Note that the other four choices are divisible by 5, but not by 3.

24. **C.** By the order of operations rules,

$$\begin{aligned}
19 + 4 \cdot 2^2 - 10 \div 5 &= 19 + 4 \cdot 4 - 10 \div 5 \\
&= 19 + 16 - 10 \div 5 \\
&= 19 + 16 - 2 \\
&= 35 - 2 \\
&= 33
\end{aligned}$$

25. **B.**

$$(-1)^4 = (-1)(-1)(-1)(-1) = 1$$
$$(-2)^3 = (-2)(-2)(-2) = -8$$
$$(-3)^2 = (-3)(-3) = 9$$

Therefore, $(-1)^4 \cdot (-2)^3 \cdot (-3)^2 = (1)(-8)(9) = -72$.

26. **D.**

$$\sqrt{252} = \sqrt{36 \cdot 7} = 6\sqrt{7}$$

27. **B.** The percent decrease from 75 to 60 is as follows:

$$\frac{75 - 60}{75} = \frac{15}{75} = \frac{1}{5} = 0.2 = 20\%$$

28. **B.**

$$1.2\,\overline{)0.0\,0.576} = 12\overline{)0.576} \quad \begin{array}{r} 0.048 \\ \underline{48} \\ 96 \\ \underline{96} \end{array}$$

29. **A.**

$$\frac{5}{16} = 5 \div 16 = 16\overline{)5.0000} \quad \begin{array}{r} 0.3125 \\ \underline{48} \\ 20 \\ \underline{16} \\ 40 \\ \underline{32} \\ 80 \\ \underline{80} \end{array}$$

30. **B.** 80% of what number is 28?

$$(0.80) \cdot x = 28$$

$$x = 28 \div 0.08 = 0.8\,\overline{)28.0} = 8\overline{)280} \quad \begin{array}{r} 35 \\ \underline{24} \\ 40 \\ \underline{40} \end{array}$$

Multiple-Choice (Select One or More Answers)

31. **C and D.** A number is prime if it is divisible by only 1 and the number itself. Since 61 is only divisible by 1 and 61 and 73 is only divisible by 1 and 73, they are prime numbers. The other numbers are divisible by some numbers other than 1 and the number itself.

32. **C, D, E, and F.**

25% of $75,000 = (0.25)($75,000) = $18,750

30% of $75,000 = (0.30)($75,000) = $22,500

Therefore, $19,000, $20,000, $21,000, and $22,000 all fall between these two values.

33. **F and G.**

75% of 33 = 0.75 × 33 = 24.75

Hence, at least 25 questions must be answered correctly to score at least 75% on the test.

34. **B and C.** Since $\frac{3}{5} = 0.6$ and $\frac{3}{4} = 0.75$, the only numbers that lie between 0.6 and 0.75 on the real number line are 0.65 and 0.7.

35. **A, D, and F.** Any number divisible by 6 must be divisible by both 2 and 3. Each of the six choices is divisible by 2 since they are all even numbers. However, only 66, 96, and 126 are divisible by 3 since the sum of their digits—6 + 6 = 12, 9 + 6 = 15, and 1 + 2 + 6 = 9—are divisible by 3.

36. **B, D, F, and G.** In the sequence, the difference between the first and second numbers is 1, the difference between the second and third numbers is 2, the difference between the third and fourth numbers is 3, and so on. Continuing this pattern, the sequence would be 2, 3, 5, 8, 12, 17, 23, 30, 38, 47, 57, 68, 80, 93, … Therefore, 23, 30, 57, and 80 would be in the sequence.

37. **A, C, D, and F.** Expanding the fraction $\dfrac{3}{8}$ to equivalent forms yields:

$$\frac{3}{8} = \frac{3 \times 2}{8 \times 2} = \frac{6}{16}$$

$$\frac{3}{8} = \frac{3 \times 5}{8 \times 5} = \frac{15}{40}$$

$$\frac{3}{8} = \frac{3 \times 10}{8 \times 10} = \frac{30}{80}$$

$$\frac{3}{8} = \frac{3 \times 8}{8 \times 8} = \frac{24}{64}$$

38. **B, D, and F.** The only numbers that are perfect squares are 16, 64, 100, and 144. Of these, $16 = 8 \times 2$, $64 = 8 \times 8$, and $144 = 8 \times 18$ are also multiples of 8.

39. **B, C, and D.** To solve, find the number of students who achieved each grade:

A: 10% of $160 = (0.10)(160) = 16$

B: 15% of $160 = (0.15)(160) = 24$

C: 40% of $160 = (0.40)(160) = 64$

D: 20% of $160 = (0.20)(160) = 32$

F: 5% of $160 = (0.05)(160) = 8$

W: 10% of $160 = (0.10)(160) = 16$

More than 20 calculus students received grades of B, C, and D.

40. **A, D, and F.** If the product of two positive integers is odd, then each of the integers must be odd. Hence 5, 11, and 19 are possible values for one of the integers.

41. **A, B, C, D, E, and F.** If the sum of two integers is negative, one of the integers could be positive, negative, or zero. Using each answer choice as an example:

$$-8 + 5 = -3$$
$$-1 + -3 = -4$$
$$0 + -3 = -3$$
$$1 + -6 = -5$$
$$3 + -7 = -4$$
$$6 + -8 = -2$$

42. A, B, and C.

$$5.0\% \text{ of } \$47 = (0.05)(\$47) = \$2.35; \ \$2.35 + \$47 = \$49.35$$

$$5.5\% \text{ of } \$47 = (0.055)(\$47) = \$2.59; \ \$2.59 + \$47 = \$49.59$$

$$6.0\% \text{ of } \$47 = (0.06)(\$47) = \$2.82; \ \$2.82 + \$47 = \$49.82$$

$$6.5\% \text{ of } \$47 = (0.065)(\$47) = \$3.06; \ \$3.06 + \$47 = \$50.06$$

$$7.0\% \text{ of } \$47 = (0.07)(\$47) = \$3.29; \ \$3.29 + \$47 = \$50.29$$

$$7.5\% \text{ of } \$47 = (0.075)(\$47) = \$3.53; \ \$3.53 + \$47 = \$50.53$$

Therefore, the sales tax rates which would keep the total cost less than \$50 are 5.0%, 5.5%, and 6.0%.

43. C and D. Since 0.394 and 0.4 are less than 0.53, and since 0.85 and 0.9 are greater than 0.842, the only decimals that lie between 0.53 and 0.842 on the real number line are 0.5314 and 0.71.

44. A and C. Expressing each fraction as a whole number or a mixed numeral yields:

$$\frac{39}{5} = 7\frac{4}{5}$$

$$\frac{75}{11} = 6\frac{9}{11}$$

$$\frac{65}{9} = 7\frac{2}{9}$$

$$\frac{20}{3} = 6\frac{2}{3}$$

$$\frac{90}{15} = 6$$

$$\frac{55}{8} = 6\frac{7}{8}$$

Hence, $\frac{39}{5}$ and $\frac{65}{9}$ are greater than 7.

45. **A, B, C, D, and F.** Expressing 0.75 as a fraction, $0.75 = \dfrac{75}{100} = \dfrac{3}{4}$.

Equivalent forms of the fraction $\dfrac{3}{4}$ are as follows:

$$\frac{3}{4} = \frac{3 \times 10}{4 \times 10} = \frac{30}{40}$$

$$\frac{3}{4} = \frac{3 \times 4}{4 \times 4} = \frac{12}{16}$$

$$\frac{3}{4} = \frac{3 \times 5}{4 \times 5} = \frac{15}{20}$$

$$\frac{3}{4} = \frac{3 \times 7}{4 \times 7} = \frac{21}{28}$$

Numeric Entry (Fill-in)

46. **63**

Since $\dfrac{7}{8} = \dfrac{\square}{72}$ and $8 \times 9 = 72$, the numerator must be $7 \times 9 = 63$.

47. **540**

Since 1 yard = 36 inches, 15 yards = $15 \times 36 = 540$ inches.

48. **5,184**

$4^3 \cdot 3^4 = 64 \cdot 81 = 5{,}184$

49. **19**

By the order of operations rules,
$$9 + 3 \cdot 5 - 10 \div 2 = 9 + 15 - 10 \div 2$$
$$= 9 + 15 - 5$$
$$= 24 - 5$$
$$= 19$$

50. **137.5**

"What percent of 8 is 11?" translates to "11 ÷ 8 = ?"

$$
\begin{array}{r}
1.375 \\
8\overline{)11.000} \\
\underline{8} \\
30 \\
\underline{24} \\
60 \\
\underline{56} \\
40 \\
\underline{40}
\end{array}
$$

$11 \div 8 = 1.375 = 137.5\%$

51. **72**

$$\sqrt{81} \times \sqrt[3]{64} \times \sqrt[3]{8} = 9 \times 4 \times 2$$
$$= 72$$

52. **83**

81 is not prime since it is divisible by 3, 9, and 27.

82 is not prime since it is an even number.

83 is only divisible by itself and 1.

53. **912**

Since 1 week = 7 days, 5 weeks = $5 \times 7 = 35$ days, and 5 weeks 3 days = $35 + 3 = 38$ days.

Since 1 day = 24 hours, 38 days = $38 \times 24 = 912$ hours.

54. 12.02

$$0.\underset{\curvearrowright}{52.})\overline{6.\underset{\curvearrowright}{25.}} = 52)\overline{625.000} \quad \overset{12.019}{}$$

$$\begin{array}{r} \underline{52} \\ 105 \\ \underline{104} \\ 100 \\ \underline{52} \\ 480 \\ \underline{468} \end{array}$$

Therefore, $6.25 \div 0.52 = 12.02$ to the nearest hundredth.

55. $\dfrac{8}{125}$

$$0.064 = \frac{64}{1,000} = \frac{64 \div 8}{1,000 \div 8} = \frac{8}{125}$$

56. 22.95

17% of $135 = 0.17 \cdot 135 = 22.95$

57. 17.5

Since 1 quart = 2 pints, 140 pints = $140 \div 2 = 70$ quarts.

Since 1 gallon = 4 quarts, 70 quarts = $70 \div 4 = 17.5$ gallons.

58. 13

The closest perfect squares to 159 are $12^2 = 144$ and $13^2 = 169$. Since 159 is closer to 169 than it is to 144, $\sqrt{159}$ is closest to $\sqrt{169} = 13$.

59. 660,000

In the number 658,143, the 5 is in the ten thousand place. Since the number immediately to the right is 5 or more, the 5 is rounded up to a 6. So 658,143 rounded to the nearest ten thousand is 660,000.

60. 0.0025

$$0.05^2 = (0.05)(0.05)$$
$$= 0.0025$$

Chapter 4

Algebra

Algebra is a key branch of mathematics that uses the basic building blocks of the four operations of arithmetic: addition, subtraction, multiplication, and division. Understanding *algebraic expressions* depends upon your knowledge of arithmetic operations, but algebra requires a different way of *thinking* and *reasoning*. Think of algebra as a language that uses mathematical statements where letters (called *variables*), such as x and y, are used to represent numbers. To solve problems using algebraic expressions, variables (unknown quantities) and numbers (known quantities) are connected to represent two or more relationships so that you can perform the arithmetic operations.

Since solving algebra problems requires knowledge of the relationship between variables and numbers, many students find learning algebra to be challenging. This is because abstract thinking skills are needed to understand interrelated connections among variables, numbers, and their operations. If you are one of these students, pace yourself as you learn new concepts, be open-minded to a different way of understanding concepts, and practice step-by-step methods as often as possible. The abstract thinking utilized in algebra requires your patience to develop solid skills.

As you review this chapter, remember that you already use algebraic skills every day, even if you are not aware of it. Any time you evaluate unknown quantities, you are using a part of your brain that accesses the skills necessary to perform algebra. For example, suppose that you need to catch a flight and want to estimate how long it will take (time = t) to get to the airport. If the airport is 30 miles from your home (distance = d), and you travel at 60 mph (rate = r), you can easily calculate in your head that it would take 30 minutes in travel time. This problem could be solved by the algebraic expression known as the time-distance formula, $r \cdot t = d$. Notice that the variable is unknown until you build connecting relationships. This is algebra!

Algebraic Topics

This chapter defines key algebraic terms, introduces important algebraic topics, and walks you through step-by-step practice examples. As you review this chapter, always keep in mind that algebraic equations are like a balance scale. The relationship of variables and numbers must be kept in balance. When you perform an operation on one side of the equal sign, you must perform the same operation on the other side of the equal sign.

Start with the following diagnostic test and then study and practice each of the major algebraic topics covered on the checklist. Chart your progress as you review each topic. To reinforce what you have learned, work the practice questions at the end of this chapter (answers and explanations are provided). The practice questions are arranged by question type to help you practice solving algebra problems that are specific to the GRE exam.

Algebra Topics You Should Know

Topic	Study Pages	Worked Examples	Further Study Required
Exponents	pp. 125–128		
Absolute value	p. 128		
Operations on algebraic expressions	pp. 128–132		
Linear equations and inequalities	pp. 132–142		
Polynomials and factoring	pp. 142–148		
Quadractic equations	pp. 148–152		
Fractional (rational) equations	pp. 152–156		
Radicals and roots	pp. 156–159		
Direct and inverse variations	p. 160		
Coordinate geometry	pp. 161–164		
Linear graphs and slope of a line	pp. 164–167		
Quadractic graphs	p. 167		
Vertex of a parabola	pp. 168–169		
Functions	pp. 169–171		

The following diagnostic test is designed to help you identify specific algebraic topics that require further concentration. After you take the diagnostic test, analyze your test results and develop a step-by-step action plan to pinpoint topics to study.

Algebra Diagnostic Test

25 Questions

Directions: Solve each problem in this section by using the information given and your own mathematical calculations.

1. Evaluate: $x^3 - 3x^2 + 6x - 19$ when $x = -2$

2. Subtract: $(12y^2 + 5yz - 6z^2) - (9y^2 - 13yz + 5z^2)$

3. Multiply: $(3a - 2)(9a^2 + 5a + 7)$

4. Simplify: $\dfrac{\left(a^2b^3\right)^4 \cdot \left(a^2b^2\right)^5}{\left(a^3b^2\right)^3}$

5. Simplify: $5\sqrt{18} + 6\sqrt{50} - 4\sqrt{98}$

6. Solve for y: $|3y - 19| = 11$

7. Solve for x: $3x - 4y + 9z = 16$

8. Solve for x and y: $3x + 4y = -29$
$$5x - 2y = -5$$

9. Solve for z: $3z + 15 \geq 7z - 29$

10. Divide: $(12y^{10} - 24y^8 + 36y^6 + 6y^4) \div 6y^2$

11. Multiply: $(5x + 4y)(3x - 4y)$

12. Factor completely: $50a^2 - 128$

13. Factor completely: $4x^4 + 8x^3 - 140x^2$

14. Simplify: $\dfrac{z^2 - 5z - 14}{2z^2 - 8}$

15. Solve for z: $\dfrac{5}{2z-5} = \dfrac{3}{3z+2}$

16. Solve for x: $x^2 - 48 = 8x$

17. Solve for x: $x^2 - 5x = 36$

18. Solve for y: $\sqrt{5y+7} = 6$

19. Add: $\dfrac{5}{x^2 z^4} + \dfrac{4}{x^3 z^3} + \dfrac{3}{x^2 z^2}$

20. Find the slope of the line passing through $(5, -6)$ and $(-7, 2)$.

21. Find the x-intercept(s) of the graph of $y = x^2 + 3x - 18$.

22. Find the slope and y-intercept of the graph of $4x - 3y = 36$.

23. If Δ is a binary operation defined as $a \Delta b = \dfrac{a^2}{a^2 + b^2}$, what is the value of $4 \Delta 6$?

24. Find three consecutive odd integers whose sum is 813.

25. How many pounds of coffee worth $7.50 per pound must be blended with coffee worth $9.50 per pound to make a mixture of 12 pounds of coffee worth $8.00 per pound?

Scoring the Diagnostic Test

The following section will assist you in scoring and analyzing your diagnostic test results. Use the answer key to score your results on the Analysis Sheet that follows. Read through the answer explanations on pages 116–123 to clarify the solutions to the problems.

Answer Key

Functions

1. -51

Operations on Algebraic Expressions

2. $3y^2 + 18yz - 11z^2$

3. $27a^3 - 3a^2 + 11a - 14$

Exponents

4. $a^9 b^{16}$

Radicals and Roots

5. $17\sqrt{2}$

Absolute Value

6. $y = 10$ or $y = \dfrac{8}{3}$, or $2\dfrac{2}{3}$

Linear Equations and Inequalities

7. $x = \dfrac{4y - 9z + 16}{3}$

8. $x = -3$ and $y = -5$

9. $z \le 11$, or $11 \ge z$

Operations on Algebraic Exponents

10. $2y^8 - 4y^6 + 6y^4 + y^2$

11. $15x^2 - 8xy - 16y^2$

Polynominals

12. $2(5a + 8)(5a - 8)$

13. $4x^2(x + 7)(x - 5)$

14. $\dfrac{z - 7}{2(z - 2)}$, or $\dfrac{z - 7}{2z - 4}$

Rational Equations

15. $\dfrac{-25}{9}$, or $-2\dfrac{7}{9}$

Quadratic and Polynomial Equations

16. $x = 12$ or $x = -4$

17. $x = 9$ or $x = -4$

Radical Equations

18. $y = \dfrac{29}{5}$, or $5\dfrac{4}{5}$

Exponents

19. $\dfrac{5x + 4z + 3xz^2}{x^3 z^4}$

Analytical Geometry

20. $-\dfrac{2}{3}$

21. $x = -6$ or $x = 3$

22. Slope $= \dfrac{4}{3}$, y-intercept $= -12$

Functions

23. $\dfrac{4}{13}$

Linear Equations and Inequalities

24. 269, 271, and 273

25. 9 pounds

Charting and Analyzing Your Diagnostic Test Results

Record your diagnostic test results in the following chart, and use these results as a guide for an effective algebra review. Mark the problems that you missed, paying particular attention to those that were missed because of a "lack of knowledge." These are the areas you will want to focus on as you study the algebra topics.

Algebra Diagnostic Test Analysis Sheet

Topic	Total Possible	Number Correct	Number Incorrect (A) Simple Mistake	(B) Misread Problem	(C) Lack of Knowledge
Functions	2				
Operations on algebraic expressions	2				
Exponents	2				
Radicals and roots	1				
Absolute value	1				
Linear equations and inequalities	5				
Operations on algebraic exponents	2				
Polynominals	3				
Rational equations	1				
Quadratic and polynominal equations	2				
Radical equations	1				
Analytical geometry	3				
Total Possible Explanations for Incorrect Answers: Columns A, B, and C					
Total Number of Answers Correct and Incorrect	25	Add the total number of correct answers here: _____	Add columns A, B, and C: _____ Total number of incorrect answers		

Algebra Diagnostic Test Answers and Explanations

Functions

1. −51

$$\text{If } x = -2, \ x^3 - 3x^2 + 6x - 19 = (-2)^3 - 3(-2)^2 + 6(-2) - 19$$
$$= -8 - 3(4) - 12 - 19$$
$$= -51$$

Operations on Algebraic Expressions

2. $3y^2 + 18yz - 11z^2$

$$\left(12y^2 + 5yz - 6z^2\right) - \left(9y^2 - 13yz + 5z^2\right) = 12y^2 + 5yz - 6z^2 - 9y^2 + 13yz - 5z^2$$
$$= 3y^2 + 18yz - 11z^2$$

3. $27a^3 - 3a^2 + 11a - 14$

$$(3a - 2)\left(9a^2 + 5a + 7\right) = (3a)\left(9a^2 + 5a + 7\right) - 2\left(9a^2 + 5a + 7\right)$$
$$= 27a^3 + 15a^2 + 21a - 18a^2 - 10a - 14$$
$$= 27a^3 - 3a^2 + 11a - 14$$

Exponents

4. $a^9 b^{16}$

$$\frac{\left(a^2 b^3\right)^4 \cdot \left(a^2 b^2\right)^5}{\left(a^3 b^2\right)^3} = \frac{\left(a^8 b^{12}\right)\left(a^{10} b^{10}\right)}{a^9 b^6}$$
$$= \frac{a^{18} b^{22}}{a^9 b^6}$$
$$= a^9 b^{16}$$

Radicals and Roots

5. $17\sqrt{2}$

$$5\sqrt{18} + 6\sqrt{50} - 4\sqrt{98} = 5\sqrt{9 \cdot 2} + 6\sqrt{25 \cdot 2} - 4\sqrt{49 \cdot 2}$$
$$= 5 \cdot 3\sqrt{2} + 6 \cdot 5\sqrt{2} - 4 \cdot 7\sqrt{2}$$
$$= 15\sqrt{2} + 30\sqrt{2} - 28\sqrt{2}$$
$$= 17\sqrt{2}$$

Absolute Value

6. $y = 10$ or $y = \dfrac{8}{3}$, or $2\dfrac{2}{3}$

Since $|3y - 19| = 11$,

$$3y - 19 = 11 \qquad \text{or} \qquad 3y - 19 = -11$$
$$3y - 19 + 19 = 11 + 19 \qquad 3y - 19 + 19 = -11 + 19$$
$$3y = 30 \qquad\qquad 3y = 8$$
$$\frac{3y}{3} = \frac{30}{3} \qquad\qquad \frac{3y}{3} = \frac{8}{3}$$
$$y = 10 \qquad\qquad y = \frac{8}{3}, \text{ or } 2\frac{2}{3}$$

Linear Equations and Inequalities

7. $x = \dfrac{4y - 9z + 16}{3}$

Solve for x: $3x - 4y + 9z = 16$

$$3x - 4y + 9z = 16$$
$$3x - 4y + 9z + 4y - 9z = 16 + 4y - 9z$$
$$3x = 4y - 9z + 16$$
$$\frac{3x}{3} = \frac{4y - 9z + 16}{3}$$
$$x = \frac{4y - 9z + 16}{3}$$

117

8. $x = -3$ and $y = -5$

$3x + 4y = -29$ and $5x - 2y = -5$

Multiply the second equation by 2:

$$3x + 4y = -29 \quad \rightarrow \quad 3x + 4y = -29$$
$$\underline{2(5x - 2y) = 2(-5)} \rightarrow \underline{10x - 4y = -10}$$

Add the resulting two equations:

$$3x + 4y = -29$$
$$\underline{10x - 4y = -10}$$
$$13x = -39$$

Solve for x: $\quad \dfrac{13x}{13} = \dfrac{-39}{13}$

$$x = -3$$

Substitute $x = -3$ in either of the original equations:

$$3x + 4y = -29 \quad \rightarrow \quad 3(-3) + 4y = -29$$
$$-9 + 4y = -29$$
$$-9 + 4y + 9 = -29 + 9$$
$$4y = -20$$
$$\dfrac{4y}{4} = \dfrac{-20}{4}$$
$$y = -5$$

9. $z \le 11$, or $11 \ge z$

$$3z + 15 \ge 7z - 29$$
$$3z + 15 - 7z \ge 7z - 29 - 7z$$
$$-4z + 15 \ge -29$$
$$-4z + 15 - 15 \ge (-29) + (-15)$$
$$-4z \ge -44$$
$$\dfrac{-4z}{-4} \le \dfrac{-44}{-4}$$
$$z \le 11, \text{ or } 11 \ge z$$

Operations on Algebraic Exponents

10. $2y^8 - 4y^6 + 6y^4 + y^2$

$$\left(12y^{10} - 24y^8 + 36y^6 + 6y^4\right) \div 6y^2$$
$$= \frac{12y^{10}}{6y^2} - \frac{24y^8}{6y^2} + \frac{36y^6}{6y^2} + \frac{6y^4}{6y^2}$$
$$= 2y^8 - 4y^6 + 6y^4 + y^2$$

11. $15x^2 - 8xy - 16y^2$

$$(5x + 4y)(3x - 4y) = 5x(3x - 4y) + 4y(3x - 4y)$$
$$= 15x^2 - 20xy + 12xy - 16y^2$$
$$= 15x^2 - 8xy - 16y^2$$

Polynominals

12. $2(5a + 8)(5a - 8)$

$$50a^2 - 128 = 2\left(25a^2 - 64\right)$$
$$= 2(5a + 8)(5a - 8)$$

13. $4x^2(x + 7)(x - 5)$

$$4x^4 + 8x^3 - 140x^2 = 4x^2\left(x^2 + 2x - 35\right)$$
$$= 4x^2(x + 7)(x - 5)$$

14. $\dfrac{z - 7}{2(z - 2)}$, or $\dfrac{z - 7}{2z - 4}$

$$\frac{z^2 - 5z - 14}{2z^2 - 8} = \frac{(z - 7)(z + 2)}{2(z^2 - 4)}$$
$$= \frac{(z - 7)\cancel{(z + 2)}}{2\cancel{(z + 2)}(z - 2)}$$
$$= \frac{z - 7}{2(z - 2)}, \text{ or } \frac{z - 7}{2z - 4}$$

Rational Equations

15. $\dfrac{-25}{9}$, or $-2\dfrac{7}{9}$

Cross multiply:

$$\frac{5}{2z-5}=\frac{3}{3z+2}$$
$$5(3z+2)=3(2z-5)$$
$$15z+10=6z-15$$
$$15z+10-6z=6z-15-6z$$
$$9z+10=-15$$
$$9z+10-10=-15-10$$
$$9z=-25$$
$$\frac{9z}{9}=\frac{-25}{9}$$
$$z=\frac{-25}{9},\ \text{or}\ -2\frac{7}{9}$$

Quadratic and Polynomial Equations

16. $x=12$ or $x=-4$

$$x^2-48=8x$$
$$x^2-48-8x=8x-8x$$
$$x^2-8x-48=0$$
$$(x-12)(x+4)=0$$
$$x-12=0 \qquad \text{or} \quad x+4=0$$
$$x=12 \qquad\qquad x=-4$$

17. $x=9$ or $x=-4$

$$x^2-5x=36$$
$$x^2-5x-36=36-36$$
$$x^2-5x-36=0$$
$$(x-9)(x+4)=0$$
$$x-9=0 \qquad \text{or} \quad x+4=0$$
$$x=9 \qquad\qquad x=-4$$

Radical Equations

18. $y = \dfrac{29}{5}$, or $5\dfrac{4}{5}$

$$\sqrt{5y+7} = 6$$

Square both sides of the equation:

$$\left(\sqrt{5y+7}\right)^2 = (6)^2$$
$$5y+7 = 36$$
$$5y+7-7 = 36-7$$
$$5y = 29$$
$$\frac{5y}{5} = \frac{29}{5}$$
$$y = \frac{29}{5}, \text{ or } 5\frac{4}{5}$$

Check by inserting $y = \dfrac{29}{5}$ into the original equation:

$$\sqrt{5y+7} = \sqrt{5\left(\frac{29}{5}\right)+7}$$
$$= \sqrt{29+7}$$
$$= \sqrt{36}$$
$$\sqrt{5y+7} = 6$$

Exponents

19. $\dfrac{5x + 4z + 3xz^2}{x^3 z^4}$

$$\frac{5}{x^2 z^4} + \frac{4}{x^3 z^3} + \frac{3}{x^2 z^2} \rightarrow \text{LCD} = x^3 z^4$$

Expand each fraction using the LCD:

$$\frac{5}{x^2 z^4} \cdot \frac{x}{x} + \frac{4}{x^3 z^3} \cdot \frac{z}{z} + \frac{3}{x^2 z^2} \cdot \frac{xz^2}{xz^2} = \frac{5x}{x^3 z^4} + \frac{4z}{x^3 z^4} + \frac{3xz^2}{x^3 z^4}$$
$$= \frac{5x + 4z + 3xz^2}{x^3 z^4}$$

Analytical Geometry

20. $-\dfrac{2}{3}$

The slope, m, of a line passing through (x_1, y_1) and (x_2, y_2) is

$$m = \frac{y_1 - y_2}{x_1 - x_2}, \text{ or } m = \frac{y_2 - y_1}{x_2 - x_1}$$

$$m = \frac{-6 - 2}{5 - (-7)} = \frac{-8}{12} = -\frac{2}{3}$$

21. $x = -6$ or $x = 3$

The x-intercepts of a graph are all x values when $y = 0$.
Since $y = x^2 + 3x - 18$,

$$x^2 + 3x - 18 = 0$$
$$(x + 6)(x - 3) = 0$$
$$x + 6 = 0 \quad \text{or} \quad x - 3 = 0$$
$$x = -6 \qquad x = 3$$

22. Slope $= \dfrac{4}{3}$, y-intercept $= -12$

A linear equation in the form $y = mx + b$ has a slope $= m$ and y-intercept $= b$.

$$\text{Since } 4x - 3y = 36,$$
$$4x - 3y - 4x = 36 - 4x$$
$$-3y = -4x + 36$$
$$\frac{-3y}{-3} = \frac{-4x}{-3} + \frac{36}{-3}$$
$$y = \frac{4}{3}x - 12$$

Hence, the slope of the line is $\dfrac{4}{3}$, and the y-intercept is -12.

Functions

23. $\dfrac{4}{13}$

$$\text{If } a\Delta b = \frac{a^2}{a^2 + b^2},$$

$$4\Delta 6 = \frac{4^2}{4^2 + 6^2} = \frac{16}{16 + 36} = \frac{16}{52} = \frac{4}{13}$$

Linear Equations and Inequalities

24. 269, 271, and 273

Let x = 1st odd integer

$x + 2$ = 2nd odd integer

$x + 4$ = 3rd odd integer

Since the sum of the three integers is 813,

$$(x) + (x + 2) + (x + 4) = 813$$
$$3x + 6 = 813$$
$$3x + 6 - 6 = 813 - 6$$
$$3x = 807$$
$$\frac{3x}{3} = \frac{807}{3}$$
$$x = 269,\ x + 2 = 271,\ x + 4 = 273$$

25. 9 pounds

Let x = pounds of $7.50 coffee

$12 - x$ = pounds of $9.50 coffee

$$7.50x + 9.50(12 - x) = 12(8.00)$$
$$7.50x + 114 - 9.50x = 96.00$$
$$-2.00x + 114 = 96$$
$$-2x + 114 - 114 = 96 - 114$$
$$-2x = -18$$
$$\frac{-2x}{-2} = \frac{-18}{-2}$$
$$x = 9$$

Hence, 9 pounds of coffee worth $7.50 per pound must be blended with 3 pounds of coffee worth $9.50 per pound.

123

Algebra Review

Algebra's Implied Multiplication

The operation of multiplication may be expressed in a variety of ways algebraically. For example, the product of 3 times y may be expressed as $3y$, with no operation symbol indicating the operation of multiplication. A raised dot and parentheses may also be used to indicate the operation of multiplication. For example, the product of 5 times 6 may be expressed as: $5 \cdot 6 = 5(6) = (5)(6) = 5 \times 6$.

Set Theory

Set theory is fundamental for most topics in modern mathematics.

Term	Definition	Examples
Set	A set is a collection of objects that are separated by a comma and grouped in braces.	$A = \{1, 2, 3, 4, 5\}$ $V = \{a, e, i, o, u\}$
Element	The objects that make up a set are called elements (or members) of the set. The symbol used for an element is $\in$. ($\notin$ means "not an element of.")	If $D = \{3, 4, 8, 9, 14, 17, 20\}$, then $4 \in D$ and $5 \notin D$.
Subset	If a set is part of or identical to another set, it is called a subset of the set. The symbol used for subset is $\subseteq$.	$\{3, 8, 9\} \subseteq \{1, 3, 6, 7, 8, 9, 10\}$ $\{a, b, c, d, e\} \subseteq \{a, b, c, d, e\}$ *Note: A proper subset $\subset$ cannot be identical to the original set.*
Empty or null set	A set with no elements is called an empty set or null set. The symbol used to represent an empty set is $\oslash$ or { }.	$\oslash$ or { }
Finite set	A set that has a countable number of elements is called a finite set.	$Y = \{2, 5, a, x, 10, z\}$ is a finite set with 6 elements.
Infinite set	A set whose elements continue indefinitely is called an infinite set. Note that three dots are used to indicate a set is infinite and follows the same pattern.	$H = \{4, 8, 12, 16, 20, 24, ...\}$

(continued)

Term	Definition	Examples
Equal sets	Sets that have exactly the same elements are called equal sets. Equal sets are not proper subsets of each other.	If $A = \{2, 5, 8, 11\}$ and $B = \{8, 2, 11, 5\}$, then $A = B$.
Equivalent sets	Sets that have the same number of elements are called equivalent sets. Note that the elements themselves do not have to be the same.	If $X = \{a, b, c, d, e\}$ and $Y = \{1, 2, 3, 4, 5\}$, then X and Y are equivalent sets.
Union	The union of two or more sets is a set containing all of the elements of those sets. The symbol used for the operation of a set union is $\cup$.	If $P = \{5, 6, 7, 8, 9, 10\}$ and $Q = \{8, 9, 10, 11, 12\}$, then $P \cup Q = \{5, 6, 7, 8, 9, 10, 11, 12\}$.
Intersection	The intersection of two or more sets is a set that contains only those elements that are common to the sets. If the sets have no elements in common, then their intersection is a null or empty set. The symbol used for the operation of set intersection is $\cap$.	If $A = \{3, 4, 5, 6, 7\}$ and $B = \{4, 6, 8, 10\}$, then $A \cap B = \{4, 6\}$. If $C = \{3, 5, 7, 9\}$ and $D = \{2, 4, 6, 8, 10\}$, then $C \cap D = \varnothing$.
Venn diagram (Euler circles)	A Venn diagram is a way to pictorially describe sets as shown in the figure. In this illustration of the Venn diagram, A represents all the elements in the smaller oval, B represents all the elements in the larger oval, and C represents all the elements that the ovals have in common.	

Exponents

An **exponent** is a number written above and to the right of a number or variable. The number or variable that the exponent is applied to is called the **base.** In the expression 5^2, the base is 5, and the exponent is 2.

Positive Integer Exponents

A **positive integer exponent** indicates the number of times the base is to be used as a factor.

Examples

  1. $3^5 = 3 \cdot 3 \cdot 3 \cdot 3 \cdot 3 = 243$

  2. $(-2)^4 = (-2)(-2)(-2)(-2) = 16$

  3. $9^1 = 9$

Zero Exponents

Any non-zero number raised to the 0 power is 1. Note that 0^0 is undefined.

Examples

  1. $6^0 = 1$

  2. $(-15)^0 = 1$

  3. $\left(\dfrac{3}{4}\right)^0 = 1$

Negative Integer Exponents

Any **negative integer exponent** can be rewritten as a positive integer exponent by changing the base to its reciprocal. In general,

$$x^{-n} = \left(\frac{1}{x}\right)^n, \text{ or } \frac{1}{x^n}.$$

Examples

  1. $8^{-2} = \left(\dfrac{1}{8}\right)^2 = \left(\dfrac{1}{8}\right)\left(\dfrac{1}{8}\right) = \dfrac{1}{64}$

  2. $\left(\dfrac{3}{4}\right)^{-3} = \left(\dfrac{4}{3}\right)^3 = \left(\dfrac{4}{3}\right)\left(\dfrac{4}{3}\right)\left(\dfrac{4}{3}\right) = \dfrac{64}{27}, \text{ or } 2\dfrac{10}{27}$

Fractional or Rational Exponents

A **fractional exponent** may be interpreted in two parts, with the numerator indicating the power and the denominator indicating the root to be applied to the base. In general, $x^{\frac{m}{n}} = \sqrt[n]{x^m}$ or $\left(\sqrt[n]{x}\right)^m$.

It is generally easier to apply the root (denominator) first, before evaluating the power (numerator).

Examples

1. $25^{\frac{3}{2}} = \left(\sqrt{25}\right)^3 = 5^3 = 5 \cdot 5 \cdot 5 = 125$

2. $8^{\frac{4}{3}} = \left(\sqrt[3]{8}\right)^4 = 2^4 = 2 \cdot 2 \cdot 2 \cdot 2 = 16$

Properties of Exponents

Addition Property: $x^m \cdot x^n = x^{m+n}$

Examples

1. $x^6 \cdot x^{-9} \cdot x^8 = x^{6+(-9)+8} = x^5$

2. $y^{-10} \cdot y^4 = y^{(-10)+4} = y^{-6} = \dfrac{1}{y^6}$

Subtraction Property: $x^m \div x^n = x^{m-n}$

Examples

1. $z^{12} \div z^4 = z^{12-4} = z^8$

2. $a^5 \div a^9 = a^{5-9} = a^{-4} = \dfrac{1}{a^4}$

Power to a Power Property: $(x^m)^n = x^{m \cdot n}$

Examples

1. $\left(y^3\right)^4 = y^{3(4)} = y^{12}$

2. $\left(z^2\right)^{-3} = z^{2(-3)} = z^{-6} = \dfrac{1}{z^6}$

Product Rule: $(a \cdot b)^n = a^n \cdot b^n$

Examples

1. $(a^3 b^4)^3 = a^{3 \cdot 3} \cdot b^{4 \cdot 3} = a^9 b^{12}$

2. $(8x^6 y^5)^2 = 8^2 \cdot x^{6 \cdot 2} \cdot y^{5 \cdot 2} = 64 x^{12} y^{10}$

Quotient Rule: $\left(\dfrac{a}{b}\right)^n = \dfrac{a^n}{b^n}$

Example

1. $\left(\dfrac{x^3}{z^4}\right)^5 = \dfrac{x^{3 \cdot 5}}{z^{4 \cdot 5}} = \dfrac{x^{15}}{z^{20}}$

Absolute Value

The **absolute value** of a number x is its distance from zero (disregarding direction). Absolute values are denoted by vertical bars placed in the front and back of a number or expression, $|x|$. Note that the absolute value of any real number is always non-negative.

Examples

1. $|15| = 15$

2. $|-8| = 8$

3. $|0| = 0$

Operations on Algebraic Expressions

Variables

A **variable** is a symbol used to denote any element of a given set—often a letter used to stand for a number. Variables are used to change word expressions into *algebraic expressions*.

Words that Signify an Operation of a Variable

Addition	sum, more than, plus
Subtraction	difference, less than, minus, remainder
Multiplication	product, times, of, twice
Division	quotient, ratio, divided by, half

Examples

Express each of the following word statements algebraically.

1. Seven increased by two times x: $7 + 2x$

2. Twice the sum of x and y: $2(x + y)$

3. The sum of twice x and y: $2x + y$

4. The product of five and the difference between x and y: $5(x - y)$

5. The ratio of x and y decreased by the quotient of w and z: $\dfrac{x}{y} - \dfrac{w}{z}$

Addition

When adding algebraic expressions, combine like or similar terms. Like terms must have the same variable(s) and the same exponent applied to the variable(s). Like terms are combined by adding the numerical coefficients of the like terms and keeping the variable(s) the same.

Examples

1. $8xy + 7yz - 3xy - 12yz = 5xy - 5yz$

2. $12a^2b + 11ab^2 + 5a^2b - 9ab^2 = 17a^2b + 2ab^2$

3. $9m^2 - 11mn + 5n^2$ cannot be simplified because there are no like terms to combine.

Subtraction

Subtracting algebraic expressions follows the same rule as addition: combine like terms. The signs of each term in the expression that follow the subtraction should be changed, and then all like terms may be combined.

Examples

1. $\left(9x^2 - 4x + 7\right) - \left(6x^2 - 8x + 11\right) = 9x^2 - 4x + 7 - 6x^2 + 8x - 11$
$$= 3x^2 + 4x - 4$$

2. $(5a - 9b - 9) - (14 + 5b - 7a) = 5a - 9b - 9 - 14 - 5b + 7a$
$$= 12a - 14b - 23$$

129

Multiplication

To multiply algebraic expressions, multiply numerical coefficients and multiply variables, applying the *addition property of exponents* if possible. Also keep in mind that each term in one expression must be multiplied by each term in the other expression. After the multiplication has been performed, combine like terms if possible.

Examples

  1. $(6x^4)(-4x^8) = -24x^{12}$

  2. $5y^2\,(8y^2 - 11y + 3) = 40y^4 - 55y^3 + 15y^2$

Sometimes referred to as the "FOIL" method, the first (F), outside (O), inside (I), and last (L) terms are multiplied to get the initial product before the like terms are combined.

  3. $(7z + 4)\,(2z - 3) = 14z^2 - 21z + 8z - 12$
$$= 14z^2 - 13z - 12$$

Often referred to as the product of a sum times a difference, the terms are identical except for the signs between them.

  4. $(8a + 5b)\,(8a - 5b) = 64a^2 - 40ab + 40ab - 25b^2$
$$= 64a^2 - 25b^2$$

The distributive property can be used to simplify more complex multiplication of algebraic expressions.

  5. $(3x - 4)\,(x^2 - 6x + 7) = 3x^3 - 18x^2 + 21x - 4x^2 + 24x - 28$
$$= 3x^3 - 22x^2 + 45x - 28$$

Division

To divide algebraic expressions, divide numerical coefficients and divide variables applying the *subtraction property of exponents* if possible. Note that division of algebraic expressions is similar to the method used in multiplication of algebraic expressions.

Examples

1. $(35x^{10}) \div (-5x^2) = -7x^8$

2. $\dfrac{24a^5b^9}{3a^8b^3} = 8a^{-3}b^6 = \dfrac{8b^6}{a^3}$

3. $\left(36z^6 - 24z^5 + 12z^4 - 18z^3\right) \div 6z^2 = \dfrac{36z^6}{6z^2} - \dfrac{24z^5}{6z^2} + \dfrac{12z^4}{6z^2} - \dfrac{18z^3}{6z^2}$

$$= 6z^4 - 4z^3 + 2z^2 - 3z$$

Evaluating Algebraic Expressions

The basic rule for evaluating an algebraic expression begins with substituting the given values for the variables using parentheses. Then perform the indicated operations following the *order of operations* rules (see page 58).

Examples

1. Evaluate: $4x^2 + 7x + 19$, if $x = -3$

$$\begin{aligned} 4x^2 + 7x + 19 &= 4(-3)^2 + 7(-3) + 19 \\ &= 4(9) - 21 + 19 \\ &= 36 - 21 + 19 \\ &= 34 \end{aligned}$$

2. Evaluate: $\dfrac{6a - 11b}{3c}$, if $a = -3$, $b = -2$, and $c = 4$

$$\begin{aligned} \dfrac{6a - 11b}{3c} &= \dfrac{6(-3) - 11(-2)}{3(4)} \\ &= \dfrac{-18 + 22}{12} \\ &= \dfrac{4}{12} \\ &= \dfrac{1}{3} \end{aligned}$$

3. Evaluate: $6yz - 2y^2$, if $y = 3$ and $z = -4$

$$6yz - 2y^2 = 6(3)(-4) - 2(3)^2$$
$$= -72 - 2(9)$$
$$= -72 - 18$$
$$= -90$$

Solving Linear Equations

Linear Equations in One Variable

To solve a linear equation, it is necessary to find all the replacement values for the variable that make the equation a true statement. An equation consists of a *left member* and a *right member* separated by an equal sign (=). The goal in solving an equation is to get the variable isolated on one side of the equation and the numerical value on the other side of the equation.

A basic rule to follow is to remember that an equation is like a balance scale. In order to maintain the balance, whatever operation is performed on one side of an equation must also be performed on the other side of the equation. Although most linear equations have only one solution, it is important to note that a linear equation may have more than one solution, or may have no solution.

Examples

1. Solve: $4x + 39 = 15$

$$4x + 39 = 15$$
$$4x + 39 - 39 = 15 - 39 \quad \text{(subtract 39 from each side)}$$
$$4x = -24$$
$$\frac{4x}{4} = \frac{-24}{4} \quad \text{(divide each side by 4)}$$
$$x = -6$$

Remember, to solve a linear equation with one variable, cancel the numbers that are added or subtracted by using the opposite operation on both sides of the equation. Then divide by the number in front of the variable to get the variable by itself.

2. Solve: $\dfrac{2}{3}y - 25 = 13$

$$\dfrac{2}{3}y - 25 = 13$$

$$\dfrac{2}{3}y - 25 + 25 = 13 + 25 \quad \text{(add 25 to each side)}$$

$$\dfrac{2}{3}y = 38$$

$$\dfrac{3}{2}\left(\dfrac{2}{3}y\right) = \dfrac{3}{2}(38) \quad \text{(divide each side by } \dfrac{2}{3}\text{, which is the}$$

$$y = \dfrac{114}{2} \qquad \text{same as multiplying each side by } \dfrac{3}{2}\text{)}$$

$$y = 57$$

3. Solve: $4z - 11 = 7z + 28$

$$4z - 11 = 7z + 28$$

$$4z - 11 - 7z = 7z + 28 - 7z \quad \text{(subtract } 7z \text{ from each side to}$$

$$-3z - 11 = 28 \qquad\qquad \text{get all the } z\text{'s on one side)}$$

$$-3z - 11 + 11 = 28 + 11 \quad \text{(add 11 to each side)}$$

$$-3z = 39$$

$$\dfrac{-3z}{-3} = \dfrac{39}{-3} \qquad \text{(divide each side by } -3\text{)}$$

$$z = -13$$

4. Solve for a: $5a + 6b = 7c$

$$5a + 6b = 7c$$

$$5a + 6b - 6b = 7c - 6b \quad \text{(subtract } 6b \text{ from both sides)}$$

$$5a = 7c - 6b$$

$$\dfrac{5a}{5} = \dfrac{7c - 6b}{5} \qquad \text{(divide each side by 5)}$$

$$a = \dfrac{7c - 6b}{5}$$

Absolute Value Linear Equations

When a linear expression is inside the absolute value symbol as part of the equation, it is referred to as an **absolute value linear equation.** The absolute value of x is written $|x|$. If $|x| = 2$, then $x = 2$ or $x = -2$ since $|2| = 2$ and $|-2| = 2$.

Examples

1. Solve: $|3z + 11| = 5$

If $|3z + 11| = 5$, then:

$$
\begin{array}{lll}
3z + 11 = 5 & \text{or} & 3z + 11 = -5 \\
3z + 11 - 11 = 5 - 11 & & 3z + 11 - 11 = -5 - 11 \\
3z = -6 & & 3z = -16 \\
\dfrac{3z}{3} = \dfrac{-6}{3} & & \dfrac{3z}{3} = \dfrac{-16}{3} \\
z = -2 & & z = -\dfrac{16}{3}, \text{ or } -5\dfrac{1}{3}
\end{array}
$$

2. Solve: $|4y + 24| = 0$

If $|4y + 24| = 0$, then

$$
\begin{aligned}
4y + 24 &= 0 \\
4y + 24 - 24 &= 0 - 24 \\
4y &= -24 \\
\frac{4y}{4} &= \frac{-24}{4} \\
y &= -6
\end{aligned}
$$

3. Solve: $|5x + 35| = -15$

Since the absolute value of a number can never be negative, the absolute value of an algebraic expression cannot equal -15. Hence, this equation has no solution. Note that replacing the variable with any real number will result in an absolute value that is a positive real number or zero.

In general, if the absolute value of a linear expression is equal to a positive number, the equation will have two solutions. If the absolute value of a linear expression is equal to zero, the equation will have only one solution. However, if the absolute value of a linear expression is equal to a negative number, the equation will have no solution.

Solving Systems of Equations in Two Variables

Solving a system of linear equations in two variables requires finding a value for both unknowns. This can be accomplished by using one of two algebraic methods:

- Elimination method
- Substitution method

Using the Elimination Method

1. Arrange the terms in each of the equations so that the variables are on one side of the equation and the constant is on the other side of the equation.
2. Multiply one or both equations by a constant so that the numeral coefficients of one of the variables are opposites of each other.
3. Add the resulting equations to eliminate one variable.
4. Solve the resulting equation for the remaining variable.
5. Substitute this value in either of the two original equations and solve for the second variable.
6. Check your answers by substituting these values in each of the original equations.

Examples

1. Solve: $3x + 5y = -4$

$$6x - 3y = 57$$

Multiply both sides of the first equation by -2:

$$-2(3x + 5y) = -2(-4) \rightarrow -6x - 10y = 8$$

Note that you are leaving the second equation as it is.

$$-2(3x+5y) = -2(-4) \rightarrow -6x-10y = 8$$
$$6x-3y = 57 \qquad\qquad \underline{6x-\ 3y = 57}$$

Now add the two equations to eliminate the x terms:

$$-6x-10y = 8$$
$$\underline{6x-\ 3y = 57}$$
$$-13y = 65$$
$$\frac{-13y}{-13} = \frac{65}{-13}$$
$$y = -5$$

Substitute $y = -5$ in the first equation:

$$3x+5y = -4$$
$$3x+5(-5) = -4$$
$$3x-25 = -4$$
$$3x-25+25 = -4+25$$
$$3x = 21$$
$$\frac{3x}{3} = \frac{21}{3}$$
$$x = 7$$

Hence, the solution is $x = 7$ and $y = -5$, which will yield a true statement when these values are substituted for x and y in each of the original equations.

2. Solve: $3x+2y = 12$
$$\underline{5x-2y = -28}$$

Since the numerical coefficients of the y variable are opposites, the equations may be added as they appear to eliminate the y terms.

$$3x + 2y = 12$$
$$5x - 2y = -28$$
$$8x = -16$$
$$\frac{8x}{8} = \frac{-16}{8}$$
$$x = -2$$

Substitute $x = -2$ in the second equation:

$$5x - 2y = -28$$
$$5(-2) - 2y = -28$$
$$-10 - 2y = -28$$
$$-10 - 2y + 10 = -28 + 10$$
$$-2y = -18$$
$$\frac{-2y}{-2} = \frac{-18}{-2}$$
$$y = 9$$

Hence the solution is $x = -2$ and $y = 9$, which will yield a true statement when these values are substituted for x and y in each of the original equations.

Special Cases

There are two special cases that sometimes occur when solving a system of equations using the elimination method:

1. If both variables are eliminated when adding the equations and the resulting equation is a true statement $0 = 0$, then the equations are, in fact, the same equation and the system has an infinite number of solutions for each of the variables.

2. If both variables are eliminated when adding the equations and the resulting equation is a false statement, then the system has no solution.

Examples

1. Solve: $x - 2y = 5$
$$-2x + 4y = 7$$

Multiply both sides of the first equation by 2. Note that you are leaving the second equation as it is:

$$2(x-2y) = 2(5) \quad \rightarrow \quad 2x - 4y = 10$$
$$-2x + 4y = 7 \qquad\qquad \underline{-2x + 4y = 7}$$

Add the two equations:

$$2x - 4y = 10$$
$$\underline{-2x + 4y = 7}$$
$$0 = 17$$

Since both variables are eliminated and the resulting statement, $0 = 17$, is false, the system has no solution. Graphically, this means that the two equations represent lines that are parallel and have no points in common.

2. Solve: $6a - 3b = 15$
$$\underline{2a - b = 5}$$

Multiply both sides of the second equation by -3 (note that you are leaving the first equation as it is):

$$6a - 3b = 15 \qquad \rightarrow \qquad 6a - 3b = 15$$
$$-3(2a - b) = -3(5) \quad \rightarrow \quad \underline{-6a + 3b = -15}$$

Add the two equations:

$$6a - 3b = 15$$
$$\underline{-6a + 3b = -15}$$
$$0 = 0$$

Since both variables are eliminated and the resulting statement, $0 = 0$, is true, the system has an infinite number of solutions. Any ordered pair of values for a and b that satisfies one of the equations will also satisfy the other equation. Graphically, this means that the two equations represent the same straight line.

Using the Substitution Method

1. Choose one of the equations and solve the equation for one of its variables in terms of the other variable.
2. Substitute this expression for the variable in the other equation.
3. Solve the equation for the remaining variable.
4. Substitute this value in either of the two original equations to find the second variable.
5. As with the elimination method, if both variables are eliminated after substituting and the resulting equation is a true statement, then the equations are the same and the system has an infinite number of solutions for each of the variables. If, on the other hand, the resulting equation is a false statement, then the system has no solution.

Examples

1. Solve: $x - 2y = -8$

$\underline{2x + 3y = 19}$

Solve the first equation for x by adding $2y$ to both sides of the equation.

$$x - 2y = -8$$
$$x - 2y + 2y = -8 + 2y$$
$$x = 2y - 8$$

Substitute $x = 2y - 8$ in the second equation:

$$2x + 3y = 19$$
$$2(2y - 8) + 3y = 19$$
$$4y - 16 + 3y = 19$$
$$7y - 16 = 19$$
$$7y - 16 + 16 = 19 + 16$$
$$7y = 35$$
$$\frac{7y}{7} = \frac{35}{7}$$
$$y = 5$$

Substitute $y = 5$ in the first equation:

$$x - 2y = -8$$
$$x - 2(5) = -8$$
$$x - 10 = -8$$
$$x - 10 + 10 = -8 + 10$$
$$x = 2$$

Hence, the solution is $x = 2$ and $y = 5$, which will yield a true statement for x and y in each of the original equations.

2. Solve: $4x + 2y = -12$
$$\underline{2x + y = \ \ \ 15}$$

Solve the second equation for y:

$$2x + y = 15$$
$$2x + y - 2x = 15 - 2x$$
$$y = 15 - 2x$$

Substitute $y = 15 - 2x$ in the first equation:

$$4x + 2y = -12$$
$$4x + 2(15 - 2x) = -12$$
$$4x + 30 - 4x = -12$$
$$30 = -12$$

Since both variables were eliminated and the resulting equation, $30 = -12$, is false, the system has no solution.

Solving Linear Inequalities in One Variable

An **inequality** consists of a *left member* and a *right member* separated by any one of four inequality symbols: >, <, ≥, or ≤. To solve an inequality means to find all values for the variable that make the inequality a *true statement*. The goal in solving an inequality is to get the variable isolated on one side of the inequality symbol and the numerical value on the other side. The method used is basically the same as the method used for solving linear equations: What is done to one side of an inequality must be done to the other side as well. **There is a special case that must be observed which requires that the inequality symbol be reversed when both sides of the inequality are multiplied or divided by a negative number.**

Examples

1. Solve: $6y - 23 > 13$

$$6y - 23 > 13$$
$$6y - 23 + 23 > 13 + 23 \quad \text{(add 23 to each side)}$$
$$6y > 36$$
$$\frac{6y}{6} > \frac{36}{6} \quad \text{(divide each side by 6)}$$
$$y > 6$$

An equivalent solution would be $6 < y$.

2. Solve: $4z - 19 \leq 7z + 26$

$$4z - 19 \leq 7z + 26$$
$$4z - 19 - 7z \leq 7z + 26 - 7z \quad \text{(subtract } 7z \text{ from each side)}$$
$$-3z - 19 \leq 26$$
$$-3z - 19 + 19 \leq 26 + 19 \quad \text{(add 19 to each side)}$$
$$-3z \leq 45$$
$$\frac{-3z}{-3} \geq \frac{45}{-3} \quad \text{(divide each side by } -3, \text{ and notice}$$
$$z \geq -15 \qquad \text{the inequality symbol is reversed)}$$

An equivalent solution would be $-15 \leq z$.

3. Solve for x: $-\dfrac{3}{8}x - 2 < 13$

$$-\dfrac{3}{8}x - 2 < 13$$

$$-\dfrac{3}{8}x - 2 + 2 < 13 + 2 \qquad \text{(add 2 to each side)}$$

$$-\dfrac{3}{8}x < 15$$

$$\left(\dfrac{\cancel{8}}{3}\right)\left(\dfrac{\cancel{3}}{\cancel{8}}x\right) > -\left(\dfrac{8}{\cancel{3}}\right)\left(\dfrac{\cancel{15}^{5}}{1}\right) \left(\begin{array}{l} \text{divide each side by } -\dfrac{3}{8}, \text{ which is the} \\[4pt] \text{same as multiplying each side by } -\dfrac{8}{3}, \\[4pt] \text{and then switch the direction of the} \\[4pt] \text{inequality} \end{array} \right)$$

$$x > -40$$

An equivalent solution would be $-40 < x$.

Polynomials and Factoring

Special types of algebraic expressions, called polynomials, occur in many algebra problems. Factoring polynomials can often simplify the process of solving what would otherwise appear to be a difficult problem.

Polynomials

A **polynomial** is an algebraic expression made up of two or more terms. Terms are separated by addition or subtraction.

Examples

1. $4z^8 + 7z^5 - 9z + 11$

2. $5x + 3y$

3. $a^2 - 5b^2$

A **monomial** is an algebraic expression made up of only one term.

Examples

1. $4y^5$

2. $3a^3b^2c^4$

A **binomial** is a polynomial with exactly two terms.

Examples

1. $5a + 3b$

2. $7x^2 - 12$

A **trinomial** is a polynomial with exactly three terms.

Examples

1. $4z^3 - 3z + 10$

2. $10a^2b^2 - 9a^2b + 8ab^2$

Polynomials are commonly written in descending order with the power of terms decreasing with each successive term. They may also be written in ascending order with the power of terms increasing with each successive term.

Operations on Polynomials

Since polynomials are algebraic expressions, the same rules apply for addition, subtraction, multiplication, and division of polynomials as for algebraic expressions.

Adding or Subtracting Polynomials

To **add or subtract polynomials,** follow the same rules as with addition and subtraction of algebraic expressions (page 129). Notice that you add or subtract the coefficients only and leave the variables the same.

Examples

1. $12x + 4x - 23x - (-3x) = [12 + 4 - 23 - (-3)]x = [12 + 4 - 23 + 3]x = -4x$

2. $(4x - 7z) - (3x - 4z) = 4x - 7z - 3x + 4z = (4 - 3)x + (-7 + 4)z = x - 3z$

143

3. $15x^2yz$
$\underline{-18x^2yz}$
$-3x^2yz$

Multiplying Polynomials

To **multiply polynomials,** multiply each term in one polynomial by each term in the other polynomial. Simplify if possible.

Examples

1. $-8(2x - y) = -8(2x) - (-8)(y)$
$= -16x + 8y$

2. $(4x + 2y)(3x - y)$
$= [(4x)(3x)] + [(4x)(-y)] + [(2y)(3x)] + [(2y)(-y)]$
$= 12x^2 - 4xy + 6xy - 2y^2$
$= 12x^2 + 2xy - 2y^2$

> **Tip:** You may want to use the "FOIL" method when multiplying a pair of bionomials together (see Example 3 on page 130).

Dividing a Polynomial by a Monomial

To **divide a polynomial by a monomial,** divide each term in the polynomial by the monomial.

Examples

1. $\dfrac{16x^2y + 18xy^3}{2xy} = \dfrac{16x^2y}{2xy} + \dfrac{18xy^3}{2xy}$

$= \left(\dfrac{16}{2}\right)\left(\dfrac{x^2}{x}\right)\left(\dfrac{y}{y}\right) + \left(\dfrac{18}{2}\right)\left(\dfrac{x}{x}\right)\left(\dfrac{y^3}{y}\right)$

$= \qquad 8x \qquad + \qquad 9y^2$

2. $(6x^2 + 2x) \div (2x) = \dfrac{6x^2 + 2x}{2x} = \dfrac{6x^2}{2x} + \dfrac{2x}{2x} = 3x + 1$

Factoring Polynomials

Factoring a polynomial means to find two or more expressions whose product is the given polynomial. This is equivalent to being given the answer to a multiplication problem and trying to determine what was multiplied to get the given product.

Factoring Out the Greatest Common Factor

1. Find the greatest common factor (GCF) of each term of the polynomial. The GCF is the largest factor that is common to each term of the polynominal.
2. Divide each term of the polynomial by the greatest common factor to obtain the second factor.

Examples

1. Factor: $15x^5 - 9x^3$

   The GCF of $15x^5$ and $9x^3$ is $3x^3$.

   Since $\dfrac{15x^5}{3x^3} = 5x^2$ and $\dfrac{9x^3}{3x^3} = 3$, $15x^5 - 9x^3 = 3x^3(5x^2 - 3)$.

2. Factor: $8y^5 + 24y^4 + 4y^3$

   The GCF of $8y^5$, $24y^4$, and $4y^3$ is $4y^3$.

   Since $\dfrac{8y^5}{4y^3} = 2y^2$, $\dfrac{24y^4}{4y^3} = 6y$, and $\dfrac{4y^3}{4y^3} = 1$,

   $8y^5 + 24y^4 + 4y^3 = 4y^3(2y^2 + 6y + 1)$.

Factoring the Difference of Two Squares

This method may be used if the given polynomial is the difference of two monomials that are perfect squares.

1. Find the square root of each of the two terms in the polynomial.
2. The factors may be expressed as the product of the sum of the two square roots times the difference of the two square roots from the previous step.

Examples

1. Factor: $9x^2 - 25$

Since $9x^2$ and 25 are both perfect squares, $9x^2 - 25 = (3x + 5)(3x - 5)$.

The factors may also be written as $(3x - 5)(3x + 5)$.

2. Factor: $49a^4 - 100b^2$

Since $49a^4$ and $100b^2$ are both perfect squares, $49a^4 - 100b^2 = (7a^2 + 10b)(7a^2 - 10b)$.

The factors may also written as $(7a^2 - 10b)(7a^2 + 10b)$.

Polynomials that Are the Sum of Two Squares

It is important to note that a polynomial that is the sum of two squares is not factorable since it is a prime polynomial.

Examples

1. $x^2 + 25$ is not factorable.

2. $16x^2 + 81$ is not factorable.

Tip: If possible, always factor out the greatest common factor (GCF) before considering the difference of two squares, or any other factoring technique.

Factoring Trinomials

When factoring trinomials of the form $ax^2 + bx + c$, take the following steps:

1. Check for a greatest common factor and factor it out if possible.
2. Consider all possible factors of the first term, ax^2, and place these factors as the first term in each of the double parentheses of the form ( )( ).
3. Consider all possible factors of the last term, c, and place these factors as the second term in each of the double parentheses.

4. Apply the "FOIL" multiplication method to each of the possible factors to determine which pair of factors will generate the correct middle term, bx.

5. Note that if the last term, c, is positive, then the last two terms in the double parentheses must both be positive or both be negative.

6. Remember to check the answer by multiplying the factors to get the original polynomial.

Examples

1. Factor: $x^2 + 5x + 6$

There are no common factors to pull out. The only factors of x^2 are $(x)(x)$, while the possible factors of $+6$ are $(1)(6)$, $(-1)(-6)$, $(2)(3)$, and $(-2)(-3)$. The correct factorization is:

$$x^2 + 5x + 6 = (x + 2)(x + 3)$$

2. Factor: $x^2 + 5x - 6$

There are no common factors to pull out. The only factors of x^2 are $(x)(x)$, while the possible factors of -6 are $(-1)(6)$, $(1)(-6)$, $(-2)(3)$, and $(2)(-3)$. The correct factorization is:

$$x^2 + 5x - 6 = (x + 6)(x - 1)$$

3. Factor: $3z^2 - 2z - 21$

There are no common factors to pull out. The only factors of $3z^2$ are $(3z)(z)$, while the possible factors of -21 are $(-1)(21)$, $(1)(-21)$, $(-3)(7)$, and $(3)(-7)$. The correct factorization is:

$$3z^2 - 2z - 21 = (3z + 7)(z - 3)$$

4. Factor: $4y^2 - 9y + 2$

There are no common factors to pull out. The possible factors of $4y^2$ are $(2y)(2y)$ and $(4y)(y)$. The possible factors of $+2$ are $(1)(2)$ and $(-1)(-2)$. The correct factorization is:

$$4y^2 - 9y + 2 = (4y - 1)(y - 2)$$

5. Factor: $3x^4 + 6x^3 - 45x^2$

The GCF of all three terms of the polynomial is $3x^2$, which should be factored out first. This yields:

$3x^4 + 6x^3 - 45x^2 = 3x^2(x^2 + 2x - 15)$

The only factors of x^2 are $(x)(x)$, while the possible factors of -15 are $(1)(-15)$, $(-1)(15)$, $(3)(-5)$, and $(-3)(5)$. The correct factorization is:

$$3x^4 + 6x^3 - 45x^2 = 3x^2\left(x^2 + 2x - 15\right)$$
$$= 3x^2(x + 5)(x - 3)$$

6. Factor: $a^2 - 7a - 12$

There are no common factors to pull out. The only factors of a^2 are $(a)(a)$, while the possible factors of -12 are $(1)(-12)$, $(-1)(12)$, $(2)(-6)$, $(-2)(6)$, $(3)(-4)$, and $(-3)(4)$. However, no combination of the factors in the double parentheses form $(\ )(\ )$ will yield a middle term of $-7a$. Hence, this polynomial is not factorable and is prime.

Solving Quadratic Equations

A **quadratic equation** is an equation that may be expressed in the form $ax^2 + bx + c = 0$, where $a \neq 0$.

Tip: The largest exponent on the variable in a quadratic equation is 2.

Using the Factoring Method

1. Express the equation in the form $ax^2 + bx + c = 0$.
2. Factor the polynomial.
3. Set each factor equal to zero.
4. Solve each of the resulting equations.
5. Check all answers in the original equation.

Examples

1. Solve: $x^2 - 24 = 5x$

$$x^2 - 24 = 5x$$
$$x^2 - 24 - 5x = 5x - 5x$$
$$x^2 - 5x - 24 = 0$$
$$(x - 8)(x + 3) = 0$$
$$x - 8 = 0 \quad \text{or} \quad x + 3 = 0$$
$$x = 8 \qquad\qquad x = -3$$

Each answer will check correctly when substituted into the original equation.

2. Solve: $2y^2 - 7y + 3 = 0$

$$2y^2 - 7y + 3 = 0$$
$$(2y - 1)(y - 3) = 0$$
$$2y - 1 = 0 \quad \text{or} \quad y - 3 = 0$$
$$2y = 1 \qquad\qquad y = 3$$
$$y = \frac{1}{2}$$

Each answer will check correctly when substituted into the original equation.

3. Solve: $9z^2 - 49 = 0$

$$9z^2 - 49 = 0$$
$$(3z + 7)(3z - 7) = 0$$
$$3z + 7 = 0 \quad \text{or} \quad 3z - 7 = 0$$
$$3z = -7 \qquad\qquad 3z = 7$$
$$z = -\frac{7}{3} \qquad\qquad z = \frac{7}{3}$$

Each answer will check correctly when substituted into the original equation.

4. Solve: $3x^2 + 2x + 8 = 2x^2 - 3x + 8$

Simplify by moving all terms to one side of the equation:

$$3x^2 + 2x + 8 = 2x^2 - 3x + 8$$
$$3x^2 + 2x + 8 - 2x^2 + 3x - 8 = 2x^2 - 3x + 8 - 2x^2 + 3x - 8$$
$$x^2 + 5x = 0$$
$$x(x + 5) = 0$$
$$x = 0 \quad \text{or} \quad x + 5 = 0$$
$$x = 0 \qquad\qquad x = -5$$

Each answer will check correctly when substituted into the original equation.

Solving Polynomial Equations (That Are Not Necessarily Quadratic Equations)

The factoring method may also be used to solve polynomial equations that are not necessarily quadratic equations.

Example

1. Solve: $3x^4 + 6x^3 - 45x^2 = 0$

$$3x^4 + 6x^3 - 45x^2 = 0$$
$$3x^2(x^2 + 2x - 15) = 0$$
$$3x^2(x + 5)(x - 3) = 0$$
$$3x^2 = 0 \quad \text{or} \quad x + 5 = 0 \quad \text{or} \quad x - 3 = 0$$
$$x^2 = 0 \qquad\qquad x = -5 \qquad\qquad x = 3$$
$$x = 0$$

Each answer will check correctly when substituted into the original equation.

Using the Quadratic Formula Method

The quadratic formula may be used to solve a quadratic equation in the form $ax^2 + bx + c = 0$, where $a \neq 0$.

This method is useful when a quadratic expression cannot be factored or when the factors are difficult to determine.

The formula is $x = \dfrac{-b \pm \sqrt{b^2 - 4ac}}{2a}$, where a, b, and c are determined after the equation is written in the form $ax^2 + bx + c = 0$. If the factoring method was used, the answers would be the same as those found using the quadratic formula.

Examples

1. Solve: $x^2 - 24 = 5x$

$$x^2 - 24 = 5x$$

$$x^2 - 24 - 5x = 5x - 5x$$

$$x^2 - 5x - 24 = 0 \rightarrow a = 1, \ b = -5, \ c = -24$$

$$x = \frac{-b \pm \sqrt{b^2 - 4ac}}{2a}$$

$$= \frac{-(-5) \pm \sqrt{(-5)^2 - 4(1)(-24)}}{2(1)}$$

$$= \frac{5 \pm \sqrt{25 + 96}}{2}$$

$$= \frac{5 \pm \sqrt{121}}{2}$$

$$= \frac{5 \pm 11}{2}$$

$$x = \frac{5 + 11}{2} = \frac{16}{2} = 8 \quad \text{or} \quad x = \frac{5 - 11}{2} = \frac{-6}{2} = -3$$

2. Solve: $9z^2 - 49 = 0$

$$9z^2 - 49 = 0 \rightarrow a = 9, \; b = 0, \; c = -49$$

$$z = \frac{-(0) \pm \sqrt{(0)^2 - 4(9)(-49)}}{2(9)}$$

$$= \frac{\pm\sqrt{1764}}{18}$$

$$= \pm\frac{42}{18}$$

$$z = \frac{42}{18} = \frac{7}{3} \;\text{ or }\; z = \frac{-42}{18} = -\frac{7}{3}$$

3. Solve: $x^2 + 5x = 0$

$$x^2 + 5x = 0 \rightarrow a = 1, \; b = 5, \; c = 0$$

$$x = \frac{-(5) \pm \sqrt{(5)^2 - 4(1)(0)}}{2(1)}$$

$$= \frac{-5 \pm \sqrt{25 - 0}}{2}$$

$$= \frac{-5 \pm 5}{2}$$

$$x = \frac{-5 + 5}{2} = \frac{0}{2} = 0 \;\text{ or }\; x = \frac{-5 - 5}{2} = \frac{-10}{2} = -5$$

Fractional (Rational) Expressions

A **fractional (rational) expression** is simply an algebraic expression containing one or more algebraic fractions. Algebraic fractions use a variable in the numerator, denominator, or both numerator and denominator, such as $\frac{3}{x}$, $\frac{x+1}{2}$, or $\frac{x^2 - x - 2}{x+1}$. Since division by 0 is impossible, variables in the denominator have certain restrictions. The denominator, can never equal 0. Therefore in $\frac{5}{x}$, $x \neq 0$; in $\frac{2}{x-3}$, $x \neq 3$; in $\frac{3}{a-b}$, $a - b \neq 0$, which implies $a \neq b$; and in $\frac{4}{a^2 b}$, $a \neq 0$ and $b \neq 0$. Be aware of these types of restrictions.

Simplifying Fractional Expressions

To *simplify algebraic fractions* first factor the numerator and the denominator and then divide common factors.

Examples

1. Simplify: $\dfrac{x^2 - 3x + 2}{3x - 6}$

$$\frac{x^2 - 3x + 2}{3x - 6} = \frac{(x-1)(x-2)}{3(x-2)} = \frac{(x-1)\,\overset{1}{\cancel{(x-2)}}}{3\cancel{(x-2)}} = \frac{(x-1)}{3}$$

2. Simplify: $\dfrac{(3x - 3)}{(4x - 4)}$

$$\frac{(3x-3)}{(4x-4)} = \frac{3(x-1)}{4(x-1)} = \frac{3\overset{1}{\cancel{(x-1)}}}{4\cancel{(x-1)}} = \frac{3}{4}$$

Warning: Do *not* divide through an addition or subtraction sign. The following is NOT allowed:

$$\frac{x+1}{x+2} \neq \frac{\cancel{x}+1}{\cancel{x}+2} \quad \text{or} \quad \frac{x+6}{6} \neq \frac{x+\cancel{6}}{\cancel{6}}$$

Multiplying Fractional Expressions

To *multiply algebraic fractions,* first factor the numerators and denominators that are polynomials and then divide where possible. Multiply the remaining numerators and denominators. *If you've divided properly, your answer will be in simplified form.*

Examples

1. $\left(\dfrac{x^3}{2y}\right)\left(\dfrac{5y^2}{6x}\right) = \dfrac{\overset{x^2}{\cancel{x^3}}}{2\cancel{y}} \cdot \dfrac{5\overset{y}{\cancel{y^2}}}{6\cancel{x}} = \dfrac{5x^2y}{12}$

2. $\left(\dfrac{x-5}{x}\right)\left(\dfrac{x+2}{x^2-2x-15}\right) = \dfrac{\overset{1}{\cancel{(x-5)}}}{x} \cdot \dfrac{x+2}{\cancel{(x-5)}(x+3)} = \dfrac{x+2}{x(x+3)}$

153

Dividing Fractional Expressions

To *divide algebraic fractions,* invert the second fraction (the divisor) and then multiply the fractions. Remember: You can divide only *after* you invert.

Examples

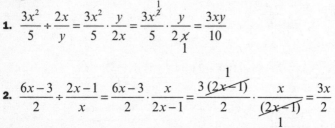

1. $\dfrac{3x^2}{5} \div \dfrac{2x}{y} = \dfrac{3x^2}{5} \cdot \dfrac{y}{2x} = \dfrac{3x^{\cancel{2}^{\,1}}}{5} \cdot \dfrac{y}{2\cancel{x}_{1}} = \dfrac{3xy}{10}$

2. $\dfrac{6x-3}{2} \div \dfrac{2x-1}{x} = \dfrac{6x-3}{2} \cdot \dfrac{x}{2x-1} = \dfrac{3\,\cancel{(2x-1)}^{\,1}}{2} \cdot \dfrac{x}{\cancel{(2x-1)}_{1}} = \dfrac{3x}{2}$

Adding or Subtracting Fractional Expressions with a Common Denominator

To *add or subtract algebraic fractions that have a common denominator,* simply keep the denominator and combine (add or subtract) the numerators. Simplify if possible.

Examples

1. $\dfrac{4}{x} + \dfrac{5}{x} = \dfrac{4+5}{x} = \dfrac{9}{x}$

2. $\dfrac{3x-2}{x+1} - \dfrac{2x-1}{x+1} = \dfrac{3x-2-(2x-1)}{x+1} = \dfrac{3x-2-2x+1}{x+1} = \dfrac{x-1}{x+1}$

Adding or Subtracting Fractional Expressions with Different Denominators

To *add or subtract algebraic fractions with different denominators*, find the least common denominator (LCD) of the fractions. Expand each fraction to an equivalent fraction whose denominator is the LCD. Combine (add or subtract) the numerators and keep the denominator the same. Simplify if possible.

Examples

1. $\dfrac{3}{x} + \dfrac{5}{x+1}$

The LCD of x and $x + 1$ is $x(x + 1)$. Expand each fraction to the LCD.

$$\begin{aligned}
\frac{3}{x} + \frac{5}{x+1} &= \frac{3(x+1)}{x(x+1)} + \frac{5x}{x(x+1)} \\
&= \frac{3(x+1) + 5x}{x(x+1)} \\
&= \frac{3x + 3 + 5x}{x(x+1)} \\
&= \frac{8x + 3}{x(x+1)}
\end{aligned}$$

2. $\dfrac{3x-2}{x^2-25} - \dfrac{5}{6x-30}$

$x^2 - 25 = (x - 5)(x + 5)$ and $6x - 30 = 6(x - 5)$.

The LCD of $(x - 5)(x + 5)$ and $6(x - 5)$ is $6(x - 5)(x + 5)$.

$$\begin{aligned}
\frac{3x-2}{x^2-25} - \frac{5}{6x-30} &= \frac{3x-2}{(x-5)(x+5)} - \frac{5}{6(x-5)} \\
&= \frac{6(3x-2)}{6(x-5)(x+5)} - \frac{5(x+5)}{6(x-5)(x+5)} \\
&= \frac{18x-12}{6(x-5)(x+5)} - \frac{5x+25}{6(x-5)(x+5)} \\
&= \frac{18x-12-5x-25}{6(x-5)(x+5)} \\
&= \frac{13x-37}{6(x-5)(x+5)}
\end{aligned}$$

Solving Fractional Equations

The method used in solving fractional equations is as follows:

1. Find the least common denominator (LCD) of all fractions in the equation.

2. Eliminate the fractions in the equation by multiplying both sides of the equation by the LCD.

3. Solve the resulting equation.

4. Check all answers in the original equation to avoid answers that cause a denominator to equal zero.

Examples

1. Solve: $\dfrac{7x}{3} - \dfrac{3x}{2} = \dfrac{5}{6}$

The LCD of 2, 3, and 6 is 6. Multiply both sides of the equation by the LCD.

$$\frac{7x}{3} - \frac{3x}{2} = \frac{5}{6}$$
$$\frac{6}{1} \cdot \frac{7x}{3} - \frac{6}{1} \cdot \frac{3x}{2} = \frac{6}{1} \cdot \frac{5}{6}$$
$$14x - 9x = 5$$
$$5x = 5$$
$$x = 1$$

2. Solve: $\dfrac{2}{z} + \dfrac{3}{4z} = \dfrac{5}{3}$

The LCD of z, $4z$, and 3 is $12z$. Multiply both sides of the equation by the LCD.

$$\frac{2}{z} + \frac{3}{4z} = \frac{5}{3}$$
$$\frac{12z}{1} \cdot \frac{2}{z} + \frac{12z}{1} \cdot \frac{3}{4z} = \frac{12z}{1} \cdot \frac{5}{3}$$
$$12 \cdot 2 + 3 \cdot 3 = 4z \cdot 5$$
$$24 + 9 = 20z$$
$$33 = 20z$$
$$z = \frac{33}{20}, \text{ or } 1\frac{13}{20}$$

Radicals and Roots

A **radical** is an indicated root of a number or algebraic expression. The symbol $\sqrt[n]{}$ is a radical sign, where n is called the **index** of the radical and the number or expression under the radical sign is called the **radicand.** For square roots, the index 2 is implied and is not indicated as part of the radical sign, written as $\sqrt{}$. The square root of a number is one of its two equal factors. The cube root of a number is one of its three equal factors, and so on. In general, the nth root of a number x, written as $\sqrt[n]{x}$, is one of its n equal factors.

Examples

1. $\sqrt{49} = 7$, since $7^2 = 49$

2. $\sqrt[3]{125} = 5$, since $5^3 = 125$

3. $\sqrt[4]{81} = 3$, since $3^4 = 81$

4. $\sqrt[5]{-32} = -2$, since $(-2)^5 = -32$

Note that an even root of a negative real number is not a real number, but an odd root of a negative real number is a negative real number.

Examples

1. $\sqrt{-64}$ is not a real number since there are no two equal factors whose product is -64.

2. $\sqrt[3]{-64} = -4$, since $(-4)^3 = -64$

Solving Radical Equations

A **radical equation** is any equation in which a variable is part of the radicand. The following is a method for solving radical equations:

1. Isolate the radical on one side of the equation.
2. Eliminate the radical by raising both sides of the equation to the nth power, where n is the index of the radical in the equation.
3. Solve the resulting equation.
4. Check all answers in the original equation.

Examples

1. Solve: $\sqrt{2x-5}+9=16$

Isolate the radical:

$$\sqrt{2x-5}+9=16$$
$$\sqrt{2x-5}+9-9=16-9$$
$$\sqrt{2x-5}=7$$

Square both sides to eliminate the radical:

$$\left(\sqrt{2x-5}\right)^2=(7)^2$$
$$2x-5=49$$
$$2x=54$$
$$x=27$$

Check the answer using $x=27$:

$$\sqrt{2x-5}+9=\sqrt{2(27)-5}+9$$
$$=\sqrt{54-5}+9$$
$$=\sqrt{49}+9$$
$$=7+9$$
$$=16$$

2. Solve: $43=39+\sqrt[3]{40-3y}$

Isolate the radical:

$$43=39+\sqrt[3]{40-3y}$$
$$43-39=39+\sqrt[3]{40-3y}-39$$
$$4=\sqrt[3]{40-3y}$$

Cube both sides to eliminate the radical:

$$(4)^3=\left(\sqrt[3]{40-3y}\right)^3$$
$$64=40-3y$$
$$24=-3y$$
$$y=-8$$

Check the answer using $y = -8$:

$$\begin{aligned}
39 + \sqrt[3]{40 - 3y} &= 39 + \sqrt[3]{40 - 3(-8)} \\
&= 39 + \sqrt[3]{40 + 24} \\
&= 39 + \sqrt[3]{64} \\
&= 39 + 4 \\
&= 43
\end{aligned}$$

3. Solve: $\sqrt{2z + 13} + 33 = 26$

Isolate the radical:

$$\begin{aligned}
\sqrt{2z + 13} + 33 &= 26 \\
\sqrt{2z + 13} + 33 - 33 &= 26 - 33 \\
\sqrt{2z + 13} &= -7
\end{aligned}$$

Square both sides to eliminate the radical:

$$\begin{aligned}
\left(\sqrt{2z + 13}\right)^2 &= (-7)^2 \\
2z + 13 &= 49 \\
2z &= 36 \\
z &= 18
\end{aligned}$$

Check the answer using $z = 18$:

$$\begin{aligned}
\sqrt{2z + 13} + 33 &= \sqrt{2(18) + 13} + 33 \\
&= \sqrt{36 + 13} + 33 \\
&= \sqrt{49} + 33 \\
&= 7 + 33 \\
&= 40 \neq 26
\end{aligned}$$

Since $z = 18$ does not check correctly when inserted into the original equation, the equation does not have a solution.

Direct and Inverse Variations

Direct Variation

If a variable y varies directly to a variable x, then $y = kx$, or $k = \dfrac{y}{x}$, where k is called the constant of variation or the constant of proportionality. It may be stated that y is directly proportional to x.

Inverse Variation

If a variable y varies inversely to x, then $y = \dfrac{k}{x}$, or $k = xy$, where k is again called the constant of variation or the constant of proportionality. It may also be stated that y is inversely proportional to x.

Examples

1. If y varies directly to x, and $y = 144$ when $x = 24$, find y when $x = 8$.

   Since y varies directly to x, $y = kx$.

   Since $y = 144$ when $x = 24$, $144 = k(24)$. Dividing both sides by 24 yields $6 = k$, or $k = 6$.

   Hence, the constant of variation $k = 6$, and $y = 6x$. When $x = 8$,

   $$\begin{aligned} y &= kx \\ &= 6x \\ &= 6(8) \\ y &= 48 \end{aligned}$$

2. If w varies inversely to z, and $w = 10$ when $z = 18$, find w when $z = 15$.

   Since w varies inversely to z, $w = \dfrac{k}{z}$

   Since $w = 10$ when $z = 18$, $\quad 10 = \dfrac{k}{18}$

   $$k = 180$$

   Hence, the constant of variation $k = 180$ and $w = \dfrac{180}{z}$.

   When $z = 15$, $\quad w = \dfrac{180}{15}$

   $$w = 12$$

160

Coordinate Geometry

Two-Dimension Coordinate System

Frequently in algebra we must work with two variables. Since each point on a number line corresponds to one (and only one) real number, two perpendicular number lines may be used to identify a pair of real numbers. The number lines are referred to as the **coordinate axes,** with the horizontal number line called the ***x*-axis** and the vertical number line called the ***y*-axis.** The point at which the two axes intersect is called the **origin.**

For each point in a plane, there is a corresponding and unique pair of real numbers x and y, where x refers to the horizontal position of the point and y identifies the vertical position of the point. This unique pair is called the **coordinates** of the point and is represented as an ordered pair (x, y). The coordinates of the origin are $(0, 0)$, with any point to the right of the origin having a positive x-coordinate, and any point to the left of the origin having a negative x-coordinate. Similarly, any point above the origin is assigned a positive y-coordinate, while any point below the origin is assigned a negative y-coordinate.

The coordinate axes separate the plane into four distinct regions called **quadrants.** The quadrants are numbered as follows:

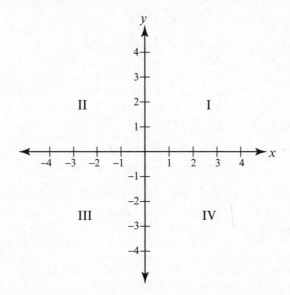

We can generalize about the x- and y-coordinates in each of the four quadrants as follows:

> In quadrant I, $x > 0$ and $y > 0$ (x and y are always positive).
>
> In quadrant II, $x < 0$ and $y > 0$ (x is always negative and y is always positive).
>
> In quadrant III, $x < 0$ and $y < 0$ (x and y are always negative).
>
> In quadrant IV, $x > 0$ and $y < 0$ (x is always positive and y is always negative).

Also note that if a point lies on the horizontal x-axis, its y-coordinate is 0, and similarly, if a point lies on the vertical y-axis, its x-coordinate is 0.

Examples

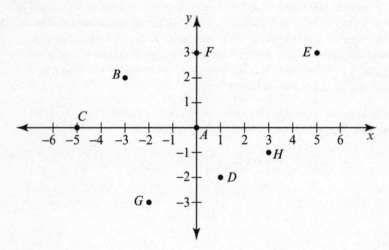

The coordinates of each of the points are:

A (0, 0)	E (5, 3)
B (−3, 2)	F (0, 3)
C (−5, 0)	G (−2, −3)
D (1, −2)	H (3, −1)

Distance and Midpoint

Given the coordinates of any two points, you can find the **distance** between them (the *length* of the segment) and the **midpoint** (the point that is located halfway between them) by using appropriate formulas.

Midpoint Formula

The point that is halfway between two given points $A(x_1, y_1)$ and $B(x_2, y_2)$ is called the midpoint, M, of segment AB. To find the coordinates of M, find the average value of the x-coordinates and the average value of the y-coordinates.

The coordinates of each midpoint M are:

$$\left(\frac{x_1 + x_2}{2},\ \frac{y_1 + y_2}{2} \right)$$

Example

1. Find the coordinates of the midpoint, M, between points $A(-4, 7)$ and $B(10, 8)$.

$$M = \left(\frac{-4+10}{2},\ \frac{7+8}{2} \right) = \left(\frac{6}{2},\ \frac{15}{2} \right) = \left(3,\ \frac{15}{2} \right)$$

Hence, the coordinates of M are $\left(3,\ \frac{15}{2} \right)$.

Distance Formula

The distance, d, between two points $A(x_1, y_1)$ and $B(x_2, y_2)$ is the same as the length of the line segment AB. The formula for finding the distance between points A and B is:

$$d = \sqrt{(x_1 - x_2)^2 + (y_1 - y_2)^2}$$

163

Note: The *order of operations rules* dictate that: (1) subtraction is performed first, (2) squaring is completed second, (3) addition is completed third, and (4) taking the square root is the last operation. Answers should always be expressed in the simplest radical form.

Examples

1. Find the distance between the points A (–8, 1) and B (–12, –2).

$$d = \sqrt{(x_1 - x_2)^2 + (y_1 - y_2)^2}$$
$$= \sqrt{(-8 - (-12))^2 + (1 - (-2))^2}$$
$$= \sqrt{(4)^2 + (3)^2}$$
$$= \sqrt{16 + 9}$$
$$= \sqrt{25}$$
$$d = 5$$

2. Find the length of the segment XY, where $X = (6, -3)$ and $Y = (16, 1)$.

$$d = \sqrt{(x_1 - x_2)^2 + (y_1 - y_2)^2}$$
$$= \sqrt{(6 - 16)^2 + (-3 - 1)^2}$$
$$= \sqrt{(-10)^2 + (-4)^2}$$
$$= \sqrt{100 + 16}$$
$$= \sqrt{116}$$
$$= \sqrt{4 \cdot 29}$$
$$d = 2\sqrt{29}$$

Linear Graphs and Slope of a Line

The graph of an equation in the form $ax + by = c$, where a and b cannot both be zero, is a straight line.

Note: In a linear equation, the largest exponent on x and y is 1.

Slope of a Line

The **slope**, m, of a line is defined as the ratio of the vertical change to the horizontal change in moving from one point on a line to any other point on the line. Since the vertical position of a point is determined by the y value and the horizontal position of a point is determined by the x value, another way to define the slope of a line is: "the ratio of the change in y values to the change in x values in moving from one point to any other point on the line."

For example: If A (x_1, y_1) and B (x_2, y_2) are any two points on a line, then the slope, m, of the line is determined by:

$$m = \frac{\text{vertical change}}{\text{horizontal change}}$$

$$m = \frac{y_1 - y_2}{x_1 - x_2} \quad \text{or} \quad m = \frac{y_2 - y_1}{x_2 - x_1}$$

Note that the order in which the y values are subtracted must be the same as the order in which the x values are subtracted.

Example

1. Find the slope of the line passing through points A $(-7, 7)$ and B $(1, -5)$.

$$m = \frac{y_1 - y_2}{x_1 - x_2}$$

$$= \frac{7 - (-5)}{-7 - 1}$$

$$= \frac{12}{-8}$$

$$m = -\frac{3}{2}$$

165

Slope-Intercept Form of a Linear Equation

When a linear equation is written in the form $y = mx + b$ with the y variable isolated, it is said to be in **slope-intercept** form for the equation of a line. The m value is the slope of the line, and the b value is the y-coordinate of the point where the line intersects the y-axis, called the **y-intercept.**

Examples

1. Find the slope and y-intercept of the line with the equation $3x + 2y = 18$.

Solve for y to express the equation in slope-intercept form:

$$3x + 2y = 18$$
$$3x + 2y - 3x = 18 - 3x$$
$$2y = -3x + 18$$
$$\frac{2y}{2} = \frac{-3x}{2} + \frac{18}{2}$$
$$y = \frac{-3}{2}x + 9$$

Hence, the slope of the line is $m = \dfrac{-3}{2}$, and the y-intercept is the point $(0, 9)$.

2. Find an equation of the line that passes through the points $(-3, 2)$ and $(6, 8)$, and express the answer in slope-intercept form.

The slope of the line passing through the two given points is:

$$m = \frac{y_1 - y_2}{x_1 - x_2}$$
$$= \frac{2 - 8}{-3 - 6}$$
$$= \frac{-6}{-9}$$
$$m = \frac{2}{3}$$

Using the slope-intercept form of a linear equation $y = mx + b$, substitute $\frac{2}{3}$ for the slope, m, and use either of the two given points to substitute for x and y. Using the first point $(-3, 2)$ and $m = \frac{2}{3}$,

$$y = mx + b$$

$$2 = \frac{2}{3}(-3) + b$$

$$2 = -2 + b$$

$$b = 4$$

The slope-intercept form, $y = mx + b$, of the equation is $y = \frac{2}{3}x + 4$.

Quadratic Graphs

The graph of an equation in the form $y = ax^2 + bx + c$ or $x = ay^2 + by + c$ (where $a \neq 0$) is a U-shaped curve called a **parabola.** The graph of an equation of the form $y = ax^2 + bx + c$ will be a parabola opening upward if $a > 0$, or a parabola opening downward if $a < 0$. Similarly, the graph of an equation in the form $x = ay^2 + by + c$ will be a parabola opening to the right if $a > 0$, or a parabola opening to the left if $a < 0$.

Examples

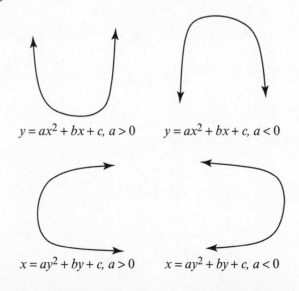

$y = ax^2 + bx + c, a > 0$ $y = ax^2 + bx + c, a < 0$

$x = ay^2 + by + c, a > 0$ $x = ay^2 + by + c, a < 0$

167

Vertex of a Parabola

A critical point on the graph of a parabola is its **vertex.** The vertex is the point where the U-shaped curve changes direction. If the quadratic equation is in the form $y = ax^2 + bx + c$, then the x-coordinate of its vertex is:

$$x = \frac{-b}{2a}$$

The y-coordinate can be determined by substituting this x value in the original equation. Similarly, if the quadratic equation is in the form $x = ay^2 + by + c$, then the y-coordinate of its vertex is:

$$y = \frac{-b}{2a}$$

and the x-coordinate can be determined by substituting this y value in the original equation.

Example

1. Find the vertex of the parabola with an equation $y = -2x^2 + 8x - 3$.

   Since the equation is in the form $y = ax^2 + bx + c$, the x-coordinate of its vertex is:

$$x = \frac{-b}{2a}$$
$$= \frac{-8}{2(-2)}$$
$$= \frac{-8}{-4}$$
$$x = 2$$

   Substituting $x = 2$ in the original equation,

$$y = -2x^2 + 8x - 3$$
$$= -2(2^2) + 8(2) - 3$$
$$= -2(4) + 16 - 3$$
$$= -8 + 16 - 3$$
$$y = 5$$

Hence, the vertex of the parabola is the point (2, 5). Also note that the parabola will open downward from its vertex since $a < 0$.

Functions

A **function** is an equation that expresses an output for any acceptable input. Often the letters f, g, or h are used to denote functions. A function is a correspondence that assigns each member of a first set to one (and only one) member of the second set. The first set is called the **domain of the function,** and the second set is called the **range of the function.**

If a variable y is a function of a variable x, write $y = f(x)$, which is read "y equals f of x" or "y equals f at x." For example:

$y = x^2 + 3$ is a function since any value of x yields one (and only one) value for y. We may write $y = f(x) = x^2 + 3$.

$x = |y|$ is not a function since one value of x, such as $x = 3$, yields two possible values of y, either $y = 3$ or $y = -3$.

Consider the function $f(x) = x^2 - 2x$. The phrase "find the value of the function when x is 6" is expressed as $f(6) = ?$.

The function is then evaluated by replacing each x with the value 6.

$$f(x) = x^2 - 2x$$
$$f(6) = (6)^2 - 2(6)$$
$$f(6) = 36 - 12$$
$$f(6) = 24$$

Examples

1. If $f(x) = x^3 - 2x^2 + 3x + 4$, find $f(3)$.

$$f(3) = (3)^3 - 2(3)^2 + 3(3) + 4$$
$$= 27 - 18 + 9 + 4$$
$$f(3) = 22$$

2. If $g(x) = 5x - 4$, find $g(4) + g(-4)$.

$$g(4) = 5(4) - 4 \text{ and } g(-4) = 5(-4) - 4$$
$$= 20 - 4 \qquad\qquad = -20 - 4$$
$$g(4) = 16 \qquad\qquad g(-4) = -24$$

Hence, $g(4) + g(-4) = 16 + (-24) = -8$.

Transformations of Functions

Transformations of a function $f(x)$ change the position of the graph of $f(x)$ but do not affect the basic shape of the graph. There are three basic types of transformations: **horizontal shifts, vertical shifts,** and **reflections.** The following generalizations represent the basic transformations on the graph of $y = f(x)$:

Basic Transformations on the Graph of $y = f(x)$

Reflection about the x-axis:	$y = -f(x)$
Reflection about the y-axis:	$y = f(-x)$
Reflection about the origin:	$y = -f(-x)$
Horizontal shift a units to the right:	$y = f(x - a)$, where $a > 0$
Horizontal shift a units to the left:	$y = f(x + a)$, where $a > 0$
Vertical shift a units upward:	$y = f(x) + a$, where $a > 0$
Vertical shift a units downward:	$y = f(x) - a$, where $a > 0$

Examples

1. If $f(x) = x^2$, how will the graph of $g(x) = x^2 + 3$ differ from the graph of $f(x)$?

   Since $g(x) = f(x) + 3$, the graph of $g(x)$ will be the graph of $f(x)$ shifted vertically upward 3 units.

2. If $f(x) = x^3$, how will the graph of $h(x) = (x - 5)^3$ differ from the graph of $f(x)$?

   Since $h(x) = f(x - 5)$, the graph of $h(x)$ will be the graph of $f(x)$ shifted horizontally 5 units to the right.

3. If $f(x) = x^4$, how will the graph of $k(x) = -x^4$ differ from the graph of $f(x)$?

   Since $k(x) = -f(x)$, the graph of $k(x)$ will be the graph of $f(x)$ reflected about the x-axis.

4. If $f(x) = \sqrt{x}$, how will the graph of $p(x) = \sqrt{x+4} - 3$ differ from the graph of $f(x)$?

Since $p(x) = f(x+4) - 3$, the graph of $p(x)$ will be the graph of $f(x)$ shifted horizontally 4 units to the left and shifted vertically downward 3 units.

Algebra Practice Questions

Now that you have reviewed algebra topics and concepts, you can practice on your own. Questions appear in four categories by question type: quantitative comparison, multiple-choice (select one answer), multiple-choice (select one or more answers), and numeric entry (fill-in). These practice questions are grouped by question type to give you a chance to practice solving problems in the same format as the GRE. The answers and explanations that follow the questions will include strategies to help you understand how to solve the problems.

General Directions: For each question, indicate the best answer, using the directions given.

- All numbers used are real numbers.
- All figures are assumed to lie in a plane unless otherwise indicated.
- Geometric figures, such as lines, circles, triangles, and quadrilaterals, are not necessarily drawn to scale. That is, you should **not** assume that quantities, such as lengths and angle measurements, are as they appear in the figure. You should assume, however, that lines shown as straight are actually straight, points on a line are in the order shown, and more generally, all geometric objects are in the relative position shown. For questions with geometric figures, you should base your answer on geometric reasoning, not on estimating or comparing quantities by sight or by measurement.
- Coordinate systems, such as xy-planes and number lines, are drawn to scale; therefore, you can read, estimate, or compare quantities in such figures by sight or by measurement.
- Graphical data presentations, such as bar graphs, pie graphs, and line graphs, are drawn to scale; therefore, you can read, estimate, or compare data values by sight or by measurement.

Answer choices in this study guide have lettered choices A, B, C, D, E, etc., for clarity, but letters will not appear on the actual exam. On the actual computer version of the exam, you will be required to click on ovals or squares to select your answer.

HELPFUL HINT
○ oval—answer will be a single choice.
☐ square box—answer will be one or more choices.

Quantitative Comparison

Directions: For questions 1 to 15, compare Quantity A and Quantity B, using additional information centered above the two quantities if such information is given. Select one of the following four answer choices for each question:

Ⓐ   Quantity A is greater.
Ⓑ   Quantity B is greater.
Ⓒ   The two quantities are equal.
Ⓓ   The relationship cannot be determined from the information given.

Three consecutive odd integers have a sum of 555.

	Quantity A	Quantity B
1.	185	the largest of the three integers

$$\frac{x-3}{3-x} = \frac{x}{3}$$

	Quantity A	Quantity B
2.	0	x

	Quantity A	Quantity B
3.	the slope of the line $3x + 4y = 12$	the slope of the line $4x + 3y = 12$

$$16^6 = 8^{z-5}$$

	Quantity A	Quantity B
4.	z	13

$3a + 2b = 1$ and $2a - 3b = -8$

Quantity A	Quantity B
a	b

5.

$z^2 - 20 = 29$

Quantity A	Quantity B
z	0

6.

$$\frac{r+s}{r} = \frac{9}{5}$$

Quantity A	Quantity B
$\dfrac{r}{s}$	1

7.

$y > 0$ and $y \neq 1$

Quantity A	Quantity B
y^5	y^4

8.

$$y = 3x^2 - 6x + 5$$

Quantity A	Quantity B
the value of x at the vertex of the graph	the value of y at the vertex of the graph

9.

$m \Delta n = \dfrac{(m-n)^2}{(m+n)^2}$ for all non-zero real numbers m and n

Quantity A	Quantity B
$9\Delta10$	$10\Delta9$

10.

$a > 0$, $b = 4a$, $c = 3b$

Quantity A	Quantity B
$\dfrac{a+b+c}{4}$	b

11.

$$x^2 < 3x \text{ and } x > 0$$

	Quantity A	**Quantity B**
12.	x	3

$$z \neq 0$$

	Quantity A	**Quantity B**
13.	$\dfrac{z^4 + z^3}{z^2}$	$\dfrac{z^4 + z^3}{z^3}$

$$\frac{5}{y+3} = \frac{4}{2y-5}$$

	Quantity A	**Quantity B**
14.	y	6

	Quantity A	**Quantity B**
15.	the distance between the points $(-5, 3)$ and $(4, -7)$	the distance between the points $(-7, 4)$ and $(3, -5)$

Multiple-Choice (Select One Answer)

Directions: Questions 16 to 30 require you to select one answer choice.

16. If $2n + 5$ is an odd integer, which of the following is an expression for the next consecutive odd integer?

Ⓐ $n + 5$
Ⓑ $n + 7$
Ⓒ $2n + 1$
Ⓓ $2n + 3$
Ⓔ $2n + 7$

17. Which of the following ordered pairs is not a point on the line
$3x - 4y - 12 = 0$?

Ⓐ $(0, -3)$
Ⓑ $(4, 0)$
Ⓒ $(-4, -6)$
Ⓓ $(-8, 3)$
Ⓔ $(12, 6)$

18. Which of the following functions of $g(x)$ would have a graph that is
the same as the graph of $f(x) = x^2$ and is shifted horizontally 3 units
to the right?

Ⓐ $g(x) = x^2 - 3$
Ⓑ $g(x) = x^2 + 3$
Ⓒ $g(x) = (x - 3)^2$
Ⓓ $g(x) = (x + 3)^2$
Ⓔ $g(x) = 3x^2$

19. Simplify: $4^4 \cdot 8^3 \cdot 16^2$

Ⓐ 512^{24}
Ⓑ 512^9
Ⓒ 16^{11}
Ⓓ 2^{576}
Ⓔ 2^{25}

20. Find the value of z if $z^2 - 8z + 15 = 15$ and $z > 0$.

Ⓐ   3
Ⓑ   5
Ⓒ   7
Ⓓ   8
Ⓔ   15

21. If y varies directly to x and $y = 1.68$ when $x = 1.2$, what is the value of y
when $x = 200$?

Ⓐ   0.28
Ⓑ   2.8
Ⓒ   28
Ⓓ   280
Ⓔ   2800

22. What is the value of n if $3m - 5n = 19$ and $2m - 4n = 16$?

  Ⓐ -5

  Ⓑ -2

  Ⓒ 2

  Ⓓ 5

  Ⓔ Cannot be determined from the information given.

23. Simplify: $\sqrt{50} + 3\sqrt{18} - \sqrt{32} + 9\sqrt{8}$

  Ⓐ $18\sqrt{2}$

  Ⓑ $28\sqrt{2}$

  Ⓒ $36\sqrt{2}$

  Ⓓ $12\sqrt{44}$

  Ⓔ $12\sqrt{108}$

24. If a point P has coordinates (a, b), which of the following guarantees that $a > b$?

  Ⓐ P lies in Quadrant I.

  Ⓑ P lies in Quadrant II.

  Ⓒ P lies in Quadrant III.

  Ⓓ P lies in Quadrant IV.

  Ⓔ P lies on the horizontal axis.

25. Simplify: $y^x \cdot y^x \cdot y^x \cdot y^x$

  Ⓐ y^{x+4}

  Ⓑ y^{4x}

  Ⓒ y^{x^4}

  Ⓓ y^{4^x}

  Ⓔ $4y^x$

26. If $ab = 55$, what is the ratio of a to b?

  Ⓐ 1 to 55

  Ⓑ 5 to 11

  Ⓒ 11 to 5

  Ⓓ 55 to 1

  Ⓔ Cannot be determined from the information given.

27. A line that passes through $(5, 0)$ and $(-3, -4)$ also passes through which of the following points?

   Ⓐ $(11, 3)$

   Ⓑ $(1, 2)$

   Ⓒ $(4, 2)$

   Ⓓ $(7, 4)$

   Ⓔ $(-1, -2)$

28. If $\dfrac{z}{3} + \dfrac{z}{6} + \dfrac{z}{12} = 21$, what is the value of z?

   Ⓐ   3

   Ⓑ   7

   Ⓒ   36

   Ⓓ   84

   Ⓔ   252

29. If m and n are positive integers such that $m^2 - n^2 = 17$, what is the value of $m^2 + n^2$?

   Ⓐ   113

   Ⓑ   128

   Ⓒ   145

   Ⓓ   289

   Ⓔ   Cannot be determined from the information given.

30. Which of the following fractions is equivalent to $\dfrac{x^2 + 2x - 24}{x^2 + 8x - 48}$?

   Ⓐ $\dfrac{1}{4}$

   Ⓑ $\dfrac{1}{2}$

   Ⓒ $\dfrac{1}{2x + 2}$

   Ⓓ $\dfrac{x - 6}{x - 12}$

   Ⓔ $\dfrac{x + 6}{x + 12}$

Multiple-Choice (Select One or More Answers)

Directions: Questions 31 to 45 require you to select one or more answer choices.

31. Which of the following points lie on the line $5x - 3y = 12$?

   Ⓐ $(0, 4)$

   Ⓑ $(3, 1)$

   Ⓒ $(0, -4)$

   Ⓓ $(3, -1)$

   Ⓔ $\left(\dfrac{2}{5}, \dfrac{-10}{3}\right)$

   Ⓕ $\left(4, \dfrac{8}{3}\right)$

32. Which of the following values of x is a solution for the equation $4x^5 + 20x^4 - 24x^3 = 0$?

   Ⓐ -6

   Ⓑ -1

   Ⓒ 0

   Ⓓ 1

   Ⓔ 4

   Ⓕ 6

33. Which of the following linear equations have the same slope?

   Ⓐ $4x + 3y = 20$

   Ⓑ $3x + 4y = 20$

   Ⓒ $4x - 3y = 20$

   Ⓓ $3x - 4y = 20$

   Ⓔ $9x + 12y = 20$

   Ⓕ $x + y = 20$

34. When a positive integer, n, is divided by 8, the remainder is 3. When n is divided by 5, the remainder is also 3. Which of the following could be the value of n?

- Ⓐ   28
- Ⓑ   43
- Ⓒ   53
- Ⓓ   68
- Ⓔ   73

35. If $|4x - 10| = 18$, which of the following could be the value of $3x + 5$?

- Ⓐ   −16
- Ⓑ   −5
- Ⓒ   −1
- Ⓓ   5
- Ⓔ   11
- Ⓕ   26

36. The graphs of which of the following equations would have a y-intercept of −3?

- Ⓐ $x + y = 3$
- Ⓑ $x + y = -3$
- Ⓒ $x - y = 3$
- Ⓓ $y - x = 3$
- Ⓔ $y = -3x$

37. Which of the following are perfect cubes?

- Ⓐ   −64
- Ⓑ   −27
- Ⓒ   1
- Ⓓ   16
- Ⓔ   64
- Ⓕ   100

38. If x and y are prime numbers less than 10, which of the following could be values of xy?

   Ⓐ   10

   Ⓑ   14

   Ⓒ   15

   Ⓓ   25

   Ⓔ   27

   Ⓕ   49

39. The graph of which of the following equations would be a parabola opening downward?

   Ⓐ $y = -5x + 4$

   Ⓑ $x = -3y^2 + 5y + 4$

   Ⓒ $y = -2x^2 + 11x - 1$

   Ⓓ $y = x - 5$

   Ⓔ $y = 3x^2 + 2x - 1$

   Ⓕ $x = 4y^2 + 1$

40. If a, b, and c are odd integers, which of the following must also be an odd integer?

   Ⓐ $a^2 - b^2$

   Ⓑ a^2b^2

   Ⓒ $a^2 + b^2$

   Ⓓ $a + c$

   Ⓔ $a^2 + b^2 + c^2$

   Ⓕ abc

41. Which of the following are prime numbers?

   Ⓐ   83

   Ⓑ   91

   Ⓒ   103

   Ⓓ   111

   Ⓔ   119

   Ⓕ   127

42. If m is an integer in the expression $x^2 + mx - 24$, which of the following could be values of m?

- Ⓐ   −10
- Ⓑ   −5
- Ⓒ   −2
- Ⓓ   2
- Ⓔ   5
- Ⓕ   10

43. Which of the following linear equations have a slope of $m < 0$?

- Ⓐ $9x + 4y = 36$
- Ⓑ $2x − 5y = 10$
- Ⓒ $x + y = 15$
- Ⓓ $x = −3$
- Ⓔ $y = −6$

44. Which of the following are equal to 2^{100}?

- Ⓐ 4^{25}
- Ⓑ 4^{50}
- Ⓒ 8^{25}
- Ⓓ 16^{25}
- Ⓔ 32^{20}

45. Which of the following values of z would be in the solution of $5z − 10 < 8z − 6$?

- Ⓐ   −8
- Ⓑ   −5
- Ⓒ   −1
- Ⓓ   0
- Ⓔ   4

Numeric Entry (Fill-in)

Directions: Questions 46 to 60 require you to solve the problem and write your answer in a box or boxes.

- Write out your answer with numerals.
- Your answer may be an integer, a decimal, or a fraction, and it may be negative.
- If a question asks for a fraction, there will be two boxes—one for the numerator and one for the denominator.
- Equivalent forms of the correct answer, such as 4.5 and 4.50, are all correct. Fractions do not need to be reduced to lowest terms.
- Write out the exact answer unless the question asks you to round your answer.

46. What is the value of x if $4x^2 + 20x + 25 = 0$? Give the answer as a fraction.

47. What is the slope of the line $3x - 6y = 25$? Give the answer as a fraction.

48. What is the value of z if $\dfrac{6}{2z-3} = \dfrac{5}{z+2}$? Give the answer as a fraction.

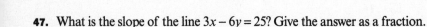

49. What is the value of $x^3 + 4y^3 - z^3$ if $x = -3, y = 2, z = -4$?

50. If $3a(4a+5)(3a-4)(a+1)(a-2)=0$, what is the smallest value of a? Give the answer as a fraction.

51. What is the value of y at the vertex of the graph of $y = 2x^2 + 4x + 9$?

52. What is value of x if $3x + 5y = 7$ and $2x + 3y = 5$?

53. What is the value of y where the graph of $4x - 3y + 24 = 0$ intersects the y-axis?

54. What is the only perfect cube between 300 and 400?

55. If $g(x) = 3x^2 - 5x + 4$, what is $g(-2)$?

56. If $x + a = 20$, $x - b = 15$, $x + c = 10$, and $x - d = 5$, what is the value of $a + b + c + d$?

57. What is the distance between the points (–3, 10) and (2, –2)?

58. If $f(x) = 2x - 5$ and $g(x) = x^2 + 3$, what is the value of $f(-2) - g(-3)$?

59. If $\dfrac{\dfrac{1}{x} + \dfrac{1}{z}}{\dfrac{1}{x} \cdot \dfrac{1}{z}} = \dfrac{4}{5}$, what is the value of $x + z$? Give the answer as a fraction.

60. If the midpoint of $\overline{AB}$ is (–2, 6) and B is the point (6, 4), what is the y value of point A?

Charting and Analyzing Your Practice Results

The first step in analyzing the practice exercises is to use the following chart to identify your strengths and areas that need further clarification. The answers and explanations following this chart will help you solve the practice problems, but you should look for trends in the types of errors (repeated errors). Look especially for low scores in *specific* topic areas. These are the areas that you may need to review again and again until the solutions become automatic.

Mark the problems that you missed and notice the topic and question type. Ask yourself, are you missing question(s) due to lack of knowledge of the topic/concept, or are you missing questions due to lack of knowledge of the question type?

Analysis/Tally Sheet

Topic	Total Possible	Number Correct	Number Incorrect		
			(A) Simple Mistake	(B) Misread Problem	(C) Lack of Knowledge
Algebraic word problems Questions 1, 16, 29, 34, 40	5				
Algebraic fractions Questions 11, 30, 59	3				
Exponents Questions 4, 8, 13, 19, 25, 37, 44, 54	8				
Absolute value and square root Questions 23, 35	2				
Algebraic expressions Questions 6, 20, 42, 46, 50	5				
Linear equations and inequalities Questions 5, 12, 22, 28, 45, 52, 56	7				
Ratios and proportions Questions 2, 7, 10, 14, 26, 48	6				
Slope Questions 3, 33, 43, 47	4				
Graphing linear and quadratic equations Questions 9, 18, 24, 36, 39, 51, 53	7				
Variations and prime numbers Questions 21, 38, 41	3				
Analytic geometry Questions 15, 17, 27, 31, 57, 60	6				

(*continued*)

Analysis/Tally Sheet (*continued*)

Topic	Total Possible	Number Correct	Number Incorrect		
			(A) Simple Mistake	(B) Misread Problem	(C) Lack of Knowledge
Functions Questions 32, 49, 55, 58	4				
Total Possible Explanations for Incorrect Answers: Columns A, B, and C					
Total Number of Answers Correct and Incorrect	60	Add the total number of correct answers here: _____	Add columns A, B, and C: _____ Total number of incorrect answers		

Answers and Explanations

Quantitative Comparison

1. B. Let the three consecutive odd integers be represented by x, $x + 2$, and $x + 4$.

Since their sum is 555,

$$(x)+(x+2)+(x+4)=555$$
$$3x+6=555$$
$$3x+6-6=555-6$$
$$3x=549$$
$$\frac{3x}{3}=\frac{549}{3}$$
$$x=183, x+2=185, x+4=187$$

2. A.

$$\frac{x-3}{3-x} = \frac{x}{3}$$

Cross multiply to get
$$3(x-3) = x(3-x)$$
$$3x - 9 = 3x - x^2$$
$$3x - 9 - 3x + x^2 = 3x - x^2 - 3x + x^2$$
$$x^2 - 9 = 0$$
$$(x-3)(x+3) = 0$$
$$x - 3 = 0 \quad \text{or} \quad x + 3 = 0$$
$$x = 3 \qquad\qquad x = -3$$

However, $x \neq 3$ since this value would yield a denominator of 0 in the fraction $\frac{x-3}{3-x}$. Hence, the solution is $x = -3$, and Quantity A has the greater value.

3. A. Express each equation in the form $y = mx + b$, where m is the slope of the line.

$$3x + 4y = 12 \qquad \text{and} \qquad 4x + 3y = 12$$
$$3x + 4y - 3x = 12 - 3x \qquad 4x + 3y - 4x = 12 - 4x$$
$$4y = -3x + 12 \qquad\qquad 3y = -4x + 12$$
$$\frac{4y}{4} = \frac{-3x}{4} + \frac{12}{4} \qquad\qquad \frac{3y}{3} = \frac{-4x}{3} + \frac{12}{3}$$
$$y = \frac{-3}{4}x + 3 \qquad\qquad y = \frac{-4}{3}x + 4$$
$$\text{Slope} = \frac{-3}{4} \qquad\qquad \text{Slope} = \frac{-4}{3}$$

Hence, Quantity A has the greater value.

4. C. Since $16 = 2^4$ and $8 = 2^3$, $16^6 = (2^4)^6 = 2^{24}$ and $8^{z-5} = (2^3)^{z-5} = 2^{3z-15}$.

Hence, $2^{3z-15} = 2^{24}$ and
$$3z - 15 = 24$$
$$3z - 15 + 15 = 24 + 15$$
$$3z = 39$$
$$\frac{3z}{3} = \frac{39}{3}$$
$$z = 13$$

Hence, the quantities are equal.

5. B.

$3a + 2b = 1$ and $2a - 3b = -8$

Multiply the first equation by 3 and the second equation by 2, then add the two equations.

$$3(3a + 2b) = 3(1) \quad \rightarrow \quad 9a + 6b = 3$$
$$\underline{2(2a - 3b) = 2(-8)} \quad \rightarrow \quad \underline{4a - 6b = -16}$$
$$13a = -13$$
$$\frac{13a}{13} = \frac{-13}{13}$$
$$a = -1$$

Substitute $a = -1$ in either of the original equations.

$$3a + 2b = 1 \rightarrow 3(-1) + 2b = 1$$
$$-3 + 2b = 1$$
$$-3 + 2b + 3 = 1 + 3$$
$$2b = 4$$
$$b = 2$$

Hence, Quantity B has the greater value.

6. D.

$$z^2 - 20 = 29$$
$$z^2 - 20 - 29 = 29 - 29$$
$$z^2 - 49 = 0$$
$$(z + 7)(z - 7) = 0$$
$$z + 7 = 0 \quad \text{or} \quad z - 7 = 0$$
$$z = -7 \qquad\qquad z = 7$$

Therefore, the relationship cannot be determined from the information given.

7. A.

$$\frac{r+s}{r} = \frac{9}{5}$$

$$\frac{r}{r} + \frac{s}{r} = \frac{9}{5}$$

$$1 + \frac{s}{r} = \frac{9}{5}$$

$$\frac{s}{r} = \frac{9}{5} - 1 = \frac{4}{5}$$

Hence, $\frac{r}{s} = \frac{5}{4}$, and Quantity A has the greater value.

8. D. If $y = 2$, then $2^5 = 32$ and $2^4 = 16$ and $y^5 > y^4$.

However, if $y = \frac{1}{2}$, then $\left(\frac{1}{2}\right)^5 = \frac{1}{32}$ and $\left(\frac{1}{2}\right)^4 = \frac{1}{16}$ and $y^5 < y^4$.

Therefore, the relationship cannot be determined from the information given.

9. B. Since the x value of the vertex of a parabola in the equation $y = ax^2 + bx + c$ is $x = \frac{-b}{2a}$, the x value for the parabola $y = 3x^2 - 6x + 5$ is $x = \frac{-(-6)}{2(3)} = \frac{6}{6} = 1$.

Substitute $x = 1$ in the original equation.

$y = 3x^2 - 6x + 5 = 3(1)^2 - 6(1) + 5 = 3 - 6 + 5 = 2$

Hence, Quantity B has the greater value.

10. C.

$$\text{Since } m\Delta n = \frac{(m-n)^2}{(m+n)^2},$$

$$9\Delta10 = \frac{(9-10)^2}{(9+10)^2} = \frac{(-1)^2}{(19)^2} = \frac{1}{361}$$

$$\text{and}$$

$$10\Delta9 = \frac{(10-9)^2}{(10+9)^2} = \frac{(1)^2}{(19)^2} = \frac{1}{361}$$

Hence, the two quantities are equal.

11. **A.** Since $a > 0$, $b = 4a$, and $c = 3b$,

$$\frac{a+b+c}{4} = \frac{a+4a+3b}{4}$$
$$= \frac{a+4a+3(4a)}{4}$$
$$= \frac{a+4a+12a}{4}$$
$$= \frac{17a}{4}, \text{ or } 4\frac{1}{4}a$$

Since $4\frac{1}{4}a > 4a = b$, Quantity A has the greater value.

12. **B.**

$$x^2 < 3x \text{ and } x > 0$$
$$x^2 - 3x < 3x - 3x$$
$$x^2 - 3x < 0$$
$$x(x-3) < 0$$

If $x(x-3) < 0$, then $x > 0$ and $x - 3 < 0$, or $x < 0$ and $x - 3 > 0$.

Since $x > 0$,

$$x - 3 < 0$$
$$x - 3 + 3 < 0 + 3$$
$$x < 3$$

Hence, Quantity B has the greater value.

13. **D.**

$$\frac{z^4 + z^3}{z^2} = \frac{z^4}{z^2} + \frac{z^3}{z^2} = z^2 + z$$
$$\text{and}$$
$$\frac{z^4 + z^3}{z^3} = \frac{z^4}{z^3} + \frac{z^3}{z^3} = z + 1$$

If $z = \dfrac{1}{2}$, then $z^2 + z = \left(\dfrac{1}{2}\right)^2 + \dfrac{1}{2} = \dfrac{1}{4} + \dfrac{1}{2} = \dfrac{3}{4}$ and

$z + 1 = \dfrac{1}{2} + 1 = 1\dfrac{1}{2}$.

Then Quantity B is larger than Quantity A. However, if $z = 2$, then $z^2 + z = (2^2) + 2 = 4 + 2 = 6$, and $z + 1 = 2 + 1 = 3$, then Quantity A is larger than Quantity B. Therefore, the answer is D; the relationship cannot be determined from the information given.

14. **A.**

$$\dfrac{5}{y+3} = \dfrac{4}{2y-5}$$

Cross multiply to get
$$5(2y-5) = 4(y+3)$$
$$10y - 25 = 4y + 12$$
$$10y - 25 - 4y = 4y + 12 - 4y$$
$$6y - 25 = 12$$
$$6y - 25 + 25 = 12 + 25$$
$$6y = 37$$
$$\dfrac{6y}{6} = \dfrac{37}{6}$$
$$y = \dfrac{37}{6}, \text{ or } 6\dfrac{1}{6}$$

Hence, Quantity A has the greater value.

15. **C.** The distance, d, between the points (x_1, y_1) and (x_2, y_2) is

$$d = \sqrt{(x_1 - x_2)^2 + (y_1 - y_2)^2}$$

The distance between the points $(-5, 3)$ and $(4, -7)$ is

$$\sqrt{(-5-4)^2 + (3-(-7))^2} = \sqrt{(-9)^2 + (10)^2} = \sqrt{81 + 100} = \sqrt{181}$$

The distance between the points $(-7, 4)$ and $(3, -5)$ is

$$\sqrt{(-7-3)^2 + (4-(-5))^2} = \sqrt{(-10)^2 + (9)^2} = \sqrt{100 + 81} = \sqrt{181}$$

Hence, the two quantities are equal.

Multiple-Choice (Select One Answer)

16. E. Since $2n + 5$ is an odd integer, the next consecutive odd integer is 2 more than $2n + 5$, or $(2n + 5) + 2 = 2n + 7$.

17. D. Substitute $x = -8$ and $y = 3$ into the original equation:

$$3x - 4y - 12 = 3(-8) - 4(3) - 12$$
$$= -24 - 12 - 12$$
$$= -48$$
$$\neq 0$$

The other four ordered pairs, $(0, -3)$, $(4, 0)$, $(-4, -6)$, and $(12, 6)$, all satisfy the original equation.

18. C. If the graph of a function $f(x)$ is shifted horizontally 3 units to the right, the new function would be expressed as $f(x - 3)$. Since $f(x) = x^2$, $g(x) = f(x - 3) = (x - 3)^2$.

19. E.

$4 = 2^2, 4^4 = (2^2)^4 = 2^8$
$8 = 2^3, 8^3 = (2^3)^3 = 2^9$
$16 = 2^4, 16^2 = (2^4)^2 = 2^8$

Therefore, $4^4 \cdot 8^3 \cdot 16^2 = 2^8 \cdot 2^9 \cdot 2^8 = 2^{25}$.

20. D.

$$z^2 - 8z + 15 = 15$$
$$z^2 - 8z + 15 - 15 = 15 - 15$$
$$z^2 - 8z = 0$$
$$z(z - 8) = 0$$
$$z = 0 \quad \text{or} \quad z - 8 = 0$$
$$z = 0 \qquad \qquad z = 8$$

Since it is given that $z > 0$, then $z = 8$ is the only solution.

21. D. Since y varies directly to x, $y = kx$, where k is the constant of the variation. If $y = 1.68$ when $x = 1.2$, then

$$y = kx \rightarrow 1.68 = 1.2k$$
$$\frac{1.68}{1.2} = \frac{1.2k}{1.2}$$
$$k = 1.4 \text{ and } y = 1.4x$$

If $x = 200$, $y = 1.4x = (1.4)(200) = 280$.

22. A. Multiply the first equation by 2 and the second equation by −3, then add the two equations:

$$2(3m-5n)=\ 2(19)\ \rightarrow\ \ 6m-10n=\ \ 38$$
$$\underline{-3(2m-4n)=-3(16)\ \rightarrow\ \ \underline{-6m+12n=-48}}$$
$$2n=-10$$
$$\frac{2n}{2}=\frac{-10}{2}$$
$$n=-5$$

23. B.

$$\sqrt{50}=\sqrt{25\cdot 2}=5\sqrt{2}$$
$$3\sqrt{18}=3\sqrt{9\cdot 2}=3\cdot 3\sqrt{2}=9\sqrt{2}$$
$$\sqrt{32}=\sqrt{16\cdot 2}=4\sqrt{2}$$
$$9\sqrt{8}=9\sqrt{4\cdot 2}=9\cdot 2\sqrt{2}=18\sqrt{2}$$

Hence, $\sqrt{50}+3\sqrt{18}-\sqrt{32}+9\sqrt{8}$
$$=5\sqrt{2}+9\sqrt{2}-4\sqrt{2}+18\sqrt{2}$$
$$=28\sqrt{2}$$

24. D. Any point in Quadrant IV will have a positive x-coordinate and a negative y-coordinate. Therefore, if the point $P(a, b)$ is in Quadrant IV, $a > b$.

25. B. $y^x\cdot y^x\cdot y^x\cdot y^x=y^{x+x+x+x}=y^{4x}$

26. E. Since there are an infinite number of values for a and b such that $ab = 55$, the ratio of a to b cannot be determined from the information given. For example, if $a = 11$ and $b = 5$, then $ab = 55$, and the ratio of a to b is $\frac{a}{b}=\frac{11}{5}$. However, if $a = 5$ and $b = 11$, then $ab = 55$, but the ratio of a to b is $\frac{a}{b}=\frac{5}{11}$.

27. A. A line that passes through (5, 0) and (−3, −4) has a slope of m.

$$m=\frac{y_1-y_2}{x_1-x_2}=\frac{0-(-4)}{5-(-3)}=\frac{4}{8}=\frac{1}{2}$$

The slope-intercept form of the equation is $y = mx + b = \dfrac{1}{2}x + b$.

Substituting the x and y values of either of the two given points, such as $(5, 0)$, yields:

$$y = \dfrac{1}{2}x + b$$

$$0 = \dfrac{1}{2}(5) + b$$

$$0 = \dfrac{5}{2} + b$$

$$b = \dfrac{-5}{2} \quad \text{and} \quad y = \dfrac{1}{2}x - \dfrac{5}{2}$$

For the point $(11, 3)$, with $x = 11$:

$$y = \dfrac{1}{2}x - \dfrac{5}{2} = \dfrac{1}{2}(11) - \dfrac{5}{2} = \dfrac{11}{2} - \dfrac{5}{2} = \dfrac{6}{2} = 3$$

Hence, the point $(11, 3)$ lies on the line that passes through $(5, 0)$ and $(-3, -4)$. None of the other points $(1, 2)$, $(4, 2)$, $(7, 4)$, or $(-1, -2)$ satisfies the equation $y = \dfrac{1}{2}x - \dfrac{5}{2}$.

28. C. Multiply the given equation through by the LCD of 12.

$$12\left(\dfrac{z}{3} + \dfrac{z}{6} + \dfrac{z}{12}\right) = 12(21)$$

$$12\left(\dfrac{z}{3}\right) + 12\left(\dfrac{z}{6}\right) + 12\left(\dfrac{z}{12}\right) = 12(21)$$

$$4z + 2z + z = 252$$

$$7z = 252$$

$$\dfrac{7z}{7} = \dfrac{252}{7}$$

$$z = 36$$

29. C. Since m and n are positive integers, m^2 and n^2 are positive integers and perfect square integers.

If $m^2 - n^2 = 17$, then $m^2 = 81$ and $n^2 = 64$ and $m^2 + n^2 = 81 + 64 = 145$.

30. E. Factor the numerator and the denominator of the given fraction:

$$\frac{x^2+2x-24}{x^2+8x-48}=\frac{(x+6)\cancel{(x-4)}}{(x+12)\cancel{(x-4)}}$$
$$=\frac{x+6}{x+12}$$

Multiple-Choice (Select One or More Answers)

31. B, C, E, and F.

For the given equation $5x-3y=12$:

At $(0, 4) \rightarrow 5(0)-3(4)=0-12=-12 \neq 12$

At $(3, 1) \rightarrow 5(3)-3(1)=15-3=12$

At $(0, -4) \rightarrow 5(0)-3(-4)=0+12=12$

At $(3, -1) \rightarrow 5(3)-3(-1)=15+3=18 \neq 12$

At $\left(\frac{2}{5}, \frac{-10}{3}\right) \rightarrow 5\left(\frac{2}{5}\right)-3\left(\frac{-10}{3}\right)=2+10=12$

At $\left(4, \frac{8}{3}\right) \rightarrow 5(4)-3\left(\frac{8}{3}\right)=20-8=12$

32. A, C, and D.

$$4x^5+20x^4-24x^3=0$$
$$4x^3\left(x^2+5x-6\right)=0$$
$$4x^3(x+6)(x-1)=0$$
$$4x^3=0 \quad \text{or} \quad x+6=0 \quad \text{or} \quad x-1=0$$
$$x=0 \qquad\qquad x=-6 \qquad\qquad x=1$$

33. B and E.

Express each equation in the form $y = mx + b$, where m is the slope of the line:

If $4x+3y=20$, then $y=\frac{-4}{3}x+\frac{20}{3}$ and $m=\frac{-4}{3}$.

If $3x+4y=20$, then $y=\frac{-3}{4}x+5$ and $m=\frac{-3}{4}$.

If $4x-3y=20$, then $y=\frac{4}{3}x-\frac{20}{3}$ and $m=\frac{4}{3}$.

If $3x - 4y = 20$, then $y = \dfrac{3}{4}x - 5$ and $m = \dfrac{3}{4}$.

If $9x + 12y = 20$, then $y = \dfrac{-9}{12}x + \dfrac{20}{12} = \dfrac{-3}{4}x + \dfrac{5}{3}$ and $m = \dfrac{-3}{4}$.

If $x + y = 20$, then $y = -x + 20$ and $m = -1$.

34. B. If 43 is divided by 8, the remainder is 3, and if 43 is divided by 5, the remainder is also 3. None of the other choices satisfies both of these conditions.

35. C and F.

If $|4x - 10| = 18$, then

$$
\begin{array}{ccc}
4x - 10 = 18 & \text{or} & 4x - 10 = -18 \\
4x - 10 + 10 = 18 + 10 & & 4x - 10 + 10 = -18 + 10 \\
4x = 28 & & 4x = -8 \\
\dfrac{4x}{4} = \dfrac{28}{4} & & \dfrac{4x}{4} = \dfrac{-8}{4} \\
x = 7 & & x = -2
\end{array}
$$

If $x = 7$, then $3x + 5 = 3(7) + 5 = 21 + 5 = 26$.

If $x = -2$, then $3x + 5 = 3(-2) + 5 = -6 + 5 = -1$.

36. B and C.

Express each equation in the form $y = mx + b$, where b is the value of the y-intercept:

If $x + y = 3$, then $y = -x + 3$ and $b = 3$.

If $x + y = -3$, then $y = -x - 3$ and $b = -3$.

If $x - y = 3$, then $y = x - 3$ and $b = -3$.

If $y - x = 3$, then $y = x + 3$ and $b = 3$.

If $y = -3x$, then $b = 0$.

37. A, B, C, and E.

$-64 = (-4)^3$, $-27 = (-3)^3$, $1 = (1)^3$, and $64 = (4)^3$

Note that 16 and 100 are perfect squares, not perfect cubes.

38. **A, B, C, D, and F.**

Since x and y are prime numbers that are less than 10, their possible values are 2, 3, 5, and 7. Among the values that xy could be are

$2 \cdot 5 = 5 \cdot 2 = 10$

$2 \cdot 7 = 7 \cdot 2 = 14$

$3 \cdot 5 = 5 \cdot 3 = 15$

$5 \cdot 5 = 25$

$7 \cdot 7 = 49$

The only factors of 27, answer choice E, are 3 and 9 or 1 and 27, which do not satisfy the given conditions for x and y.

39. **C.** The graph of a parabola of the form $y = ax^2 + bx + c$ (where $a \neq 0$) will open downward if $a < 0$. The only equation satisfying this condition is $y = -2x^2 + 11x - 1$. Note that $x = -3y^2 + 5y + 4$ will be a parabola opening to the left.

40. **B, E, and F.**

a^2b^2 is an odd integer since both a^2 and b^2 are odd and the product of two odd integers is odd.

$a^2 + b^2 + c^2$ is an odd integer since a^2 is odd, b^2 is odd, and c^2 are odd and the sum of three odd integers is odd.

abc is odd since the product of three odd integers is odd.

$a^2 - b^2$, $a^2 + b^2$, and $a + c$ are all even integers.

41. **A, C, and F.**

83, 103, and 127 are prime numbers since their only factors are 1 and the number itself.

91 is not prime since $7 \cdot 13 = 91$

111 is not prime since $3 \cdot 37 = 111$

119 is not prime since $7 \cdot 17 = 119$

42. **A, B, C, D, E, and F.**

If $m = -10$, $x^2 + mx - 24 = x^2 - 10x - 24 = (x - 12)(x + 2)$.

If $m = -5$, $x^2 + mx - 24 = x^2 - 5x - 24 = (x - 8)(x + 3)$.

If $m = -2$, $x^2 + mx - 24 = x^2 - 2x - 24 = (x - 6)(x + 4)$.

If $m = 2$, $x^2 + mx - 24 = x^2 + 2x - 24 = (x + 6)(x - 4)$.

If $m = 5$, $x^2 + mx - 24 = x^2 + 5x - 24 = (x + 8)(x - 3)$.

If $m = 10$, $x^2 + mx - 24 = x^2 + 10x - 24 = (x + 12)(x - 2)$.

43. **A and C.**

Express each equation in the form $y = mx + b$, where m is the slope of the line:

If $9x + 4y = 36$, then $y = \dfrac{-9}{4}x + 9$ and $m = \dfrac{-9}{4}$.

If $2x - 5y = 10$, then $y = \dfrac{2}{5}x - 2$ and $m = \dfrac{2}{5}$.

If $x + y = 15$, then $y = -x + 15$ and $m = -1$.

If $x = -3$, then the line is a vertical line and the slope is undefined.

If $y = -6$, then the line is a horizontal line and the slope $m = 0$.

44. **B, D, and E.**

$4^{25} = (2^2)^{25} = 2^{50}$

$4^{50} = (2^2)^{50} = 2^{100}$

$8^{25} = (2^3)^{25} = 2^{75}$

$16^{25} = (2^4)^{25} = 2^{100}$

$32^{20} = (2^5)^{20} = 2^{100}$

45. **C, D, and E.**

$$5z - 10 < 8z - 6$$
$$5z - 10 - 8z < 8z - 6 - 8z$$
$$-3z - 10 < -6$$
$$-3z - 10 + 10 < -6 + 10$$
$$-3z < 4$$
$$\frac{-3z}{-3} > \frac{4}{-3}$$
$$z > \frac{-4}{3}$$

Hence, -1, 0, and 4 are in the solution of $5z - 10 < 8z - 6$.

Numeric Entry (Fill-in)

46. $\dfrac{-5}{2}$

$$4x^2 + 20x + 25 = 0$$
$$(2x+5)(2x+5) = 0$$
$$\text{or}$$
$$(2x+5)^2 = 0$$
$$2x+5 = 0$$
$$2x+5-5 = 0-5$$
$$2x = -5$$
$$\frac{2x}{2} = \frac{-5}{2}$$
$$x = \frac{-5}{2}$$

47. $\dfrac{1}{2}$

Express the equation in the form $y = mx + b$, where m is the slope of the line:

$$3x - 6y = 25$$
$$3x - 6y - 3x = 25 - 3x$$
$$-6y = -3x + 25$$
$$\frac{-6y}{-6} = \frac{-3x}{-6} + \frac{25}{-6}$$
$$y = \frac{1}{2}x - \frac{25}{6} \text{ and the slope } m = \frac{1}{2}$$

48. $\dfrac{27}{4}$

$$\frac{6}{2z-3} = \frac{5}{z+2}$$

Cross multiply
$$6(z+2) = 5(2z-3)$$
$$6z + 12 = 10z - 15$$
$$6z + 12 - 10z = 10z - 15 - 10z$$
$$-4z + 12 = -15$$
$$-4z + 12 - 12 = -15 - 12$$
$$-4z = -27$$
$$\frac{-4z}{-4} = \frac{-27}{-4}$$
$$z = \frac{27}{4}$$

49. 69

If $x = -3$, $y = 2$, and $z = -4$, then

$$\begin{aligned}
x^3 + 4y^3 - z^3 &= (-3)^3 + 4(2)^3 - (-4)^3 \\
&= -27 + 4(8) - (-64) \\
&= -27 + 32 + 64 \\
&= 69
\end{aligned}$$

50. $\dfrac{-5}{4}$

If $3a(4a + 5)(3a - 4)(a + 1)(a - 2) = 0$, then $3a = 0$, or $4a + 5 = 0$, or $3a - 4 = 0$, or $a + 1 = 0$, or $a - 2 = 0$. That means

$$a = 0 \quad \text{or} \quad a = \frac{-5}{4} \quad \text{or} \quad a = \frac{4}{3} \quad \text{or} \quad a = -1 \quad \text{or} \quad a = 2$$

Hence, the smallest possible value of a is $\dfrac{-5}{4}$.

51. 7

The x value at the vertex of a parabola with equation $y = ax^2 + bx + c$ (where $a \neq 0$) is $x = \dfrac{-b}{2a}$.

For the parabola $y = 2x^2 + 4x + 9$, $x = \dfrac{-b}{2a} = \dfrac{-4}{2(2)} = \dfrac{-4}{4} = -1$.

Substitute $x = -1$ into the given equation:

$$\begin{aligned}
y &= 2x^2 + 4x + 9 \\
&= 2(-1)^2 + 4(-1) + 9 \\
&= 2(1) - 4 + 9 \\
&= 2 - 4 + 9 \\
y &= 7
\end{aligned}$$

52. 4

Multiply the first equation by 3 and the second equation by -5:

$$\begin{aligned}
3(3x + 5y) &= 3(7) \quad \rightarrow \quad 9x + 15y = 21 \\
-5(2x + 3y) &= -5(5) \quad \rightarrow \quad \underline{-10x - 15y = -25} \\
& \qquad\qquad\qquad\qquad\quad -x \qquad\quad = -4 \ \text{ and } \ x = 4
\end{aligned}$$

53. 8

If a graph intersects the y-axis, then $x = 0$ at that point.
Since $4x - 3y + 24 = 0$, if $x = 0$:

$$4x - 3y + 24 = 0$$
$$4(0) - 3y + 24 = 0$$
$$-3y + 24 = 0$$
$$-3y + 24 - 24 = 0 - 24$$
$$-3y = -24$$
$$\frac{-3y}{-3} = \frac{-24}{-3}$$
$$y = 8$$

54. 343

Since $6^3 = 216$, $7^3 = 343$, and $8^3 = 512$, the only perfect cube between 300 and 400 is 343.

55. 26

$$\text{If } g(x) = 3x^2 - 5x + 4, \ g(-2) = 3(-2)^2 - 5(-2) + 4$$
$$= 3(4) + 10 + 4$$
$$= 26$$

56. 10

Since $x + a = 20$ and $x - b = 15$,

$$(x + a) - (x - b) = 20 - 15$$
$$x + a - x + b = 5$$
$$a + b = 5$$

Since $x + c = 10$ and $x - d = 5$,

$$(x + c) - (x - d) = 10 - 5$$
$$x + c - x + d = 5$$
$$c + d = 5$$

Hence, $a + b + c + d = 5 + 5 = 10$.

57. 13

The distance, d, between the points (x_1, y_1) and (x_2, y_2) is

$$d = \sqrt{(x_1 - x_2)^2 + (y_1 - y_2)^2}$$

The distance, d, between the points $(-3, 10)$ and $(2, -2)$ is

$$\begin{aligned}
d &= \sqrt{(-3 - 2)^2 + (10 - (-2))^2} \\
&= \sqrt{(-5)^2 + (12)^2} \\
&= \sqrt{25 + 144} \\
&= \sqrt{169} \\
d &= 13
\end{aligned}$$

58. −21

Since $f(x) = 2x - 5, f(-2) = 2(-2) - 5 = -4 - 5 = -9$
Since $g(x) = x^2 + 3, g(-3) = (-3)^2 + 3 = 9 + 3 = 12$
Therefore, $f(-2) - g(-3) = -9 - 12 = -21$

59. $\dfrac{4}{5}$

$$\frac{\dfrac{1}{x} + \dfrac{1}{z}}{\dfrac{1}{x} \cdot \dfrac{1}{z}} = \frac{\dfrac{1}{x} \cdot \dfrac{z}{z} + \dfrac{1}{z} \cdot \dfrac{x}{x}}{\dfrac{1}{xz}} = \frac{4}{5}$$

$$\frac{\dfrac{z}{xz} + \dfrac{x}{xz}}{\dfrac{1}{xz}} \cdot \frac{xz}{xz} = \frac{4}{5}$$

$$\frac{\dfrac{z}{xz} \cdot xz + \dfrac{x}{xz} \cdot xz}{\dfrac{1}{xz} \cdot xz} = \frac{4}{5}$$

$$\frac{z + x}{1} = \frac{4}{5}$$

$$x + z = \frac{4}{5}$$

Another solution could be:

$$\frac{\dfrac{1}{x}+\dfrac{1}{z}}{\dfrac{1}{x}\cdot\dfrac{1}{z}}=\frac{4}{5}$$

$$\frac{1}{x}+\frac{1}{z}=\frac{1}{xz}\left(\frac{4}{5}\right) \quad \left(\text{multiply by the denominator } \frac{1}{xz}\right)$$

$$\frac{z+x}{xz}=\frac{4}{5xz} \quad \text{(get LCD of } xz \text{ on left side)}$$

$$5xz(z+x)=4(xz) \quad \text{(cross multiply)}$$

$$z+x=\frac{4xz}{5xz} \quad \text{(divide by } 5xz)$$

$$x+z=\frac{4}{5} \quad \text{(simplify)}$$

60. **8**

The midpoint, M, between two points (x_1, y_1) and (x_2, y_2) is

$$M\left\{\frac{x_1+x_2}{2},\ \frac{y_1+y_2}{2}\right\}$$

Since the midpoint of $\overline{AB}$ is $(-2, 6)$ and endpoint B is the point $(6, 4)$, the y value of point A can be determined by

$$\frac{y+4}{2}=6$$

$$\frac{y+4}{2}\cdot 2=6\cdot 2$$

$$y+4=12$$

$$y+4-4=12-4$$

$$y=8$$

Chapter 5

Geometry

The word "geometry" literally means "Earth's measurement," and its concepts have been studied for thousands of years. The GRE tests your ability to apply measurement and geometric concepts to solve problems within the context of math logic. You will be asked to apply your knowledge of mathematical relationships among geometric shapes, angles, and other configurations.

As you approach geometry problems on the GRE, keep in mind that the visual illustrations of geometric figures are *not* necessarily drawn to scale. However, lines shown in the figures are straight, and points on the line are in the order shown. Some shapes may appear larger, while others may appear smaller. When selecting the answer choice, you should always base your answer on geometric logic, and not on estimating or comparing quantities by sight.

Geometry Topics You Should Know

Topic	Study Pages	Worked Examples	Further Study Required
Lines, segments, rays, angles, and congruence	pp. 225–231		
Triangles: perimeter, area, and angle measure	pp. 234–244		
Pythagorean theorem	pp. 240–241		
Polygons: perimeter, area, and angle measure of quadrilaterals and other polygons	pp. 231–234 pp. 244–254		
Circles: circumference, radius, diameter, area, and arcs	pp. 254–260		
Solid geometry: volume and surface area	pp. 260–264		

The following diagnostic test is designed to help you identify specific geometry topics that require further concentration. After you take the diagnostic test, analyze your test results and develop a step-by-step action plan to pinpoint topics to study.

Geometry Diagnostic Test

25 Questions

Directions: Solve each problem in this section by using the information given and your own mathematical calculations.

1. If $\angle A = 59°$ and $\angle B = 58°$ in $\triangle ABC$, what is the longest side of the triangle?

2. In the following figure, $\ell_1 \parallel \ell_2$ and $\angle 1 = 70°$. Find the measure of $\angle 2$.

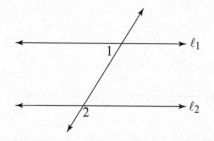

3. Find the sum of the interior angles of a polygon with 15 sides.

4. Find the measure of one of the interior angles of a regular decagon.

5. In $\triangle XYZ$, $\overline{XZ} \perp \overline{YZ}$, $XZ = 24$, and $XY = 26$. Find the length of $\overline{YZ}$.

6. In the following figure, find the area of the given $\triangle ABC$.

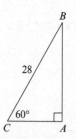

7. In the following figure, $MP = NP$ and $\angle N = 57°$. Find the measure of $\angle 1$.

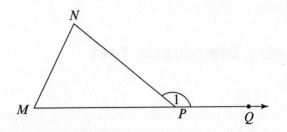

8. An isosceles right triangle has a leg whose length is 15. Find the length of its hypotenuse.

9. In the following figure, find the area of trapezoid $ABCD$.

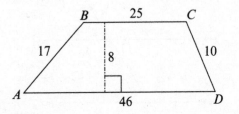

10. Find the area of a parallelogram whose sides have lengths of 18 and 22, with a base angle of 30°.

11. Find the area of a rhombus whose diagonals have lengths of 25 and 30.

12. Find the area of a rectangle if one of its sides has the length of 30 and one of its diagonals has the length of 34.

13. Find the perimeter of a square whose diagonal has the length of $19\sqrt{2}$.

14. If $\triangle ABC \sim \triangle XYZ$, with $XY = 20$, $YZ = 25$, $XZ = 30$, and $AC = 24$, find the perimeter of $\triangle ABC$.

15. In the following figure, $\angle BAC = 37°$ and $\angle DAE = 61°$. Find the measure of $\angle CAD$.

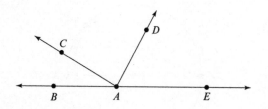

16. An angle has a measure that is four times the measure of its supplement. Find the measure of the larger angle.

17. A right triangle has a leg with a length of 12 and a hypotenuse with a length of 16. Find the length of its other leg.

18. Find the area of an equilateral triangle whose sides have a length of 30.

19. Find the area of a circle whose circumference is 28π and express the answer in terms of π.

20. In the following circle, X is a point on the circle and $\angle X = 50°$. Find the measure of $\overparen{YXZ}$.

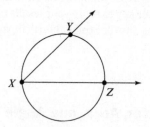

21. In the following circle with center C, $\angle C = 80°$. Find the measure of $\angle DAB$.

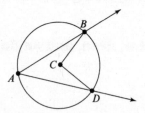

207

22. In the circle below with center C, $XY = 12$ and $YZ = 16$. Find the area of the circle.

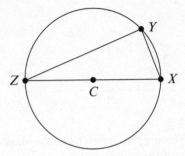

23. Find the surface area of a box with square faces, with sides of length 12 inches if the box has no top.

24. Find the volume of a right circular cylinder with a radius of 6 inches and a height of 14 inches.

25. Find the volume of a cardboard box whose base is a rectangle of 3 feet by 4 feet and whose height is 2 feet.

Scoring the Diagnostic Test

The following section will assist you in scoring and analyzing your diagnostic test results. Use the answer key to score your results on the Analysis Sheet that follows. Read through the answer explanations on pages 211–225 to clarify the solutions to the problems.

Answer Key

Triangles: Perimeter, Area, and Angle Measure

1. $\overline{AB}$

Lines, Segments, Rays, Angles, and Congruence

2. 110°

Polygons: Perimeter, Area, and Angle Measure

3. 2340°

4. 144°

Pythagorean Theorem

5. 10

Polygons: Perimeter, Area, and Angle Measure

6. $98\sqrt{3}$

Triangles: Perimeter, Area, and Angle Measure

7. 114°

Pythagorean Theorem

8. $15\sqrt{2}$

Polygons: Perimeter, Area, and Angle Measure

9. 284

10. 198

11. 375

12. 480

13. 76

Lines, Segments, Rays, Angles, and Congruence

14. 60

15. 82°

16. 144°

Pythagorean Theorem

17. $4\sqrt{7}$

Polygons: Perimeter, Area, and Angle Measure

18. $225\sqrt{3}$

Circles: Circumference, Area, and Arcs

19. 196π

20. 260°

21. 40°

22. 100π

Solid Geometry: Volume and Surface Area

23. 720 square inches

24. 504π cubic inches

25. 24 cubic feet

Charting and Analyzing Your Diagnostic Test Results

Record your diagnostic test results in the following chart and use these results as a guide for an effective geometry review. Mark the problems that you missed, paying particular attention to those that were missed because of a "lack of knowledge." These are the areas you will want to focus on as you study the geometry topics.

Geometry Diagnostic Test Analysis Sheet

Topic	Total Possible	Number Correct	Number Incorrect		
			(A) Simple Mistake	(B) Misread Problem	(C) Lack of Knowledge
Lines, segments, rays, angles, and congruence	4				
Triangles: perimeter, area, and angle measure	2				
Pythagorean theorem	3				
Polygons: perimeter, area, and angle measure of quadrilaterals and other polygons	9				
Circles: circumference, area, and arcs	4				
Solid geometry: volume and surface area	3				
Total Possible Explanations for Incorrect Answers: Columns A, B, and C					
Total Number of Answers Correct and Incorrect	25	Add the total number of correct answers here: _____	Add columns A, B, and C: _____ Total number of incorrect answers		

Geometry Diagnostic Test Answers and Explanations

Triangles: Perimeter, Area, and Angle Measure

1. $\overline{AB}$

Since $\angle A = 59°$ and $\angle B = 58°$ in $\triangle ABC$, $\angle C = 63°$ (the sum of the angles in a triangle equals $180°$). In any triangle, the longest side is opposite the largest angle, so the side opposite $\angle C$ is the longest side of the triangle, which is $\overline{AB}$.

Lines, Segments, Rays, Angles, and Congruence

2. $110°$

Since $\ell_1 \parallel \ell_2$, alternate interior angles are equal and $\angle 1 = \angle 3 = 70°$. Since $\angle 2$ and $\angle 3$ form a straight line, they are supplementary and

$$\angle 2 + \angle 3 = 180°$$
$$\angle 2 + 70° = 180°$$
$$\angle 2 = 180° - 70°$$
$$\angle 2 = 110°$$

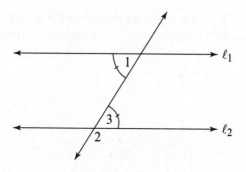

Polygons: Perimeter, Area, and Angle Measure

3. **2340°**

The sum of the interior angles of a polygon with n sides is $(n-2) \cdot 180°$. For a 15-sided polygon, the sum of the interior angles is

$$(n-2) \cdot 180° = (15-2) \cdot 180°$$
$$= 13 \cdot 180°$$
$$= 2340°$$

4. **144°**

A regular polygon is a polygon with all sides equal in length and all angles equal in measure. A regular decagon will have ten equal sides and angles. The sum of the interior angles in any decagon is

$$(10-2) \cdot 180° = 8 \cdot 180° = 1440°$$

Since there are ten equal angles in a regular decagon, each interior angle will have a measure of

$$1440° \div 10 = 144°$$

Pythagorean Theorem

5. **10**

Since $\overline{XZ} \perp \overline{YZ}$, $\angle Z$ is a right angle and $\triangle XYZ$ is a right triangle, where $\overline{XY}$ is the hypotenuse and $\overline{XZ}$ is a leg of the triangle.

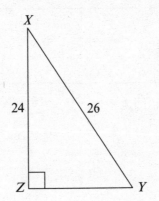

By the Pythagorean theorem,

$$(XZ)^2 + (YZ)^2 = (XY)^2$$
$$24^2 + (YZ)^2 = 26^2$$
$$576 + (YZ)^2 = 676$$
$$(YZ)^2 = 100$$
$$YZ = \sqrt{100}$$
$$YZ = 10$$

Polygons: Perimeter, Area, and Angle Measure

6. $98\sqrt{3}$

Since $\angle A$ is a right angle, $\angle A = 90°$, $\angle C = 60°$, and $\angle B = 30°$. In a 30°-60°-90° triangle, the side opposite the 30° angle is half of the hypotenuse, and the side opposite the 60° angle is half of the hypotenuse times $\sqrt{3}$.

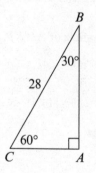

In $\triangle ABC$,

$$AC = \frac{1}{2}(BC) = \frac{1}{2}(28) = 14$$
$$AB = \frac{1}{2}(BC) \cdot \sqrt{3} = \frac{1}{2}(28) \cdot \sqrt{3} = 14\sqrt{3}$$

The area A of $\triangle ABC$ with base b and height h is

$$A = \frac{1}{2}bh$$
$$A = \frac{1}{2}(14)(14\sqrt{3})$$
$$= 7(14\sqrt{3})$$
$$A = 98\sqrt{3}$$

Triangles: Perimeter, Area, and Angle Measure

7. **114°**

   Since $MP = NP$, $\triangle MNP$ is an isosceles triangle with $\angle M = \angle N = 57°$.

   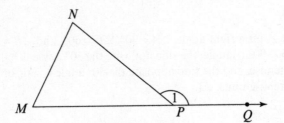

   Since $\angle 1$ is an exterior angle of $\triangle MNP$,

   $$\angle 1 = \angle M + \angle N$$
   $$= 57° + 57°$$
   $$\angle 1 = 114°$$

Pythagorean Theorem

8. **$15\sqrt{2}$**

   In an isosceles right triangle, the hypotenuse has a length equal to the length of the leg times $\sqrt{2}$. Since the given leg has a length of 15, the length of the hypotenuse is $15\sqrt{2}$.

   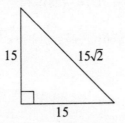

Polygons: Perimeter, Area, and Angle Measure

9. **284**

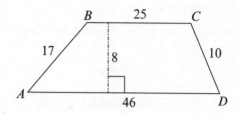

The area A of a trapezoid with bases b_1 and b_2 and height h is

$$
\begin{aligned}
A &= \frac{1}{2}h(b_1 + b_2) \\
&= \frac{1}{2}(8)(46 + 25) \\
&= (4)(71) \\
A &= 284
\end{aligned}
$$

10. **198**

The area A of a parallelogram with base b and height h is $A = bh$.

The height is drawn to form a 30°-60°-90° right triangle with a hypotenuse of length 18. The height h will have a length equal to one-half the hypotenuse: $\frac{1}{2}(18) = 9$.

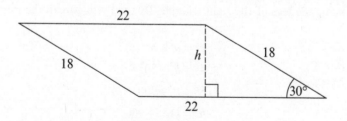

The area A of the parallelogram is

$$
\begin{aligned}
A &= bh \\
&= (22)(9) \\
A &= 198
\end{aligned}
$$

11. 375

Since the diagonals d_1 and d_2 of a rhombus are perpendicular, the area A of a rhombus is $A = \dfrac{1}{2} d_1 \cdot d_2$.

The area A of a rhombus whose diagonals have lengths of 25 and 30 is

$$\begin{aligned} A &= \frac{1}{2} d_1 d_2 \\ &= \frac{1}{2}(25)(30) \\ &= \frac{1}{2}(750) \\ A &= 375 \end{aligned}$$

12. 480

The area A of a rectangle with base b and height h is $A = bh$.

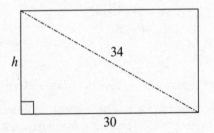

The diagonal of the rectangle forms two congruent right triangles, with the diagonal being the hypotenuse and the sides of the rectangle being the legs of the right triangle. By the Pythagorean theorem,

$$\begin{aligned} c^2 &= a^2 + b^2 \\ 34^2 &= h^2 + 30^2 \\ 1156 &= h^2 + 900 \\ h^2 &= 1156 - 900 \\ h^2 &= 256 \\ h &= \sqrt{256} \\ h &= 16 \end{aligned}$$

Hence, the area A of the rectangle is

$$A = b \cdot h$$
$$= (30)(16)$$
$$A = 480$$

13. 76

The perimeter P of a square with sides of length s is $P = 4 \cdot s$.

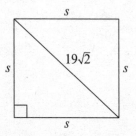

The diagonal of a square forms two isosceles right triangles whose hypotenuse is equal to the length of the legs times $\sqrt{2}$. Since the hypotenuse has a length of $19\sqrt{2}$, the length of each of the legs is 19, which is the same as each side of the square. The perimeter P of the square is

$$P = 4 \cdot s$$
$$= 4(19)$$
$$= 76$$

Lines, Segments, Rays, Angles, and Congruence

14. 60

Since $\triangle ABC \sim \triangle XYZ$, their corresponding sides are proportional and $\dfrac{AB}{XY} = \dfrac{BC}{YZ} = \dfrac{AC}{XZ}$.

The perimeter P of $\triangle ABC$ is $P = AB + BC + AC$.

To find AB,

$$\frac{AB}{XY} = \frac{AC}{XZ}$$

$$\frac{AB}{20} = \frac{24}{30}$$

$$30(AB) = (20)(24)$$

$$30(AB) = 480$$

$$AB = \frac{480}{30}$$

$$AB = 16$$

To find BC,

$$\frac{BC}{YZ} = \frac{AC}{XZ}$$

$$\frac{BC}{25} = \frac{24}{30}$$

$$30(BC) = (25)(24)$$

$$30(BC) = 600$$

$$BC = \frac{600}{30}$$

$$BC = 20$$

Hence, the perimeter P of $\triangle ABC$ is

$$P = AB + BC + AC$$
$$= 16 + 20 + 24$$
$$P = 60$$

An alternate solution would be:

Since the perimeters of similar triangles have the same ratio as the ratio of their corresponding sides

$$\frac{\text{perimeter of } \triangle ABC}{\text{perimeter of } \triangle XYZ} = \frac{AC}{XZ} = \frac{24}{30} = \frac{4}{5}$$

The perimeter of $\triangle XYZ = XY + XY + XZ$
$$= 20 + 25 + 30$$
$$= 75$$

Hence,

$$\frac{\text{perimeter of } \triangle ABC}{\text{perimeter of } \triangle XYZ} = \frac{4}{5}$$

$$\frac{\text{perimeter of } \triangle ABC}{75} = \frac{4}{5}$$

$$\text{perimeter of } \triangle ABC = \frac{4}{5} \cdot 75$$

$$= \frac{4 \cdot \overset{15}{\cancel{75}}}{\cancel{5}}$$

$$= 60$$

15. 82°

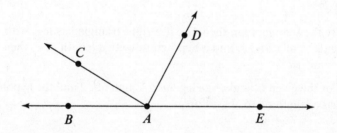

Since the three angles $\angle BAC$, $\angle CAD$, and $\angle DAE$ form a straight line, their sum is 180° and

$$\angle BAC + \angle CAD + \angle DAE = 180°$$
$$37° + \angle CAD + 61° = 180°$$
$$\angle CAD + 98° = 180°$$
$$\angle CAD = 180° - 98°$$
$$\angle CAD = 82°$$

16. **144°**

    Two angles are supplementary if their sum is 180°.

    Let x = the measure of the smaller angle.

    $4x$ = the measure of the larger angle.

    $$x + 4x = 180°$$
    $$5x = 180°$$
    $$\frac{5x}{5} = \frac{180°}{5}$$
    $$x = 36°$$
    $$4x = 4 \cdot 36° = 144°$$

Pythagorean Theorem

17. $4\sqrt{7}$

    By the Pythagorean theorem, if a right triangle has legs with lengths of a and b, and a hypotenuse with a length of c, then $c^2 = a^2 + b^2$.

    For the given triangle, one leg has a length of 12 and the hypotenuse has a length of 16. Therefore,

    $$16^2 = 12^2 + b^2$$
    $$256 = 144 + b^2$$
    $$b^2 = 256 - 144$$
    $$b^2 = 112$$
    $$b = \sqrt{112} = \sqrt{16 \cdot 7}$$
    $$b = 4\sqrt{7}$$

Polygons: Perimeter, Area, and Angle Measure

18. $225\sqrt{3}$

    An equilateral triangle is also an equiangular triangle whose angles each have a measure of 60°. Any height drawn to one of its sides forms two 30°-60°-90° triangles with the hypotenuse having a length of 30. The height h is opposite the 60° angle and has a length equal to half of the hypotenuse times $\sqrt{3}$: $h = \dfrac{1}{2}(30) \cdot \sqrt{3} = 15\sqrt{3}$.

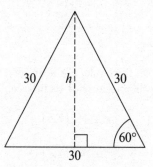

The area A of the triangle is

$$
\begin{aligned}
A &= \frac{1}{2}bh \\
&= \frac{1}{2}(30)\left(15\sqrt{3}\right) \\
&= (15)\left(15\sqrt{3}\right) \\
A &= 225\sqrt{3}
\end{aligned}
$$

Circles: Circumference, Area, and Arcs

19. **196π**

   The area A of a circle with radius r is $A = \pi r^2$.

   The circumference C of a circle with diameter d is $C = \pi d$.

   Since the circumference of the circle is 28π,

$$
\begin{aligned}
C &= \pi d \\
28\pi &= \pi d \\
\frac{28\pi}{\pi} &= \frac{\pi d}{\pi} \\
d &= 28
\end{aligned}
$$

   If the diameter of a circle is 28, its radius r is half the diameter:

$$
r = \frac{1}{2}d = \frac{1}{2}(28) = 14
$$

The area A of the circle is

$$A = \pi r^2$$
$$= \pi \left(14^2\right)$$
$$A = 196\pi$$

20. 260°

Since X is a point on the circle, $\angle X$ is an inscribed angle whose measure is half of the measure of its intercepted arc, $\widehat{YZ}$:

$$\angle X = \frac{1}{2}\left(\widehat{YZ}\right)$$
$$50° = \frac{1}{2}\left(\widehat{YZ}\right)$$
$$2 \cdot 50° = 2 \cdot \frac{1}{2}\left(\widehat{YZ}\right)$$
$$\widehat{YZ} = 100°$$

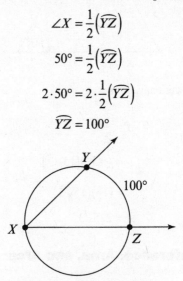

Since a circle is an arc whose measure is 360°,

$$\widehat{YXZ} = 360° - \widehat{YZ}$$
$$= 360° - 100°$$
$$\widehat{YXZ} = 260°$$

21. 40°

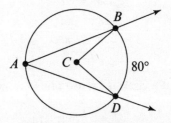

Since C is the center of the circle, $\angle C$ is a central angle whose measure is equal to the measure of its intercepted arc, $\overset{\frown}{BD}$: $\angle C = \overset{\frown}{BD} = 80°$.

$\angle DAB$ is an inscribed angle whose measure is half of the measure of its intercepted arc, $\overset{\frown}{BD}$.

$$\angle DAB = \frac{1}{2}\left(\overset{\frown}{BD}\right)$$
$$= \frac{1}{2}(80°)$$
$$\angle DAB = 40°$$

22. 100π

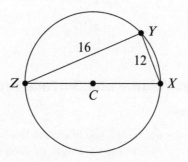

Since C is the center of the circle, $\overline{XZ}$ is a diameter that divides the circle into two semicircles whose measures are 180°. $\angle Y$ is an inscribed angle whose measure is half of the measure of its intercepted arc, $\overset{\frown}{XZ}$.

$$\angle Y = \frac{1}{2}\left(\overset{\frown}{XZ}\right)$$
$$= \frac{1}{2}(180°)$$
$$\angle Y = 90°$$

Therefore, ΔXYZ is a right triangle with legs whose lengths are 12 and 16. By the Pythagorean theorem,

$$(XZ)^2 = (XY)^2 + (YZ)^2$$
$$= (12)^2 + (16)^2$$
$$= 144 + 256$$
$$(XZ)^2 = 400$$
$$XZ = \sqrt{400} = 20$$

Hence, the circle has a diameter with a length of 20 and a radius with a length of 10. The area A of the circle is

$$A = \pi r^2$$
$$= \pi(10^2)$$
$$A = 100\pi$$

Solid Geometry: Volume and Surface Area

23. 720 square inches

Since the box does not have a top, there are five square faces, each with an area $A = s^2$, where s is the length of each side of the square. The surface area SA of the box is

$$SA = 5x^2$$
$$= 5(12^2)$$
$$= 5(144)$$
$$SA = 720 \text{ square inches}$$

24. 504π cubic inches

The volume V of a right circular cylinder with radius r and height h is $V = \pi r^2 h$.

For the given cylinder with a radius of 6 inches and height of 14 inches, the volume V is

$$V = \pi(6^2)(14)$$
$$= \pi(36)(14)$$
$$V = 504\pi \text{ cubic inches}$$

25. **24 cubic feet**

The volume V of a rectangular solid with length l, width w, and height h is $V = lwh$.

For the given box with length of 4 feet, width of 3 feet, and height of 2 feet, the volume V is

$V = (4)(3)(2)$

$V = 24$ cubic feet

Geometry Review

Basic Geometry Terms

Point

A **point** is an idea about a location in space. It has no length, no width, and no depth. It is usually named by an uppercase letter and identified by a dot.

Line (Straight Line)

A **line** is a set of points that continues indefinitely in both directions. On the GRE, a line is always considered to be straight. A line has one dimension, length, but its length cannot be measured. A line consists of an infinite number of points and is named by any two points on it. The symbol $\leftrightarrow$ is used to represent a line:

$$\text{line } AB = \overleftrightarrow{AB} = \overleftrightarrow{BA} = \text{line } BA$$

Ray

A **ray** is a set of points on a line that has a definite endpoint, called its **vertex,** and continues indefinitely in one direction only. A ray has one dimension, length, but its length cannot be measured. The symbol $\rightarrow$ is used to represent a ray:

$$\text{ray } AB = \overrightarrow{AB} \neq \overrightarrow{BA} = \text{ray } BA$$

Note that $\overrightarrow{AB}$ and $\overrightarrow{BA}$ are not the same rays since they do not have the same vertex.

Line Segment (Segment)

A **line segment** is a set of points on a line that has two distinct endpoints. A line segment is named by its two endpoints. A line segment has one dimension, length, and its length *can* be measured. The symbol ‾ is used to represent a line segment:

$$\text{line segment } AB = \overline{AB} = \overline{BA} = \text{line segment } BA$$

A line segment AB is sometimes referred to simply as segment AB.

> **Note: On the GRE, a notation of *line segment* and its *length* may expressed in the same way (with no bar above *AB*). Therefore, it is important to recognize the context of the expression that is being referenced to determine the meaning.**

A **midpoint** of a line segment is the halfway point, or the point equidistant from the endpoints.

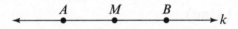

If $AM = MB$, then M is the midpoint of $\overline{AB}$. In the previous sentence, the AM and MB are considered to be lengths, and the $\overline{AB}$ is considered to be the segment itself.

Plane

A **plane** is a flat surface consisting of an infinite number of points. A plane has only two dimensions, length and width, neither of which can be measured.

Angle

An **angle** is formed by the union of two rays (or two lines that intersect at a point) with a common endpoint called the **vertex** of the angle. The rays are called the **sides** of the angle, and an angle is measured in units called **degrees** (°) from 0 to 360. The number of degrees indicates the size of the angle. The symbol $\angle$ is used to represent an angle, and the vertex letter may be used to identify the angle being referenced. However, if there is more than one angle with the same vertex, a three-letter method may be used to identify the angle, with the vertex as the middle letter.

Example

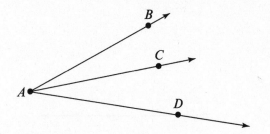

1. There are three angles in the given figure, each with a vertex at A.

   The two smaller angles are

   $$\angle BAC = \angle CAB \text{ and } \angle CAD = \angle DAC$$

   The largest angle is

   $$\angle BAD = \angle DAB$$

   Note that writing $\angle A$ would be inconclusive, since there are three angles with vertex A.

Types of Angles

There are two groups of angles: single angles (acute, right, obtuse, and straight) and pairs of angles (adjacent, complementary, supplementary, vertical, alternate interior, and alternate exterior). Let's start with single angles.

Single Angles

The four types of single angles are detailed below.

Acute Angle

An **acute angle** is an angle whose measure is between 0° and 90°.

Right Angle

A **right angle** is an angle whose measure is 90°. If two rays form a right angle, the rays are said to be perpendicular, and conversely, if two rays are perpendicular, the angle formed is a right angle. The symbol for perpendicular is ⊥. In the following figure, the small square symbol in the interior of the angle means it is a right angle. Angle T is a right angle.

Example

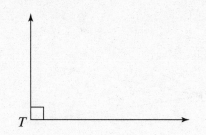

Obtuse Angle

An **obtuse angle** is an angle whose measure is between 90° and 180°.

Straight Angle

A **straight angle** is an angle whose measure is 180°.

Example

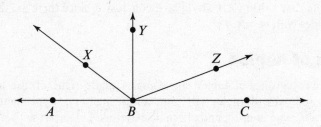

1. Given the figure with $\overleftrightarrow{AC}$ and $\overrightarrow{BY} \perp \overleftrightarrow{AC}$,

$\angle ABX$, $\angle XBY$, $\angle YBZ$, and $\angle ZBC$ are acute angles.

$\angle XBC$ and $\angle ZBA$ are obtuse angles.

$\angle ABY$ and $\angle YBC$ are right angles.

$$\text{Given } \overrightarrow{BY} \perp \overleftrightarrow{AC}$$
$$\text{means } \angle YBC = 90°$$
$$\angle YBA = 90°$$

$\angle ABC$ is a straight angle.

Pairs of Angles

The six types of pairs of angles are detailed below.

Adjacent Angles

Adjacent angles are two angles that have the same vertex, share a common side, and do not overlap.

Example

  1. In the previous figure, $\angle XBY$ and $\angle YBZ$ are one pair of adjacent angles.

Complementary Angles

Complementary angles are two angles whose sum is 90°.

Example

  1. In the previous figure, $\angle YBZ$ and $\angle ZBC$ are complementary angles.

Supplementary Angles

Supplementary angles are two angles whose sum is 180°.

Example

  1. In the previous figure, $\angle ABZ$ and $\angle ZBC$ are supplementary angles.

Vertical Angles

Vertical angles are two angles that have the same vertex and whose sides are opposite rays. These are sometimes referred to as opposite angles as well. One important property of vertical angles is that they will always be equal.

Example

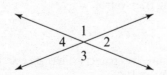

  1. In the figure, $\angle 1$ and $\angle 3$ are vertical angles and $\angle 2$ and $\angle 4$ are vertical angles.

Hence, $\angle 1 = \angle 3$ and $\angle 2 = \angle 4$.

Note that there are also four pairs of supplementary angles:

$\angle 1$ and $\angle 2$, $\angle 2$ and $\angle 3$, $\angle 3$ and $\angle 4$, and $\angle 4$ and $\angle 1$.

Alternate Interior Angles

If two lines are intersected by a third line (called a **transversal**), then two pairs of **alternate interior angles** are formed. These angles will be inside the two lines and on alternative sides of the transversal.

Example

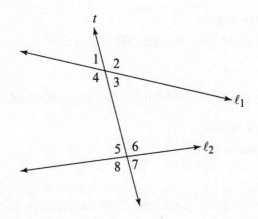

1. In the figure, lines ℓ_1 and ℓ_2 are intersected by the transversal, t, forming two pairs of alternative interior angles: $\angle 3$ and $\angle 5$, and $\angle 4$ and $\angle 6$.

Alternate Exterior Angles

If two lines are intersected by a transversal, then two pairs of **alternate exterior angles** are formed. These angles will be outside the two lines and on alternate sides of the transversal.

Example

1. In the previous figure, two pairs of alternate exterior angles are formed: $\angle 1$ and $\angle 7$, and $\angle 2$ and $\angle 8$.

It should be noted that there are also four pairs of vertical angles and eight pairs of supplementary angles in the previous figure.

A special case occurs when the two lines, ℓ_1 and ℓ_2, are parallel $\left(\ell_1 \parallel \ell_2\right)$ and are intersected by a transversal. In this situation, each pair of alternate interior angles is equal and each pair of alternate exterior angles is equal.

Examples

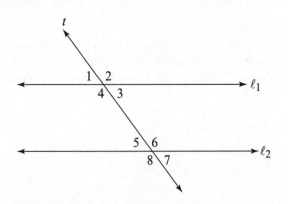

1. In the preceding figure, $\ell_1 \parallel \ell_2$ and are cut by transversal t.

   Hence, the alternate interior angles are equal: $\angle 3 = \angle 5$ and $\angle 4 = \angle 6$.

   The alternate exterior angles are equal as well: $\angle 1 = \angle 7$ and $\angle 2 = \angle 8$.

   It should be noted that if the measure of any one of the angles is given, then the measures of each of the remaining seven angles can be determined. Also, note again that there are four pairs of vertical angles and eight pairs of supplementary angles in the figure.

2. In the previous figure, if $\angle 2 = 130°$, find the measure of the remaining seven angles.

   $\angle 2 = \angle 4 = \angle 6 = \angle 8 = 130°$

   $\angle 1 = \angle 3 = \angle 5 = \angle 7 = 50°$

Polygons

Basic Terms

A **polygon** is a *closed plane figure* made up of line segments that intersect only at their endpoints. *Poly* means "many" and *gon* means "sides." Thus, polygon means "many sides." The segments are called the **sides** of

231

the polygon, and any two sides with a common endpoint form an angle of the polygon.

The endpoint of any side is called a **vertex** of the polygon, and the number of sides, angles, and vertices is always the same in any polygon. A segment whose endpoints are two non-adjacent vertices is called a **diagonal** of the polygon.

The minimum number of sides, angles, or vertices of a polygon is three. There is not a maximum number of sides, angles, or vertices. A **regular polygon** is a polygon in which all sides have the same length and all angles have the same measure.

Example

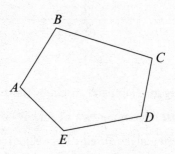

1. In the figure, polygon *ABCDE* has five vertices, five angles, and five sides.

    The *vertices* are *A*, *B*, *C*, *D*, and *E*.

    The *angles* are ∠*A*, ∠*B*, ∠*C*, ∠*D*, and ∠*E*.

    The *sides* are $\overline{AB}$, $\overline{BC}$, $\overline{CD}$, $\overline{DE}$, and $\overline{AE}$.

    The *diagonals* (not drawn) would be $\overline{AC}$, $\overline{AD}$, $\overline{BD}$, $\overline{BE}$, and $\overline{CE}$.

Convex polygons are polygons such that regardless of what side is extended, the polygon always remains on one side of the extension. The GRE only deals with convex polygons. Convex polygons and their generic names are illustrated in the figures that follow in the "Special Polygons" section.

Special Polygons

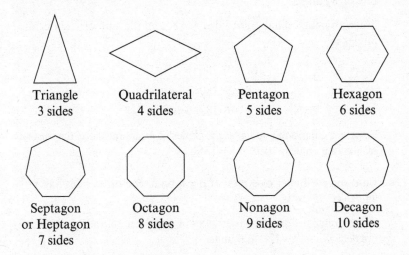

Triangle
3 sides

Quadrilateral
4 sides

Pentagon
5 sides

Hexagon
6 sides

Septagon
or Heptagon
7 sides

Octagon
8 sides

Nonagon
9 sides

Decagon
10 sides

Sum of the Angles in a Polygon

The sum of the interior angles in a polygon may be determined by $(n-2)\cdot 180°$, where n is the number of sides, angles, or vertices of the polygon.

Examples

1. Find the sum of the interior angles of a triangle.

Since a triangle has three sides, $n = 3$, and the sum of its interior angles is

$$(n-2)\cdot 180° =$$
$$(3-2)\cdot 180° = 180°$$

2. Find the sum of the interior angles of a hexagon. Since a hexagon has six sides, $n = 6$, and the sum of the interior angles is

$$(n-2)\cdot 180° =$$
$$(6-2)\cdot 180° =$$
$$4\cdot 180° = 720°$$

233

3. A stop sign has the shape of a regular octagon. Find the measure of one of its angles.

Since an octagon has eight sides, $n = 8$, and the sum of its interior angles is

$$(n-2) \cdot 180° =$$
$$(8-2) \cdot 180° =$$
$$6 \cdot 180° = 1080°$$

Since a regular octagon has eight angles of equal measure, the measure of any one angle is $1080° \div 8 = 135°$.

4. Find the perimeter of a regular decagon if one of its sides has a length of 12 units.

Since a regular decagon has 10 sides of equal length, the perimeter of the decagon is $10 \cdot 12 = 120$ units.

Triangles

General Properties

A **triangle** is a polygon with three sides, angles, and vertices. The symbol for a triangle is Δ.

The sum of the interior angles in any triangle is $180°$.

If the sides of a triangle have lengths a, b, and c, then the perimeter P is $P = a + b + c$.

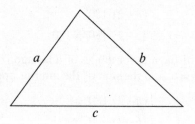

Altitude or Height

A segment drawn from any vertex of a triangle perpendicular to the opposite side or the extension of the opposite side is called an **altitude** or **height** of the triangle.

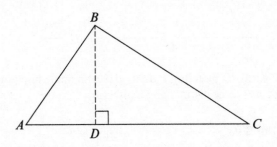

Given $\triangle ABC$ with $\overline{BD} \perp \overline{AC}$, $\overline{BD}$ is an altitude or height of $\triangle ABC$. Every triangle has three distinct heights.

Median

A segment drawn from any vertex of a triangle to the midpoint of the opposite side is called a **median** of the triangle.

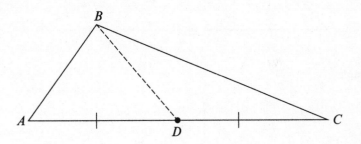

Given $\triangle ABC$ with $AD = CD$, $\overline{BD}$ is a median of $\triangle ABC$. Every triangle has three distinct medians.

Angle Bisector

A segment drawn from any vertex of a triangle that bisects the angle at that vertex is called an **angle bisector** of the triangle.

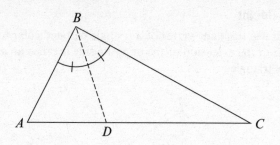

Given $\triangle ABC$ with $\overline{BD}$ bisecting $\angle ABC$, $\overline{BD}$ is an angle bisector of $\triangle ABC$. Every triangle has three distinct angle bisectors.

Area of a Triangle

The formula for the area A of a triangle is $A = \dfrac{1}{2}bh$, where the base b is any one of the sides of the triangle and h is the altitude, or height drawn to the base.

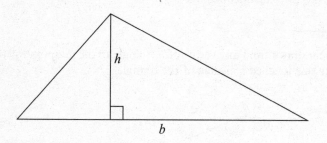

Example

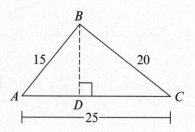

1. Find the perimeter P and the area of $\triangle ABC$ above, where $BD = 12$ and $\overline{BD} \perp \overline{AC}$.

The perimeter P of $\triangle ABC$ is the sum of the lengths of its sides: $15 + 20 + 25 = 60$.

$$\text{The area of } \triangle ABC = \frac{1}{2}bh$$
$$= \frac{1}{2}(AC)(BD)$$
$$= \frac{1}{2}(25)(12)$$
$$= 150$$

Triangle Inequality Theorem

This theorem states that the sum of the lengths of any two sides of a triangle must be greater than the length of the remaining side.

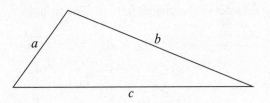

In the preceding figure,

$a + b > c$

$a + c > b$

$b + c > a$

Exterior Angle Theorem

If one side of a triangle is extended in either direction, an exterior angle is formed. This theorem states that an exterior angle of a triangle is equal to the sum of the two remote interior angles of the triangle.

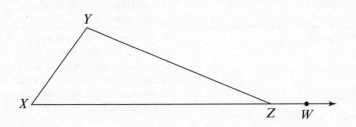

In the preceding figure, $\angle YZW = \angle X + \angle Y$. Note that every triangle has six possible exterior angles.

Opposite Angles and Opposite Sides

The largest (or smallest) side of a triangle is opposite its largest (or smallest) angle, respectively; conversely, the largest (or smallest) angle of a triangle is opposite its largest (or smallest) side. If two sides of a triangle are equal, then the angles opposite these sides are equal; conversely, if two angles of a triangle are equal, then the sides opposite these angles are equal.

Example

1. Arrange the sides of the triangle from smallest to largest.

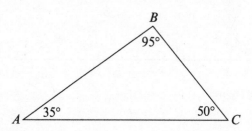

Since $\angle A$ is the smallest angle of $\triangle ABC$, the smallest side of $\triangle ABC$ is $\overline{BC}$ opposite $\angle A = 35°$. The next larger side is $\overline{AB}$, opposite $\angle C = 50°$. $\angle B = 95°$ is the largest angle of $\triangle ABC$, so the side opposite $\angle B$, $\overline{AC}$, is the largest side of $\triangle ABC$.

Types of Triangles

Triangle	Description
Acute triangle	A triangle in which all three angles are acute angles.
Right triangle	A triangle with one right angle. The two sides that form the right angle are called legs, and the side opposite the right angle is called the hypotenuse. Note that the hypotenuse must be the longest side in a right triangle since it is opposite the largest angle.

(*continued*)

Triangle	Description
Obtuse triangle	A triangle with one obtuse angle.
Scalene triangle	A triangle with no equal sides and no equal angles.
Isosceles triangle	A triangle with two equal sides and two equal angles. Remember that the equal angles must be opposite the equal sides, and the equal sides must be opposite the equal angles.
Equilateral triangle	A triangle with all three sides equal in length. Since all three angles must also be equal, this is also called an equiangular triangle, with each of its angles having a measure of 60°.

Equilateral, Isosceles, Equiangular, and Acute

Isosceles and Acute

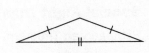

Isosceles and Obtuse

Isosceles and Right

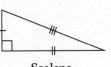

Scalene and Right

Scalene and Obtuse

In any triangle, if two of its sides have equal length, then the angles opposite those sides have equal measure; if any two angles in a triangle have equal measure, then the sides opposite those angles have equal length. If all three sides in a triangle are equal, then all three angles in the triangle are equal and vice versa. In any triangle, if one side is longer than another side, then the angle opposite the longer side will be greater than the angle opposite the shorter side and vice versa.

Examples of Common Triangles

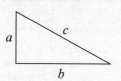

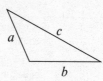

If $c^2 = a^2 + b^2$, then the triangle is a **right triangle** and the angle opposite c is 90°.

If $c^2 > a^2 + b^2$, then the triangle is an **obtuse triangle** and the angle opposite c is greater than 90°.

If $c^2 < a^2 + b^2$, then the triangle is an **acute triangle** and the angle opposite c is less than 90°.

The converse is also true.

The converse is also true.

The converse is also true.

If the angle opposite c is 90°, the triangle is a right triangle and $c^2 = a^2 + b^2$.

If the angle opposite c is greater than 90°, the triangle is an obtuse triangle and $c^2 > a^2 + b^2$.

If the angle opposite c is less than 90°, the triangle is an acute triangle and $c^2 < a^2 + b^2$.

Special Right Triangle Theorems

Pythagorean Theorem

In any right triangle, the sum of the squares of the two legs is equal to the square of the hypotenuse.

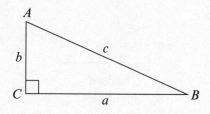

In right $\triangle ABC$, $c^2 = a^2 + b^2$.

In any right triangle, if the lengths of any two sides are known, then the length of the third side can be determined using the Pythagorean theorem.

Examples

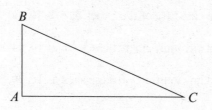

1. In $\triangle ABC$, $\overline{AB} \perp \overline{AC}$, $AC = 15$, and $BC = 17$. Find AB.

Since $\overline{AB} \perp \overline{AC}$, $\triangle ABC$ is a right triangle with legs $\overline{AB}$ and $\overline{AC}$ and hypotenuse $\overline{BC}$.

$$(AB)^2 + (AC)^2 = (BC)^2$$
$$(AB)^2 + (15)^2 = (17)^2$$
$$(AB)^2 + 225 = 289$$
$$(AB)^2 = 289 - 225$$
$$(AB)^2 = 64$$
$$AB = \sqrt{64} = 8$$

2. The legs of a right triangle have lengths of 6 and 9. Find the length of the hypotenuse.

$$c^2 = a^2 + b^2$$
$$c^2 = (6)^2 + (9)^2$$
$$c^2 = 36 + 81$$
$$c^2 = 117$$
$$c = \sqrt{117}$$
$$c = \sqrt{9 \cdot 13}$$
$$c = 3\sqrt{13}$$

Pythagorean Triples

It is useful to note that certain integer values work in the Pythagorean theorem and these integers are called **Pythagorean triples.** Any multiples of these triples will also satisfy the Pythagorean theorem.

Examples

1. 3, 4, 5 and any multiple of these such as 6, 8, 10 and 9, 12, 15

2. 5, 12, 13 and any multiple of these such as 10, 24, 26 and 15, 36, 39

3. 8, 15, 17 and any multiple of these such as 16, 30, 34 and 24, 45, 51

The 30°-60°-90° Right Triangle Theorem

In a right triangle whose acute angles measure 30° and 60°, the leg opposite the 30° angle equals half the hypotenuse, and the leg opposite the 60° angle equals half the hypotenuse times the square root of 3.

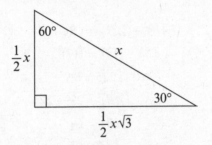

In the preceding triangle, the hypotenuse has length x, the leg opposite the 30° angle has length $\frac{1}{2}x$, and the leg opposite the 60° angle has length $\frac{1}{2}x\sqrt{3}$. In a 30°-60°-90° right triangle, if the length of any one side is known, then the lengths of the remaining two sides can be determined.

Example

1. The hypotenuse of a right triangle has length 24, and one of its angles measures 60°. Find the area of the triangle.

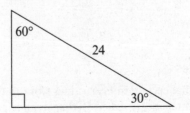

In the right triangle, since one of its acute angles is 60°, the other acute angle must be 30°, and it is a 30°-60°-90° right triangle. The side opposite the 30° angle is $\frac{1}{2} \cdot 24 = 12$, and the side opposite the 60° angle is $\frac{1}{2}(24)\left(\sqrt{3}\right) = 12\sqrt{3}$. Since the legs of a right triangle are perpendicular, one leg can be considered a base, while the other leg is an altitude or height of the triangle. Using the area formula for a triangle

$$\text{Area} = \frac{1}{2}bh$$
$$= \frac{1}{2}\left(12\sqrt{3}\right)(12)$$
$$= \frac{1}{2}\left(144\sqrt{3}\right)$$
$$\text{Area} = 72\sqrt{3}$$

The 45°-45°-90° Right Triangle Theorem

Also known as the **isosceles right triangle theorem,** this is a right triangle whose acute angles measure 45°. The hypotenuse will have a length equal to the length of either leg times the square root of 2.

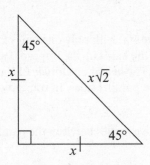

In the triangle, the legs have length x and the hypotenuse has length $x\sqrt{2}$.

Example

1. If the length of the longest side of an isosceles right triangle is $18\sqrt{2}$, find the lengths of the two remaining sides of the triangle.

Since the triangle is an isosceles right triangle, its acute angles measure 45° and the longest side must be the hypotenuse. If the hypotenuse of a 45°-45°-90° right triangle is $18\sqrt{2}$, then the length of each of its legs is 18.

Quadrilaterals

General Properties

A **quadrilateral** is a polygon with four sides, angles, and vertices. A quadrilateral has two diagonals. The sum of the interior angles in a quadrilateral is 360°. If the sides of a quadrilateral have lengths a, b, c, and d, then the perimeter P is $P = a + b + c + d$.

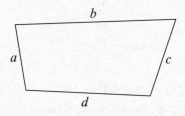

Types of Quadrilaterals

Trapezoid

A **trapezoid** is a quadrilateral with only one pair of parallel sides. The parallel sides are called the **bases** of the trapezoid and the non-parallel sides are called the **legs.** The **height** or **altitude** of a trapezoid is a segment perpendicular to the two parallel sides. In trapezoids, the following are true:

- Any two consecutive angles between the parallel sides are supplementary.
- In an **isosceles trapezoid,** the legs are equal.

Area of a Trapezoid

The area A of a trapezoid is $A = \dfrac{1}{2} h (b_1 + b_2)$, where h is the altitude or height and b_1 and b_2 are the bases of the trapezoid.

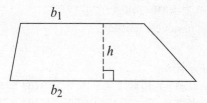

Example

1. Find the perimeter and area of the following trapezoid.

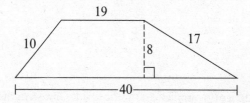

The perimeter P of the trapezoid is the sum of the lengths of its sides:

$P = 10 + 19 + 17 + 40$

$P = 86$

The area A of the trapezoid is

$$A = \frac{1}{2}h(b_1 + b_2)$$
$$= \frac{1}{2}(8)(19 + 40)$$
$$= 4(59)$$
$$A = 236$$

Parallelogram

A **parallelogram** is a quadrilateral with opposite sides that are parallel. In parallelograms, the following are true:

- Opposite sides are equal.
- Opposite angles are equal.

- Consecutive angles are supplementary.
- The diagonals bisect each other.

Area of a Parallelogram

The area A of a parallelogram is $A = b \cdot h$, where the base b is any one of the sides of the parallelogram and the height h is the height or altitude to that side.

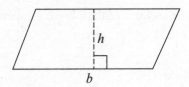

Example

1. Find the area of a parallelogram whose sides have lengths of 20 and 36 and with one of its angles having a measure of 30°.

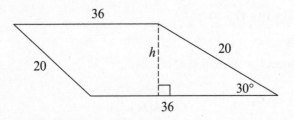

In the figure, the base of the parallelogram is 36 and the height is 10 since it is opposite the 30° angle and is equal to one-half the length of the hypotenuse of a 30°-60°-90° triangle. The area A is

$$A = b \cdot h$$
$$= (36)(10)$$
$$A = 360$$

Rectangle

A **rectangle** is a parallelogram with four right angles. In rectangles, the following are true:

- Opposite sides are equal.
- Consecutive angles are supplementary.

- The diagonals bisect each other.
- The diagonals are equal.

Area of a Rectangle

The area of a rectangle is $A = b \cdot h$, where b is the base (any one of its sides) and h is the height or altitude (any side adjacent to the base) of the rectangle. Another formula that is sometimes used for the area is $A = l \cdot w$, where l is the length and w is the width of the rectangle.

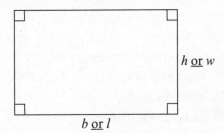

h <u>or</u> w

b <u>or</u> l

Example

1. Find the area of a rectangle with a base length of 24 and a diagonal length of 26.

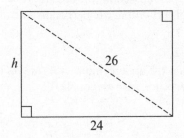

The height h can be determined using the Pythagorean theorem.

$$c^2 = a^2 + b^2$$
$$26^2 = h^2 + 24^2$$
$$676 = h^2 + 576$$
$$h^2 = 676 - 576$$
$$h^2 = 100$$
$$h = \sqrt{100} = 10$$

The area A of the rectangle is

$$A = b \cdot h$$
$$= (24)(10)$$
$$A = 240$$

Rhombus

A **rhombus** is a parallelogram with four equal sides. In rhombuses, the following are true:

- Opposite angles are equal.
- Consecutive angles are supplementary.
- The diagonals bisect each other.
- The diagonals bisect the angles.
- The diagonals are perpendicular.

It should be noted that all angles of a rhombus are not necessarily equal.

Area of a Rhombus
Since a rhombus is a parallelogram, the area A is $A = b \cdot h$. Also, since the diagonals d_1 and d_2 of a rhombus are perpendicular, an alternate formula for the area A is $A = \frac{1}{2} d_1 \cdot d_2$.

It should be noted that the area formula, $A = \frac{1}{2} d_1 \cdot d_2$, may be used for any quadrilateral with perpendicular diagonals.

Example

1. Find the area of a rhombus whose diagonals have lengths of 18 and 24.

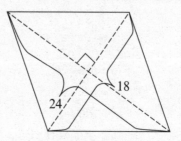

Since the diagonals of a rhombus are perpendicular, the area A is

$$A = \frac{1}{2}d_1 \cdot d_2$$
$$= \frac{1}{2}(18)(24)$$
$$A = 216$$

Square

A **square** is a rectangle and a rhombus. In squares, the following are true:

- All four sides are equal.
- All four angles are right angles, and thus all angles are equal.
- Consecutive angles are supplementary.
- The diagonals are perpendicular.
- The diagonals bisect each other.
- The diagonals bisect the angles.

Area of a Square

The area of a square is $A = s^2$, where s is the length of one of the four equal sides of the square. Since the diagonals d of a square are equal and perpendicular, an alternate formula for the area A is $A = \frac{1}{2}d \cdot d = \frac{1}{2}d^2$.

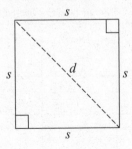

Example

1. Find the perimeter and area of a square with a diagonal length of $20\sqrt{2}$.

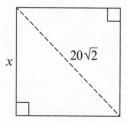

Since a diagonal of a square forms two isosceles right triangles, the two legs of the triangle will each have a length 20, which is also the length of each side of the square.

The perimeter P of the square is $P = 4 \cdot x = 4 \cdot 20 = 80$. The area A of the square is $A = x^2 = 20^2 = 400$. The area could also be found using

$$A = \frac{1}{2}d^2 = \frac{1}{2}\left(20\sqrt{2}\right)^2 = \frac{1}{2}(800) = 400.$$

Summary of the Properties of Quadrilaterals

The following table summarizes the properties of the special types of quadrilaterals.

Property	Trapezoid	Parallelogram	Rectangle	Rhombus	Square
Four sides, angles, and vertices	✓	✓	✓	✓	✓
Opposite sides are parallel		✓	✓	✓	✓
Opposite sides are equal		✓	✓	✓	✓
Opposite angles are equal		✓	✓	✓	✓

(*continued*)

Property	Trapezoid	Parallelogram	Rectangle	Rhombus	Square
Consecutive angles are supplementary		✓	✓	✓	✓
Diagonals bisect each other		✓	✓	✓	✓
Diagonals bisect the angles				✓	✓
Diagonals are equal			✓		✓
Diagonals are perpendicular				✓	✓
All sides are equal				✓	✓
All angles are equal			✓		✓
Sum of interior angles is 360°	✓	✓	✓	✓	✓

Congruent Polygons

Two polygons are said to be **congruent** if they are exactly the same shape and size. Their corresponding angles are equal in measure, and their corresponding sides are equal in length. The symbol for congruence is ≅.

Examples

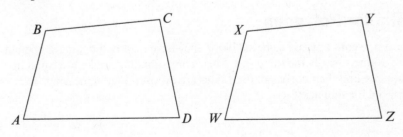

1. In the figures, if quadrilateral $ABCD \cong$ quadrilateral $WXYZ$, then the following are true:

$$\angle A = \angle W \quad \text{and} \quad AB = WX$$
$$\angle B = \angle X \quad\quad\quad BC = XY$$
$$\angle C = \angle Y \quad\quad\quad CD = YZ$$
$$\angle D = \angle Z \quad\quad\quad AD = WZ$$

2. Given: $\triangle MNQ \cong \triangle RST$ with $\angle R = 58°$ and $\angle S = 95°$. Find the measures of all three angles in $\triangle MNQ$.

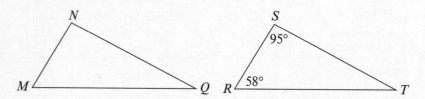

In $\triangle RST$, $\angle R + \angle S + \angle T = 180°$
$$58° + 95° + \angle T = 180°$$
$$153° + \angle T = 180°$$
$$\angle T = 27°$$

Since $\triangle MNQ \cong \triangle RST$,
$$\angle M = \angle R = 58°$$
$$\angle N = \angle S = 95°$$
$$\text{and } \angle Q = \angle T = 27°$$

Similar Polygons

Two polygons are said to be **similar** if they have exactly the same shape but are not necessarily the same size. Their corresponding angles are equal in measure and their corresponding sides are proportional in measure. The symbol for similarity is ~.

Examples

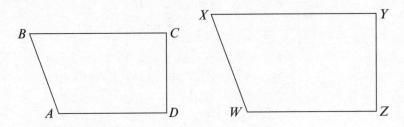

1. In the figures above, if quadrilateral $ABCD \sim$ quadrilateral $WXYZ$, then the following are true:

$\angle A = \angle W$

$\angle B = \angle X$

$\angle C = \angle Y$

$\angle D = \angle Z$

and $\dfrac{AB}{WX} = \dfrac{BC}{XY} = \dfrac{CD}{YZ} = \dfrac{AD}{WZ}$

or $\dfrac{WX}{AB} = \dfrac{XY}{BC} = \dfrac{YZ}{CD} = \dfrac{WZ}{AD}$

2. Given: $\triangle RST \sim \triangle DEF$ with $RS = 24$, $ST = 30$, $RT = 36$, and $DE = 32$. Find the perimeter of $\triangle DEF$.

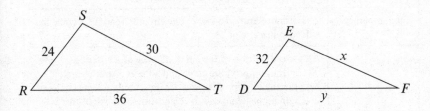

Since $\triangle RST \sim DEF$, their corresponding sides are proportional and

$$\frac{RS}{DE} = \frac{ST}{EF} = \frac{RT}{DF}.$$

$$\frac{RS}{DE} = \frac{ST}{EF} \quad \text{and} \quad \frac{RS}{DE} = \frac{RT}{DF}$$

$$\frac{24}{32} = \frac{30}{x} \qquad \qquad \frac{24}{32} = \frac{36}{y}$$

$$24 \cdot x = 32 \cdot 30 \qquad 24 \cdot y = 32 \cdot 36$$

$$24x = 960 \qquad \qquad 24y = 1152$$

$$x = \frac{960}{24} \qquad \qquad y = \frac{1152}{24}$$

$$x = 40 \qquad \qquad y = 48$$

Hence, the perimeter of $\triangle DEF = 32 + 40 + 48 = 120$.

Circles

A **circle** is the set of all points in a plane that are the same distance from a fixed point that is called the center of the circle.

Basic Terms

Radius	A radius of a circle is a segment whose endpoints are the center of a circle and any point on the circle.
Chord	A chord is a line segment whose endpoints are any two points on a circle.
Diameter	A diameter is a chord that passes through the center of a circle. In any circle, all diameters have the same length. The diameter of a circle is the longest chord of a circle and is equal to two times the length of the radius.
Circumference	The distance around a circle. The circumference of a circle has a degree measure of 360°.
Arc	An arc is a portion of the circumference of a circle consisting of two endpoints on the circle and all points on the circle between these endpoints. Arcs are measured in degree units or in length units. In *degrees*, it is a portion of the 360° that is a full rotation. In *length*, it is a portion of the circumference, which is the distance around the circle. The symbol for an arc $\overset{\frown}{AB}$ is used to denote the arc between points A and B. It is in the *context of use* that you would know whether the measure is intended to be a degree measure or a length measure.

Semicircle	An arc that is equal to one-half of the circumference of a circle and has a measure of 180°.
Minor arc	An arc whose measure is less than 180°.
Major arc	An arc whose measure is greater than 180°.
Tangent	A line that intersects a circle at exactly one point. That point is referred to as *the point of tangency*. When a diameter or a radius meets a tangent at the point of tangency, they form a 90° angle.
Secant	A line that intersects a circle at two points.
Concentric circles	Circles that have the same center.

Illustration of Terms

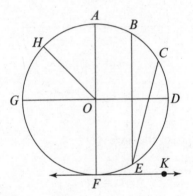

The preceding diagram is of circle O. (A circle is named by its center.) Points A, B, C, D, E, F, G, and H lie on the circle. The radii shown are $\overline{OA}$, $\overline{OD}$, $\overline{OF}$, $\overline{OG}$, and $\overline{OH}$. The diameters shown are $\overline{AF}$ and $\overline{DG}$. $DG = 2(OH)$. Chords shown that are not diameters are $\overline{BE}$ and $\overline{CE}$.

The shortest path along the circle from point E to point E is $\overarc{AE}$. The longest path along the circle from point A to point E can be shown by $\overarc{AFE}$. Some of the central angles shown are $\angle AOD$, $\angle DOF$, $\angle FOG$, $\angle FOH$, $\angle GOH$, $\angle GOA$, and $\angle HOA$. In degrees, $\overarc{AH} = \angle AOH$ and $\overarc{ADH} = 360° - \angle AOH$.

Line FK is tangent to circle O. The point of tangency is F. $\angle AFK = 90°$.

Circumference and Area of a Circle

The circumference C of a circle with a diameter d and radius r is $C = \pi \cdot d$ or $C = 2\pi r$, where $\pi \approx 3.14$ or $\pi \approx \dfrac{22}{7}$. In many cases, the circumference may be expressed in terms of π with no decimal or fractional approximation. The area A of a circle with a radius r is $A = \pi r^2$, where $\pi \approx 3.14$ or $\pi \approx \dfrac{22}{7}$.

Example

1. Find the circumference and area of a circle whose diameter is 28 and express each one in terms of π.

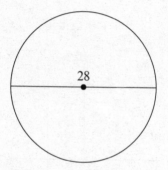

The circumference of the circle is

$$C = \pi d$$
$$= \pi(28)$$
$$C = 28\pi$$

Since the diameter of the circle is 28, the radius is 14 and the area of the circle is

$$A = \pi r^2$$
$$A = \pi\left(14^2\right)$$
$$A = 196\pi$$

Special Angles

Central Angle

A **central angle** is an angle whose vertex is the center of the circle. The degree measure of a central angle is the same as that of the arc that it intercepts on the circle.

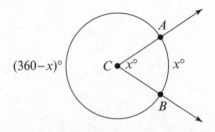

In the circle with center C, $\angle ACB$ is a central angle, and the measure of minor arc $\overset{\frown}{AB} = x° = \angle ACB$. Note that the measure of the major arc $\overset{\frown}{AB} = (360 - x)°$.

Inscribed Angle

An **inscribed angle** is an angle whose vertex is on the circle and whose sides intersect the circle at two other points. The measure of an inscribed angle is half the measure of the arc it intercepts on the circle.

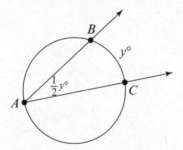

In the circle, $\angle BAC$ is an inscribed angle that intercepts $\overset{\frown}{BC}$ whose measure is $y°$. The measure of the inscribed angle $\angle BAC = \frac{1}{2}\left(\overset{\frown}{BC}\right) = \frac{1}{2}y°$. An equivalent statement about the relationship between an inscribed angle and its intercepted arc is that the measure of the intercepted arc is twice the measure of the inscribed angle.

Secant-Tangent Angle

A **secant-tangent angle** is an angle whose vertex is on the circle with one side of the angle intersecting the circle at another point, while the other side of the angle has no other points on the circle. The measure of a secant-tangent angle is half the measure of the arc it intercepts on the circle.

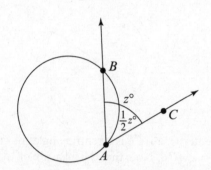

In the circle, $\angle BAC$ is a secant-tangent angle that intercepts $\overset{\frown}{AB}$ whose measure is $z°$. The measure of this secant-tangent angle $\angle BAC = \frac{1}{2}\overset{\frown}{AB} = \frac{1}{2}z°$. It may also be said that the measure of the intercepted arc is twice the measure of the secant-tangent angle.

Examples

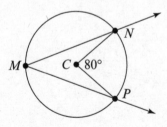

1. If the circle above has a center at C and $\angle C = 80°$, find the measure of $\angle NMP$.

   Since $\angle C$ is a central angle, the measure of the intercept arc $\overset{\frown}{NP} = 80°$. Since $\angle NMP$ is an inscribed angle, its measure is half the measure of its intercept arc $\overset{\frown}{NP}$.

$$\angle NMP = \frac{1}{2}\left(\widehat{NP}\right)$$
$$= \frac{1}{2}(80°)$$
$$\angle NMP = 40°$$

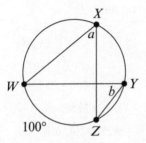

2. Given the circle above with chords $\overline{WX}$, $\overline{XZ}$, $\overline{YZ}$, and $\overline{WY}$, where $\widehat{WZ} = 100°$, find the measure of $\angle a$ and $\angle b$.

Both $\angle a$ and $\angle b$ are inscribed angles whose measures are one-half the measure of their intercepted arc $\widehat{WZ}$. Hence,

$$\angle a = \frac{1}{2}\left(\widehat{WZ}\right) \text{ and } \angle b = \frac{1}{2}\left(\widehat{WZ}\right)$$
$$= \frac{1}{2}(100°) \qquad = \frac{1}{2}(100°)$$
$$\angle a = 50° \qquad \angle b = 50°$$

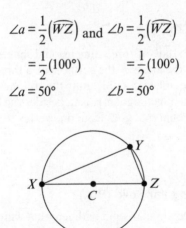

3. Given the circle above with center C, where $XY = 30$ and $YZ = 16$, find the area of the circle.

To determine the area of a circle, the radius or diameter must be known. $\angle XYZ$ is an inscribed angle whose intercepted arc is a semicircle, since $\overline{XZ}$ is the diameter of the circle. The measure of the inscribed angle is half the measure of its intercepted arc. Therefore, $\angle XYZ = \frac{1}{2}\left(\widehat{XZ}\right) = \frac{1}{2}(180°) = 90°$, and ΔXYZ is a right triangle.

By the Pythagorean theorem

$$
\begin{aligned}
(XZ)^2 &= (XY)^2 + (YZ)^2 \\
&= (30)^2 + (16)^2 \\
&= 900 + 256 \\
(XZ)^2 &= 1156 \\
XZ &= \sqrt{1156} \\
XZ &= 34
\end{aligned}
$$

The diameter of the circle is 34. Hence, the radius of the circle is 17, and the area is

$$
\begin{aligned}
A &= \pi r^2 \\
&= \pi(17)^2 \\
A &= 289\pi
\end{aligned}
$$

Solid Geometry

Solid geometry is the study of three-dimensional shapes in space. **Surface area** is the sum of all the areas of the surfaces of a three-dimensional figure. **Volume** is the number of cubic units that fill the interior of a three-dimensional figure. In a rectangular prism, besides the length, width, and height, there is a diagonal that goes from one vertex to the extreme opposite vertex.

Volume

Volume of a Rectangular Solid (Box)

The volume V of a rectangular solid with length l, width w, and height h is $V = l \cdot w \cdot h$.

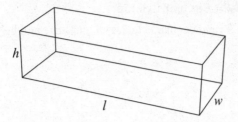

Example

1. Find the volume of a shipping box whose base is a rectangle 3 feet by 6 feet and whose height is 4 feet.

$$V = l \cdot w \cdot h$$
$$= 6 \cdot 3 \cdot 4$$
$$V = 72 \text{ cubic feet}$$

Volume of a Cube

Since the length, width, and height of a cube are all equal, the volume V of a cube whose side has length x is $V = x^3$.

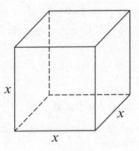

Example

1. Find the volume of a cube whose height is 9 inches.

$$V = x^3$$
$$= 9^3$$
$$V = 729 \text{ cubic inches}$$

Volume of a Right Circular Cylinder

The volume V of a right circular cylinder with radius r and height h is $V = \pi r^2 h$.

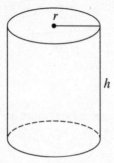

Example

1. Find the volume of a beverage can with a radius of 2 inches and a height of 6 inches.

$$V = \pi r^2 h$$
$$= \pi(2^2)(6)$$
$$= \pi(4)(6)$$
$$V = 24\pi \text{ cubic inches}$$

Surface Area

Surface Area of a Rectangular Solid

The surface area SA of a rectangular solid with length l, width w, and height h is $SA = 2lh + 2wh + 2lw$.

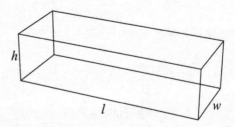

If the rectangular solid is open at the top, then the surface area SA is $SA = 2lh + 2wh + lw$.

Since each of the faces of a rectangular solid is a rectangle, their areas are determined using the area formula for a rectangle.

Example

1. Find the surface area of a cardboard box with no top whose base is a rectangle 12 inches by 24 inches and whose height is 8 inches.

$$SA = 2lh + 2wh + lw$$
$$= 2(24)(8) + 2(12)(8) + (12)(24)$$
$$= 384 + 192 + 288$$
$$SA = 864 \text{ square inches}$$

Surface Area of a Cube

The surface area SA of a cube whose side has length x is $SA = 6x^2$.

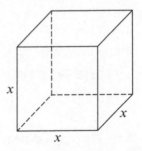

Since each of the six faces is a square with sides of length x, the area of each face is x^2. If the cube has an open top, then its surface area SA is $SA = 5x^2$.

Example

1. Find the surface area of a cube whose height is 4 feet.

$$SA = 6x^2$$
$$= 6(4^2)$$
$$= 6(16)$$
$$SA = 96 \text{ square feet}$$

Surface Area of a Right Circular Cylinder

The surface area SA of a right circular cylinder with radius r and height h is $SA = 2\pi r^2 + 2\pi rh$.

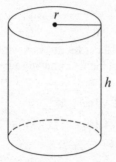

If the cylinder is *open* at the top, then its surface area SA is $SA = \pi r^2 + 2\pi rh$.

Example

1. Find the surface area of a beverage can with a radius of 2 inches and a height of 6 inches.

$$SA = 2\pi r^2 + 2\pi rh$$
$$= 2\pi\left(2^2\right) + 2\pi(2)(6)$$
$$= 2\pi(4) + 24\pi$$
$$= 8\pi + 24\pi$$
$$SA = 32\pi \text{ square inches}$$

Geometry Practice Questions

Now that you have reviewed geometry topics and concepts, you can practice on your own. Questions appear in four categories by question type: quantitative comparison, multiple-choice (select one answer), multiple-choice (select one or more answers), and numeric entry (fill-in). These practice questions are grouped by question type to give you a chance to practice solving problems in the same format as the GRE. The answers and explanations that follow the questions will include strategies to help you understand how to solve the problems.

General Directions: For each question, indicate the best answer, using the directions given.

- All numbers used are real numbers.

- All figures are assumed to lie in a plane unless otherwise indicated.

- Geometric figures, such as lines, circles, triangles, and quadrilaterals, are not necessarily drawn to scale. That is, you should **not** assume that quantities, such as lengths and angle measurements, are as they appear in the figure. You should assume, however, that lines shown as straight are actually straight, points on a line are in the order shown, and more generally, all geometric objects are in the relative position shown. For questions with geometric figures, you should base your answer on geometric reasoning, not on estimating or comparing quantities by sight or by measurement.

- Coordinate systems, such as xy-planes and number lines, are drawn to scale; therefore, you can read, estimate, or compare quantities in such figures by sight or by measurement.

- Graphical data presentations, such as bar graphs, pie graphs, and line graphs, are drawn to scale; therefore, you can read, estimate, or compare data values by sight or by measurement.

Answer choices in this study guide have lettered choices A, B, C, D, E, etc., for clarity, but letters will not appear on the actual exam. On the actual computer version of the exam, you will be required to click on ovals or squares to select your answer.

HELPFUL HINT

○ oval—answer will be a single choice.

☐ square box—answer will be one or more choices.

Quantitative Comparison

Directions: For questions 1 to 15, compare Quantity A and Quantity B, using additional information centered above the two quantities if such information is given. Select one of the following four answer choices for each question:

- Ⓐ   Quantity A is greater.
- Ⓑ   Quantity B is greater.
- Ⓒ   The two quantities are equal.
- Ⓓ   The relationship cannot be determined from the information given.

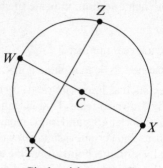

Circle with center C

1.

Quantity A	Quantity B
WX	YZ

	Quantity A	Quantity B
2.	the length of diagonal $\overline{AC}$ in rectangle $ABCD$	the length of diagonal $\overline{BD}$ in rectangle $ABCD$

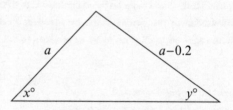

3.

Quantity A	Quantity B
x	y

	Quantity A	Quantity B
4.	the length of a side of square $MNPQ$	the length of a diagonal of square $MNPQ$

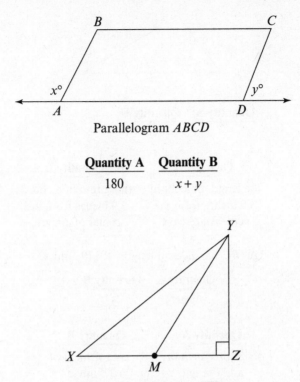

Parallelogram *ABCD*

5.

Quantity A	**Quantity B**
180	$x + y$

M is the midpoint of $\overline{XZ}$

6.

Quantity A	**Quantity B**
the area of $\triangle XYM$	the area of $\triangle MYZ$

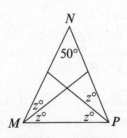

7.

Quantity A	**Quantity B**
35	z

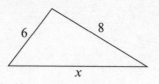

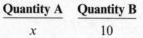

8.

Quantity A	Quantity B
x	10

9.

Quantity A	Quantity B
the length of a chord 3.8 inches from the center of circle C	the length of a chord 3.9 inches from the center of circle C

$\triangle ABC$ has sides of lengths 10, 19, and x.

10.

Quantity A	Quantity B
8	x

11.

Quantity A	Quantity B
the supplement of a 127° angle	the complement of a 37° angle

12.

Quantity A	Quantity B
the area of a triangle with sides of lengths 20, 20, and 24	the area of a triangle with sides of lengths 17, 17, and 30

13.

Quantity A	Quantity B
the measure of $\angle D$ in parallelogram $ABCD$ if $\angle A = 80°$	the measure of $\angle Z$ in trapezoid $WXYZ$ if $\angle W = 80°$

14.

Quantity A	Quantity B
the perimeter of a regular octagon with sides of length 14	the perimeter of a regular hexagon with sides of length 19

Quantity A	Quantity B
15. the sum of the interior angles of parallelogram $WXYZ$	the sum of the interior angles of trapezoid $MNPQ$

Multiple-Choice (Select One Answer)

Directions: Questions 16 to 30 require you to select one answer choice.

16. Two sides of a triangle have lengths of 8 and 15. Which of the following could NOT be the length of the third side?

   Ⓐ 7
   Ⓑ 9
   Ⓒ 11
   Ⓓ 13
   Ⓔ 15

17. What is the height of a trapezoid with base lengths of 15 and 20 if the area of the trapezoid is 280?

   Ⓐ 4
   Ⓑ 8
   Ⓒ 14
   Ⓓ 16
   Ⓔ $18\frac{2}{3}$

18. What is the degree measure of the smallest angle of a triangle if its angles are in the ratio 2:3:4?

   Ⓐ 10
   Ⓑ 20
   Ⓒ 40
   Ⓓ 60
   Ⓔ 80

19. What is the degree measure of one of the angles of a regular polygon with 15 sides?

   Ⓐ 24
   Ⓑ 120
   Ⓒ 150
   Ⓓ 156
   Ⓔ 240

20. What is the perimeter of a square whose area is 150?

Ⓐ $10\sqrt{6}$

Ⓑ $20\sqrt{6}$

Ⓒ 60

Ⓓ 120

Ⓔ 300

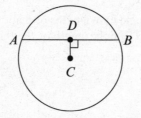

21. If C is the center of the preceding circle, whose radius is 13 and $CD = 5$, what is the length of chord $\overline{AB}$?

Ⓐ 8

Ⓑ 12

Ⓒ 16

Ⓓ 24

Ⓔ Cannot be determined from the information given.

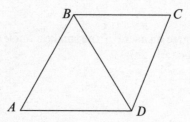

22. In the preceding rhombus $ABCD$, $AB = 40$ and $\angle A = 60°$. What is the length of diagonal $\overline{BD}$?

Ⓐ 20

Ⓑ 25

Ⓒ 30

Ⓓ 35

Ⓔ 40

23. If the length of the hypotenuse of a right triangle is 20 and one of its legs is 16, what is the area of the triangle?

Ⓐ 96

Ⓑ 120

Ⓒ 160

Ⓓ 192

Ⓔ 240

24. If $\triangle RST \sim \triangle XYZ$ and $\angle X = 53°$ and $\angle Y = 48°$, what is the degree measure of $\angle T$?

Ⓐ 48

Ⓑ 53

Ⓒ 79

Ⓓ 101

Ⓔ Cannot be determined from the given information.

25. What is the area of an equilateral triangle whose sides have a length of 24?

Ⓐ $72\sqrt{3}$

Ⓑ 144

Ⓒ $144\sqrt{3}$

Ⓓ 288

Ⓔ $288\sqrt{3}$

26. What is the volume in cubic inches of a right circular cylinder with a height of 10 inches and a diameter of 6 inches?

Ⓐ 90π

Ⓑ 120π

Ⓒ 300π

Ⓓ 360π

Ⓔ 600π

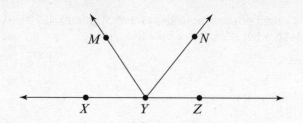

27. In the preceding figure, $\angle NYZ = 50°$ and $\overline{MY}$ bisects $\angle XYN$. What is the degree measure of $\angle XYM$?

    Ⓐ 50
    Ⓑ 55
    Ⓒ 65
    Ⓓ 75
    Ⓔ 80

28. If the diameter of circle X is 4 times the diameter of circle Y, what is the ratio of the area of circle X to the area of circle Y?

    Ⓐ 2:1
    Ⓑ 4:1
    Ⓒ 8:1
    Ⓓ 12:1
    Ⓔ 16:1

29. In the parallelogram $PQRS$, the ratio of the measure of $\angle R$ to $\angle S$ is $\dfrac{2}{3}$. What is the degree measure of $\angle S$?

    Ⓐ 36
    Ⓑ 72
    Ⓒ 90
    Ⓓ 108
    Ⓔ 144

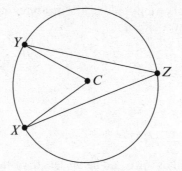

30. In the preceding circle with center C, $\overset{\frown}{XZY} = 280°$. What is the measure in degrees of $\angle Z$?

    Ⓐ   20

    Ⓑ   40

    Ⓒ   60

    Ⓓ   80

    Ⓔ   140

Multiple-Choice (Select One or More Answers)

Directions: Questions 31 to 45 require you to select one or more answer choices.

31. If a triangle has two sides of lengths 10 and 20, which of the following could be the length of the third side?

    Ⓐ   5

    Ⓑ   10

    Ⓒ   15

    Ⓓ   20

    Ⓔ   25

    Ⓕ   30

32. If a circle has a radius of 8, which of the following could represent the length of a chord of the circle?

    Ⓐ   2

    Ⓑ   4

    Ⓒ   8

    Ⓓ   12

    Ⓔ   16

    Ⓕ   20

33. Which of the following could be the measures in degrees of the acute angles of a right triangle?

- Ⓐ 45, 45
- Ⓑ 30, 60
- Ⓒ 25, 75
- Ⓓ 35, 45
- Ⓔ 42, 48
- Ⓕ 10, 80

34. Which of the following could be the length of the side of a square whose diagonal is less than 35?

- Ⓐ 10
- Ⓑ 20
- Ⓒ 30
- Ⓓ 40
- Ⓔ 50

35. Which of the following could represent the sides in a 30°-60°-90° right triangle?

- Ⓐ 3, 4, 5
- Ⓑ 5, 5√3, 10
- Ⓒ 3, 6, 9
- Ⓓ 12, 12√3, 24
- Ⓔ 5, 12, 13

36. For a parallelogram $WXYZ$, which of the following must be true?

- Ⓐ $\angle W = \angle X$
- Ⓑ $\angle X = \angle Z$
- Ⓒ $XY = WZ$
- Ⓓ $XZ = WY$
- Ⓔ $\angle Y$ and $\angle Z$ are supplementary angles.

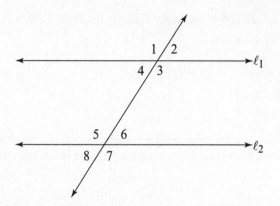

37. If $\ell_1 \parallel \ell_2$ in the preceding figure, which of the following pairs of angles have the same measure?

- Ⓐ $\angle 1, \angle 5$
- Ⓑ $\angle 2, \angle 4$
- Ⓒ $\angle 1, \angle 8$
- Ⓓ $\angle 6, \angle 7$
- Ⓔ $\angle 3, \angle 5$
- Ⓕ $\angle 2, \angle 8$

38. In rhombus $PQRS$, which of the following must be true?

- Ⓐ $\angle P = \angle Q$
- Ⓑ $\overline{QR} \perp \overline{RS}$
- Ⓒ $PR = QS$
- Ⓓ $\angle Q = \angle S$
- Ⓔ $\overline{PR} \perp \overline{QS}$

39. If $\triangle QRS \sim \triangle TUV$, which of the following must be true?

- Ⓐ $\angle R = \angle U$
- Ⓑ $QR = TU$
- Ⓒ $\angle Q = \angle V$
- Ⓓ $\dfrac{QR}{TU} = \dfrac{RS}{UV}$
- Ⓔ $\dfrac{QS}{TV} = \dfrac{UV}{RS}$

40. Which of the following triples satisfies the Pythagorean theorem?

- Ⓐ 5, 8, 9
- Ⓑ 8, 15, 17
- Ⓒ 1, 2, 3
- Ⓓ 12, 16, 20
- Ⓔ 10, 24, 26

41. Which of the following could represent the number of sides in a regular polygon if each angle of the polygon is less than 150°?

- Ⓐ 6
- Ⓑ 8
- Ⓒ 10
- Ⓓ 12
- Ⓔ 16
- Ⓕ 20

42. For a trapezoid $WXYZ$, which of the following MUST be true?

- Ⓐ $\overline{WX} \parallel \overline{YZ}$
- Ⓑ $XY = WZ$
- Ⓒ $\overline{YZ} \perp \overline{WZ}$
- Ⓓ $\angle X = \angle Z$
- Ⓔ $\angle W + \angle X + \angle Y + \angle Z = 360°$

43. Which of the following could represent the sides in an isosceles right triangle?

- Ⓐ 4, 4, 8
- Ⓑ 5, 5, $5\sqrt{2}$
- Ⓒ $\sqrt{2}$, $\sqrt{2}$, 2
- Ⓓ 7, 7, 14
- Ⓔ 3, 4, 5
- Ⓕ 1, 1, $\sqrt{2}$

44. If one side of an isosceles triangle has a length of 12, which of the following could be the lengths of the remaining sides?

- Ⓐ 12, 10
- Ⓑ 12, 20
- Ⓒ 12, 30
- Ⓓ 6, 6
- Ⓔ 8, 8

45. Which of the following could represent the radius of a circle if its circumference must be less than 90?

- Ⓐ 5
- Ⓑ 10
- Ⓒ 15
- Ⓓ 20
- Ⓔ 25
- Ⓕ 30

Numeric Entry (Fill-in)

Directions: Questions 46 to 60 require you to solve the problem and write your answer in a box or boxes.

- Write out your answer with numerals.

- Your answer may be an integer, a decimal, or a fraction, and it may be negative.

- If a question asks for a fraction, there will be two boxes—one for the numerator and one for the denominator.

- Equivalent forms of the correct answer, such as 4.5 and 4.50, are all correct. Fractions do not need to be reduced to lowest terms.

- Write out the exact answer unless the question asks you to round your answer.

46. What is the sum in degrees of the interior angles of a polygon with 14 sides?

47. In $\triangle ABC$, $\overline{AB} \perp \overline{BC}$, $BC = 30$, and $AC = 34$. What is the length of $\overline{AB}$?

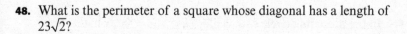

48. What is the perimeter of a square whose diagonal has a length of $23\sqrt{2}$?

49. What is the area of an isosceles triangle whose base has a length of 24 and whose legs have a length of 13?

50. What is the area of a rhombus that has a perimeter of 40 and one diagonal with a length of 12?

51. What is the surface area in square feet of a box with no top, whose base is a rectangle 4 feet by 5 feet and whose height is 2 feet?

52. Find the measure in degrees of the largest angle of a trapezoid if the angles have a ratio of 1:2:3:4.

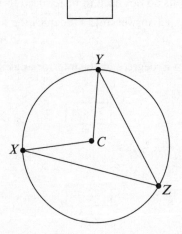

53. In the preceding circle with center C, if $\angle Z = 55°$, what is the measure in degrees of $\angle XCY$?

54. What is the measure in degrees of the smaller of two supplementary angles if one angle is 12 less than three times the measure of the other angle?

55. What is the perimeter of a rectangle if one of its sides has a length of 24 and its diagonals have a length of 30?

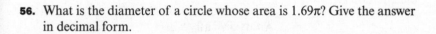

56. What is the diameter of a circle whose area is 1.69π? Give the answer in decimal form.

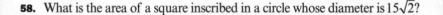

57. What is the height of a trapezoid whose area is 416 and whose bases have lengths of 19 and 45?

58. What is the area of a square inscribed in a circle whose diameter is $15\sqrt{2}$?

59. If $\triangle XYZ \sim \triangle PQR$ with $XY = 12$, $YZ = 20$, $XZ = 24$, and $PR = 30$, what is the perimeter of $\triangle PQR$?

60. What is the measure in degrees of each angle of a regular polygon with 16 sides? Give the answer in decimal form.

Charting and Analyzing Your Practice Results

The first step in analyzing the practice exercises is to use the following chart to identify your strengths and areas that need further clarification. The answers and explanations following this chart will help you solve the practice problems, but you should look for trends in the types of errors (repeated errors). Look especially for low scores in *specific* topic areas. These are the areas that you may need to review again and again until the solutions become automatic.

Mark the problems that you missed and notice the topic and question type. Ask yourself, are you missing question(s) due to lack of knowledge of the topic/concept, or are you missing questions due to lack of knowledge of the question type?

Analysis/Tally Sheet

Topic	Total Possible	Number Correct	Number Incorrect		
			(A) Simple Mistake	(B) Misread Problem	(C) Lack of Knowledge
Lines, segments, rays, angles, and congruence Questions 1, 2, 4, 5, 9, 11, 13, 15, 18, 19, 22, 24, 27, 29, 31, 33, 34, 36, 37, 38, 39, 41, 42, 46, 52, 54, 60	27				
Triangles: perimeter, area, and angle measure Questions 3, 7, 8, 10, 16, 35, 43, 44	8				
Pythagorean theorem Questions 21, 23, 40, 47	4				
Polygons: perimeter, area, and measure of quadrilaterals and other polygons Questions 6, 12, 14, 17, 20, 25, 48, 49, 50, 55, 57, 58, 59	13				

(continued)

Analysis/Tally Sheet (*continued*)

Topic	Total Possible	Number Correct	Number Incorrect (A) Simple Mistake	(B) Misread Problem	(C) Lack of Knowledge
Circles: circumference, area, and arcs Questions 28, 30, 32, 45, 53, 56	6				
Solid geometry: volume and surface area Questions 26, 51	2				
Total Possible Explanations for Incorrect Answers: Columns A, B, and C					
Total Number of Answers Correct and Incorrect	60	Add the total number of correct answers here: ___	Add columns A, B, and C: _____ Total number of incorrect answers		

Answers and Explanations

Quantitative Comparison

1. A.

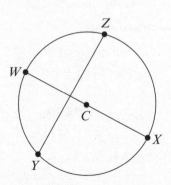

Since $\overline{WX}$ passes through the center of the circle, $\overline{WX}$ is the diameter of the circle, which is also the longest chord of the circle. Since $\overline{YZ}$ does not pass through the center, it is shorter than a diameter. Hence, Quantity A has the greater value.

2. **C.** Since the diagonals in a rectangle are always equal, $AC = BD$ and the two quantities are equal.

3. **B.** In a triangle, the larger of two angles is opposite the larger of the two sides opposite the angles. Since $a > a - 0.2$, the angle opposite the side with length a is the larger of the two angles. Hence, Quantity B has the greater value.

4. **B.** In a square, the length of a diagonal is equal to $\sqrt{2}$ times the length of a side of the square. Therefore, a diagonal of the square is longer than the length of a side of the square and Quantity B has the greater value.

5. **C.**

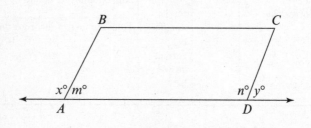

Since consecutive angles in a parallelogram are supplementary, $m + n = 180$. Since $\overleftrightarrow{AD}$ is a straight line, adjacent angles x and m are supplementary, and adjacent angles n and y are supplementary: $x + m = 180$ and $n + y = 180$.

Adding the two equations yields

$$x + m + n + y = 180 + 180$$
$$x + (m + n) + y = 360$$
$$x + 180 + y = 360$$
$$x + 180 + y - 180 = 360 - 180$$
$$x + y = 180$$

Hence, the two quantities are equal.

6. C.

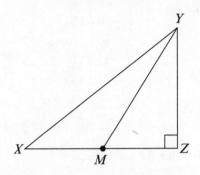

The area A_1 of $\Delta XYM = \frac{1}{2}bh = \frac{1}{2}(XM)(YZ)$.

The area A_2 of $\Delta MYZ = \frac{1}{2}bh = \frac{1}{2}(MZ)(YZ)$.

Since M is the midpoint of $\overline{XZ}$, $XM = MZ$ and

$A_1 = \frac{1}{2}(XM)(YZ) = \frac{1}{2}(MZ)(YZ) = A_2$. Hence, the two quantities are equal.

7. A.

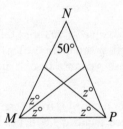

In ΔMNP, the base angles are equal, $\angle M = \angle P$.

Since the sum of the angles in a triangle is $180°$,

$$\angle M + \angle N + \angle P = 180°$$
$$2z + 50 + 2z = 180$$
$$4z + 50 = 180$$
$$4z + 50 - 50 = 180 - 50$$
$$4z = 130$$
$$\frac{4z}{4} = \frac{130}{4}$$
$$z = \frac{65}{2}, \text{ or } 32\frac{1}{2}$$

Hence, Quantity A has the greater value.

8. D.

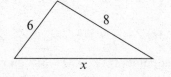

Since nothing is known about the angle measures in the triangle, the only conclusion regarding x is that

$$8 - 6 < x < 8 + 6$$
$$2 < x < 14$$

Although $x = 10$ is a possible value for x, this will only be the case when the sides of length 6 and 8 are the legs of a right triangle. Therefore, the relationship cannot be determined from the information given.

9. A. In a circle, the closer a chord is to the center of the circle, the longer the chord. Hence, a chord 3.8 inches from the center is longer than a chord 3.9 inches from the center of the circle and Quantity A has the greater value.

10. B. If a triangle has sides with lengths of 10, 19, and x, the triangle inequality theorem requires that

$$19 - 10 < x < 19 + 10$$
$$9 < x < 29$$

Hence, Quantity B has the greater value.

11. **C.** Since supplementary angles are two angles whose sum is 180°, the supplement of a 127° angle has a measure of $180° - 127° = 53°$. Since complementary angles are two angles whose sum is 90°, the complement of a 37° angle has a measure of $90° - 37° = 53°$. Hence, the two quantities are equal.

12. **A.** Since each of the triangles has two equal sides, they are isosceles triangles and the height drawn to the base of the triangles will bisect the base.

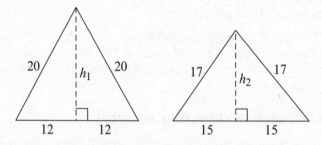

By the Pythagorean theorem

$$12^2 + h_1^2 = 20^2 \quad \text{and} \quad 15^2 + h_2^2 = 17^2$$
$$144 + h_1^2 = 400 \qquad\qquad 225 + h_2^2 = 289$$
$$h_1^2 = 400 - 144 \qquad\qquad h_2^2 = 289 - 225$$
$$h_1^2 = 256 \qquad\qquad\qquad h_2^2 = 64$$
$$h_1 = \sqrt{256} \qquad\qquad\qquad h_2 = \sqrt{64}$$
$$h_1 = 16 \qquad\qquad\qquad\quad h_2 = 8$$

The areas A_1 and A_2 of the triangles are

$$A_1 = \frac{1}{2}bh_1 \quad \text{and} \quad A_2 = \frac{1}{2}bh_2$$
$$= \frac{1}{2}(24)(16) \qquad = \frac{1}{2}(30)(8)$$
$$A_1 = 192 \qquad\qquad A_2 = 120$$

Hence, Quantity A has the greater value.

13. **D.** In a parallelogram, consecutive angles $\angle A$ and $\angle D$ are supplementary, so $\angle D = 100°$. However, in a trapezoid, consecutive angles are not necessarily supplementary, so knowing that $\angle W = 80°$ does not result in consecutive $\angle Z$ being supplementary. Therefore, the relationship cannot be determined from the information given.

14. **B.** Since a regular octagon has eight equal sides, the perimeter of a regular octagon with sides having a length of 14 is $8 \cdot 14 = 112$. Since a regular hexagon has six equal sides, the perimeter of a regular hexagon with sides having a length of 19 is $6 \cdot 19 = 114$. Hence, Quantity B has the greater value.

15. **C.** The sum of the interior angles in any quadrilateral is $360°$. Since trapezoid $MNPQ$ and parallelogram $WXYZ$ are quadrilaterals, the sum of the interior angles in each figure is $360°$. Hence, the two quantities are equal.

Multiple-Choice (Select One Answer)

16. **A.** If a triangle has two sides with lengths of 8 and 15, the triangle inequality theorem requires that the third side x have a length of

$$15 - 8 < x < 15 + 8$$
$$7 < x < 23$$

Hence, the length of the third side cannot be 7.

17. **D.** The area A of a trapezoid with height h and bases b_1 and b_2 is

$$A = \frac{1}{2}h(b_1 + b_2)$$

$$280 = \frac{1}{2}h(15 + 20)$$

$$280 = \frac{1}{2}h(35)$$

$$2 \cdot 280 = 2 \cdot \frac{1}{2}h(35)$$

$$560 = 35h$$

$$\frac{560}{35} = \frac{35h}{35}$$

$$16 = h$$

The height of the trapezoid is 16.

18. C.

$$2x = \text{smallest angle}$$
$$3x = \text{second angle}$$
$$4x = \text{third angle}$$

Since the sum of the angles in a triangle is 180°,

$$2x + 3x + 4x = 180°$$
$$9x = 180°$$
$$\frac{9x}{9} = \frac{180°}{9}$$
$$x = 20°$$

Hence, the smallest angle of the triangle has a measure of $2x = 2(20°) = 40°$.

19. D. The sum of the interior angles in a polygon with n sides is $(n - 2) \cdot 180°$. For a polygon with 15 sides, the sum of the interior angles is $(15 - 2) \cdot 180° = 13 \cdot 180° = 2340°$.

Since a regular polygon with 15 sides has angles with the same measure, the measure of one of its angles is $2340° \div 15 = 156°$.

20. B. The area A of a square with sides of length x is

$$A = x^2$$
$$150 = x^2$$
$$x = \sqrt{150} = \sqrt{25 \cdot 6}$$
$$x = 5\sqrt{6}$$

The perimeter P of a square with sides of length x is

$$P = 4x$$
$$= 4\left(5\sqrt{6}\right)$$
$$P = 20\sqrt{6}$$

21. D.

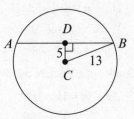

Draw radius $\overline{BC}$ and a right triangle, $\triangle BCD$, is formed. Using the Pythagorean theorem

$$(CD)^2 + (BD)^2 = (BC)^2$$
$$5^2 + (BD)^2 = 13^2$$
$$25 + (BD)^2 = 169$$
$$(BD)^2 = 169 - 25$$
$$(BD)^2 = 144$$
$$BD = \sqrt{144} = 12$$

Since $AD = BD$, $AD = 12$ and $AB = AD + BD = 12 + 12 = 24$.

22. E.

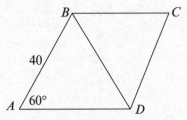

Since a rhombus has four equal sides, $AB = BC = CD = AD = 40$.

Since $AB = AD$ in $\triangle ABD$, the angles opposite these sides, $\angle ABD$ and $\angle ADB$, are equal.

Since $\angle A = 60°$ and $\angle A + \angle ABD + \angle ADB = 180°$, $\angle ABD = \angle ADB = 60°$ and $\triangle ABD$ is an equilateral triangle with sides of length 40. Hence, $AB = AD = BD = 40$.

23. A.

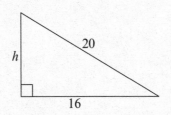

By the Pythagorean theorem

$$h^2 + 16^2 = 20^2$$
$$h^2 + 256 = 400$$
$$h^2 = 400 - 256$$
$$h^2 = 144$$
$$h = \sqrt{144} = 12$$

The area A of a triangle is

$$A = \frac{1}{2}bh$$
$$= \frac{1}{2}(16)(12)$$
$$A = 96$$

24. C. Since the sum of the angles in a triangle is $180°$, in $\triangle XYZ$

$$\angle X + \angle Y + \angle Z = 180°$$
$$53° + 48° + \angle Z = 180°$$
$$101° + \angle Z = 180°$$
$$\angle Z = 180° - 101°$$
$$\angle Z = 79°$$

Since $\triangle RST \sim \triangle XYZ$ and corresponding angles in similar triangles are equal

$\angle R = \angle X = 53°$
$\angle S = \angle Y = 48°$
$\angle T = \angle Z = 79°$

25. C.

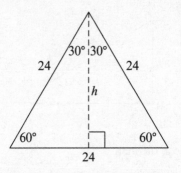

Since all three sides and all three angles in an equilateral triangle are equal, each side in the given triangle has length 24 and each angle measures 60°. A height drawn to the base of the triangle forms two 30°-60°-90° right triangles with a hypotenuse of 24. Since the side opposite the 60° angle is one-half the hypotenuse times $\sqrt{3}$, the height h is $12\sqrt{3}$. The area A of the triangle is

$$A = \frac{1}{2}bh$$
$$= \frac{1}{2}(24)\left(12\sqrt{3}\right)$$
$$A = 144\sqrt{3}$$

26. A. The volume V of a right circular cylinder with height h and radius r is

$$V = \pi r^2 h$$
$$= \pi\left(3^2\right)(10)$$
$$= \pi(9)(10)$$
$$V = 90\pi$$

27. C.

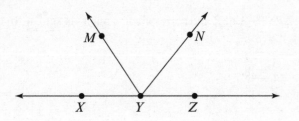

Since $\overleftrightarrow{XY}$ is a straight line

$$\angle XYM + \angle MYN + \angle NYZ = 180°$$
$$\angle XYM + \angle MYN + 50° = 180°$$
$$\angle XYM + \angle MYN = 180° - 50°$$
$$\angle XYM + \angle MYN = 130°$$

Since $\overleftrightarrow{MY}$ bisects $\angle XYN$, $\angle XYM = \angle MYN$ and

$$\angle XYM + \angle MYN = 130°$$
$$\angle XYM + \angle XYM = 130°$$
$$2 \cdot \angle XYM = 130°$$
$$\angle XYM = \frac{130°}{2}$$
$$\angle XYM = 65°$$

28. **E.** If the diameter of circle X is 4 times the diameter of circle Y, then the radius of circle X is 4 times the radius of circle Y.

Let z = the radius of circle Y and $4z$ = the radius of circle X.

The area A_1 of circle X is $A_1 = \pi r^2 = \pi(4z)^2 = 16\pi z^2$.

The area A_2 of circle Y is $A_2 = \pi r^2 = \pi(z^2) = \pi z^2$.

The ratio of A_1 to A_2 is $\dfrac{A_1}{A_2} = \dfrac{16\pi z^2}{\pi z^2} = \dfrac{16}{1} = 16:1$.

29. **D.** Let $2x$ = the measure of $\angle R$ and $3x$ = the measure of $\angle S$. Since consecutive angles in a parallelogram are supplementary and $\angle R$ and $\angle S$ are consecutive angles in parallelogram $PQRS$

$$\angle R + \angle S = 180°$$
$$2x + 3x = 180°$$
$$5x = 180°$$
$$\frac{5x}{5} = \frac{180°}{5}$$
$$x = 36°$$

Hence, the measure of $\angle S$ is $3x = 3(36°) = 108°$.

30. B. Since the degree measure of a circle is $360°$ and $\widehat{XZY} = 280°$, then $\widehat{XY} = 360° - \widehat{XZY} = 360° - 280° = 80°$.

The measure of an inscribed angle $\angle Z$ is equal to half the measure of its intercepted arc $\widehat{XY}$. Therefore, $\angle Z = \frac{1}{2}\widehat{XY} = \frac{1}{2}(80°) = 40°$.

Multiple-Choice (Select One or More Answers)

31. C, D, and E. If a triangle has two sides with lengths of 10 and 20, the triangle inequality theorem requires that the third side x have a length of

$$20 - 10 < x < 20 + 10$$
$$10 < x < 30$$

Hence, the third side could have a length of 15, 20, or 25.

32. A, B, C, D, and E. A chord of a circle may have any length greater than 0 up to and including the length of the diameter of the circle. Since the radius of the given circle is 8, its diameter is 16, which is the longest chord of the circle.

33. A, B, E, and F. Since the sum of the angles in any triangle is $180°$, the acute angles of a right triangle must be complementary (sum of $90°$).

A. $45 + 45 = 90$

B. $30 + 60 = 90$

C. $25 + 75 \neq 90$

D. $35 + 45 \neq 90$

E. $42 + 48 = 90$

F. $10 + 80 = 90$

34. A and B. If a square has sides of length x, then the length of its diagonals is $x\sqrt{2}$.

Since $\sqrt{2} \approx 1.4$,

A. $10\sqrt{2} < 35$

B. $20\sqrt{2} < 35$

C. $30\sqrt{2} > 35$

D. $40\sqrt{2} > 35$

E. $50\sqrt{2} > 35$

35. B and D. In a 30°-60°-90° right triangle, the side opposite the 30° angle is half the hypotenuse and the side opposite the 60° angle is half the hypotenuse times $\sqrt{3}$. If the hypotenuse is 10, then the side opposite the 30° angle is $\frac{1}{2}(10) = 5$ and the side opposite the 60° angle is $\frac{1}{2}(10) \cdot \sqrt{3} = 5\sqrt{3}$. If the hypotenuse is 24, then the side opposite the 30° angle is $\frac{1}{2}(24) = 12$ and the side opposite the 60° angle is $\frac{1}{2}(24) \cdot \sqrt{3} = 12\sqrt{3}$. None of the other answer choices satisfy the 30°-60°-90° right triangle property.

36. B, C, and E. In the parallelogram $WXYZ$, $\angle X = \angle Z$ since opposite angles are equal and $XY = WZ$ since opposite sides are equal. Also, $\angle Y$ and $\angle Z$ are supplementary since consecutive angles in a parallelogram are supplementary.

37. A, B, E, and F.

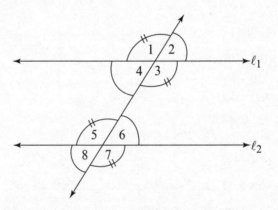

Since $\ell_1 \parallel \ell_2$, alternate interior angles are equal: $\angle 4 = \angle 6$ and $\angle 3 = \angle 5$. Alternate exterior angles are equal: $\angle 1 = \angle 7$ and $\angle 2 = \angle 8$. Vertical angles are equal: $\angle 1 = \angle 3$, $\angle 2 = \angle 4$, $\angle 5 = \angle 7$, and $\angle 6 = \angle 8$. Hence, $\angle 1 = \angle 3 = \angle 5 = \angle 7$ and $\angle 2 = \angle 4 = \angle 6 = \angle 8$.

38. D and E. In a rhombus $PQRS$, $\angle Q = \angle S$ since opposite angles are equal, and $\overline{PR} \perp \overline{QS}$ since the diagonals of a rhombus are perpendicular.

39. **A and D.** If $\triangle QRS \sim \triangle TUV$, corresponding angles are equal and corresponding sides are proportional. Hence $\angle Q = \angle T$, $\angle R = \angle U$, $\angle S = \angle V$, and $\dfrac{QR}{TU} = \dfrac{RS}{UV} = \dfrac{QS}{TV}$.

40. **B, D, and E.** The Pythagorean theorem states that the sum of the squares of the legs of a right triangle is equal to the square of the hypotenuse.

A. $5^2 + 8^2 = 9^2$

$\qquad 25 + 64 = 81$

$\qquad\qquad 89 \neq 81$

B. $8^2 + 15^2 = 17^2$

$\qquad 64 + 225 = 289$

$\qquad\qquad 289 = 289$

C. $1^2 + 2^2 = 3^2$

$\qquad 1 + 4 = 9$

$\qquad\quad 5 \neq 9$

D. $12^2 + 16^2 = 20^2$

$\qquad 144 + 256 = 400$

$\qquad\qquad 400 = 400$

E. $10^2 + 24^2 = 26^2$

$\qquad 100 + 576 = 676$

$\qquad\qquad 676 = 676$

Only choices B, D, and E satisfy the Pythagorean theorem.

41. **A, B, and C.** The sum of the interior angles in a polygon with n sides is $(n-2) \cdot 180°$. A regular polygon with n sides will have n equal sides and n equal angles. The measure of any one of the angles will be $\dfrac{(n-2) \cdot 180°}{n}$.

$$\text{For } n = 6: \frac{(6-2) \cdot 180°}{6} = \frac{4 \cdot 180°}{6} = \frac{720°}{6} = 120°$$

$$\text{For } n = 8: \frac{(8-2) \cdot 180°}{8} = \frac{6 \cdot 180°}{8} = \frac{1080°}{8} = 135°$$

For $n = 10$: $\dfrac{(10-2)\cdot 180°}{10} = \dfrac{8\cdot 180°}{10} = \dfrac{1440°}{10} = 144°$

None of the other answer choices will work.

42. **E.** In a trapezoid $WXYZ$, the sum of its angles must be 360°. Note that even though a trapezoid must have one pair of parallel sides, it is not obvious whether they would be $\overline{WX}$ and $\overline{YZ}$, or $\overline{XY}$ and $\overline{WZ}$.

43. **B, C, and F.** In an isosceles right triangle, the hypotenuse is equal to the length of one of its legs times $\sqrt{2}$.

B. If the legs have length 5 and 5, the hypotenuse would have length $5\sqrt{2}$.

C. If the legs have length $\sqrt{2}$ and $\sqrt{2}$, the hypotenuse would have length $\sqrt{2}\cdot\sqrt{2} = \sqrt{4} = 2$.

F. If the legs have lengths 1 and 1, the hypotenuse would have length $1\cdot\sqrt{2} = \sqrt{2}$.

None of the other answer choices will work.

44. **A, B, and E.** The triangle inequality theorem states that the sum of any two sides of a triangle must be greater than the third side.

A. For a triangle with sides 12, 10, 12 this is true.

B. For a triangle with sides 12, 20, 12 this is true.

C. For a triangle with sides 12, 30, 12 $\rightarrow$ 12 + 12 < 30.

D. For a triangle with sides 6, 6, 12 $\rightarrow$ 6 + 6 = 12

E. For a triangle with sides 8, 8, 12 this is true.

45. **A and B.** The circumference of a circle with radius r is $C = 2\pi r$, where $\pi \approx 3.14$.

A. For $r = 5$, $C = 2(5)\pi = 10\pi \approx 31.4 < 90$

B. For $r = 10$, $C = 2(10)\pi = 20\pi \approx 62.8 < 90$

C. For $r = 15$, $C = 2(15)\pi = 30\pi \approx 94.2 > 90$

D. For $r = 20$, $C = 2(20)\pi = 40\pi \approx 125.6 > 90$

E. For $r = 25$, $C = 2(25)\pi = 50\pi \approx 157 > 90$

F. For $r = 30$, $C = 2(30)\pi = 60\pi \approx 188.4 > 90$

Numeric Entry (Fill-in)

46. **2160**

The sum of the interior angles in a polygon with n sides is $(n-2) \cdot 180°$. The sum of the interior angles in a polygon with 14 sides is $(n-2) \cdot 180° = (14-2) \cdot 180° = 12 \cdot 180° = 2160°$.

47. **16**

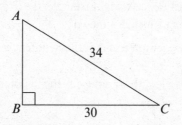

By the Pythagorean theorem

$$(AB)^2 + (BC)^2 = (AC)^2$$
$$(AB)^2 + (30)^2 = (34)^2$$
$$(AB)^2 + 900 = 1156$$
$$(AB)^2 = 1156 - 900$$
$$(AB)^2 = 256$$
$$AB = \sqrt{256}$$
$$AB = 16$$

48. **92**

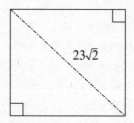

If a square has sides of length x, then the length of its diagonals is $x\sqrt{2}$. For the given square

$$x\sqrt{2} = 23\sqrt{2}$$

$$\frac{x\sqrt{2}}{\sqrt{2}} = \frac{23\sqrt{2}}{\sqrt{2}}$$

$$x = 23$$

The perimeter P of a square with sides of length x is $P = 4x$.
For the given square, $P = 4(23) = 92$.

49. **60**

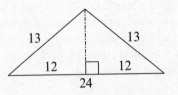

The height drawn to the base of an isosceles triangle will bisect the base. In the given triangle, the base will be bisected into two segments, each with a length of 12. By the Pythagorean theorem

$$h^2 + 12^2 = 13^2$$

$$h^2 + 144 = 169$$

$$h^2 = 169 - 144$$

$$h^2 = 25$$

$$h = \sqrt{25} = 5$$

The area A of a triangle with height h and base b is

$$A = \frac{1}{2}bh$$

$$= \frac{1}{2}(24)(5)$$

$$A = 60$$

50. **96**

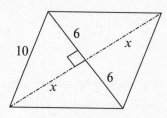

Since all four sides of a rhombus are equal and its perimeter is 40, each side must have a length of $40 \div 4 = 10$. Since the diagonals of a rhombus are perpendicular and bisect each other, the given diagonal is divided into two equal segments with length 6 and the two diagonals form four right triangles, each with a leg of length 6 and a hypotenuse of length 10.

By the Pythagorean theorem

$$x^2 + 6^2 = 10^2$$
$$x^2 + 36 = 100$$
$$x^2 = 100 - 36$$
$$x^2 = 64$$
$$x = \sqrt{64} = 8$$

The other diagonal of the rhombus has length $8 \times 2 = 16$.

The area A of a rhombus with diagonal d_1 and d_2 is

$$A = \frac{1}{2} d_1 \cdot d_2$$
$$= \frac{1}{2}(12)(16)$$
$$A = 96$$

Another solution is to figure the area of each of the four small triangles made by the intersecting diagonals. Each has an area of

$$A = \frac{1}{2}bh$$
$$= \frac{1}{2}(6)(8)$$
$$= 3 \cdot 8$$
$$A = 24$$

The area of the rhombus is $4 \cdot 24 = 96$.

51. 56

The area A_1 of the rectangular base is $A_1 = l \cdot w = 4 \cdot 5 = 20$ square feet.

The area A_2 of the front (and back) face is $A_2 = l \cdot h = 5 \cdot 2 = 10$ square feet.

The area A_3 of each of the side faces is $A_3 = w \cdot h = 4 \cdot 2 = 8$ square feet.

The surface area SA of all five faces is $SA = 20 + 10 + 10 + 8 + 8 = 56$ square feet.

52. 144

$$\text{Let } x = \text{1st angle of the trapezoid}$$
$$2x = \text{2nd angle of the trapezoid}$$
$$3x = \text{3rd angle of the trapezoid}$$
$$4x = \text{4th angle of the trapezoid}$$

Since the sum of the angles in a quadrilateral is $360°$

$$x + 2x + 3x + 4x = 360°$$
$$10x = 360°$$
$$\frac{10x}{10} = \frac{360°}{10}$$
$$x = 36°$$
$$4x = 4 \cdot 36° = 144°$$

53. 110

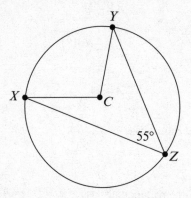

The measure of an inscribed angle $\angle Z$ is equal to half the measure of its intercepted arc $\overset{\frown}{XY}$. Hence, $\overset{\frown}{XY} = 2 \cdot \angle Z = 2 \cdot 55° = 110°$. The measure of a central angle $\angle XCY$ is equal to the measure of its intercepted arc $\overset{\frown}{XY}$. Hence, $\angle XCY = \overset{\frown}{XY} = 110°$.

54. 48

$$\text{Let} \quad x = \text{1st angle}$$
$$3x - 12 = \text{2nd angle}$$

Since supplementary angles are two angles whose sum is 180°

$$x + 3x - 12 = 180°$$
$$4x - 12 = 180°$$
$$4x = 180° + 12$$
$$4x = 192°$$
$$\frac{4x}{4} = \frac{192°}{4}$$
$$x = 48°$$

55. 84

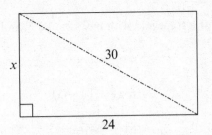

Since a rectangle is a quadrilateral with four right angles, a diagonal of a rectangle divides the figure into two right triangles. In the given figure, the right triangle has a base of 24 and a hypotenuse of 30. By the Pythagorean theorem

$$x^2 + 24^2 = 30^2$$
$$x^2 + 576 = 900$$
$$x^2 = 900 - 576$$
$$x^2 = 324$$
$$x = \sqrt{324} = 18$$

The perimeter P of a rectangle with a base b and a height h is

$$P = 2b + 2h$$
$$= 2(24) + 2(18)$$
$$= 48 + 36$$
$$P = 84$$

56. 2.6

The area A of a circle with radius r is $A = \pi r^2$.
For the given circle with area of 1.69π,

$$1.69\pi = \pi r^2$$
$$\frac{1.69\pi}{\pi} = \frac{\pi r^2}{\pi}$$
$$1.69 = r^2$$
$$r = \sqrt{1.69}$$
$$r = 1.3$$

Since the diameter d of a circle is two times the length of its radius, $d = 2 \cdot r = 2(1.3) = 2.6$.

57. 13

The area A of a trapezoid with bases b_1 and b_2 and a height h is

$$A = \frac{1}{2}h(b_1 + b_2)$$

$$416 = \frac{1}{2}h(19 + 45)$$

$$416 = \frac{1}{2}(64)h$$

$$416 = 32h$$

$$\frac{416}{32} = \frac{32h}{32}$$

$$h = 13$$

58. 225

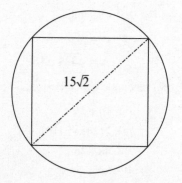

Since the square is inscribed in the circle, the diameter of the circle is the same as the diagonal of the square. The diagonal of a square is equal to the length of a side of the square times $\sqrt{2}$. In a square whose diagonal is $15\sqrt{2}$, the length of a side x is

$$x\sqrt{2} = 15\sqrt{2}$$

$$\frac{x\sqrt{2}}{\sqrt{2}} = \frac{15\sqrt{2}}{\sqrt{2}}$$

$$x = 15$$

The area A of a square with sides of length x is $A = x^2 = 15^2 = 225$.

59. 70

Since $\triangle XYZ \sim \triangle PQR$, their corresponding sides are proportional and

$$\frac{XY}{PQ} = \frac{YZ}{QR} = \frac{XZ}{PR}.$$

Given that $XY = 12$, $YZ = 20$, $XZ = 24$, and $PR = 30$,

$$\frac{XY}{PQ} = \frac{XZ}{PR} \qquad \text{and} \qquad \frac{YZ}{QR} = \frac{XZ}{PR}$$

$$\frac{12}{PQ} = \frac{24}{30} \qquad\qquad \frac{20}{QR} = \frac{24}{30}$$

$$24 \cdot PQ = (12)(30) \qquad 24 \cdot QR = (20)(30)$$

$$24 \cdot PQ = 360 \qquad\qquad 24 \cdot QR = 600$$

$$\frac{24 \cdot PQ}{24} = \frac{360}{24} \qquad\qquad \frac{24 \cdot QR}{24} = \frac{600}{24}$$

$$PQ = 15 \qquad\qquad QR = 25$$

The perimeter C of $\triangle PQR$ is

$$C = PQ + QR + PR$$
$$= 15 + 25 + 30$$
$$C = 70$$

60. 157.5

The sum of the interior angles in a polygon with n sides is $(n-2) \cdot 180°$. The sum of the interior angles in a polygon with 16 sides is $(n-2) \cdot 180° = (16-2) \cdot 180° = 14 \cdot 180° = 2520°$.

A regular polygon with n sides will have n equal angles and n equal sides. The measure of any one of the angles is equal to the sum of its interior angles divided by n. For a regular polygon with 16 sides, each angle will have a measure of $2520° \div 16 = 157.5°$.

Chapter 6

Data Analysis

GRE data analysis questions appear in a unique format compared to other Quantitative Reasoning questions. These types of questions require some knowledge of basic statistics. You must reason analytically and make sound decisions regarding multiple variations of data in order to solve problems. A solid understanding of arithmetic will help you answer these types of questions, but you must also be able to draw upon your ability to reason logically under time constraints. As you make inferences from the information presented, you will gather, organize, and interpret data in order to draw conclusions and answer the questions.

Start with the diagnostic test that follows and then study and practice each of the major data analysis topics covered on the following checklist. Chart your progress as you review each topic. Use the list to check off topics as you review them. As you evaluate your understanding of each topic area, pinpoint areas that require further study by placing a check mark next to the topic. Continue to measure your progress and refer to this list as often as necessary.

To reinforce what you have learned, work the practice questions at the end of this chapter (answer explanations are provided). The practice questions are arranged by question type to help you practice solving data analysis problems that are specific to the GRE exam.

Data Analysis Topics You Should Know

Topic	Study Pages	Worked Examples	Further Study Required
Basic statistics: mean, median, mode, and range	pp. 318–319		
Standard deviation	pp. 319–320		
Variance	p. 320		
Counting methods	p. 324		
Factorials, combinations, and permutations	pp. 324–329		
Probability	pp. 329–333		

The following diagnostic test is designed to help you identify specific data analysis topics that require further concentration. After you take the diagnostic test, analyze your test results and develop a step-by-step action plan to pinpoint topics to study.

Data Analysis Diagnostic Test

25 Questions

Directions: Solve each problem in this section by using the information given and your own mathematical calculations.

1. Find the mean of 27, 30, 28, 22, 25, and 28.

2. Find the median of 63, 80, 85, 74, 71, 83, 53, and 82.

3. Find the mode of 18, 19, 13, 17, 18, 16, and 20.

4. Find the mode of 8, 10, 3, 6, 8, 9, 7, and 3.

5. Find the mode of 16, 13, 20, 18, 11, 19, 15, 14, and 17.

6. A student has test scores of 83, 95, 91, 86, and 92. What score is needed on the sixth test for the student to have an average of 90?

7. Evaluate: 7!

8. Evaluate: $\dfrac{14!}{10! \cdot 4!}$

9. Simplify: $\dfrac{(n+1)!}{(n-2)!}$

10. How many different 4-letter groups can be formed using the letters in the word "problematic"?

11. How many 4-person committees can be formed from a total of 9 people?

12. In how many different orders may 6 people be seated in a row?

13. From a group of 7 mathematicians and 7 biologists, a committee of 7 is chosen and must include 4 mathematicians. In how many ways can this be done?

14. How many 4-digit numbers can be formed using the digits 0 through 9 if no digit may be repeated once it has been used?

15. A box contains all 26 letters of the alphabet. What is the probability that the first 2 letters drawn are the letters a, b, c, d, e, or f?

16. Three cards are drawn from a deck of 52 cards. What is the probability that all 3 cards are aces?

17. One bag contains 5 white marbles and 4 black marbles. A second bag contains 4 white marbles and 5 black marbles. If 1 marble is drawn from each bag, what is the probability that both marbles are black?

18. In the previous problem, what is the probability that 1 marble drawn from each bag is white and 1 marble is black?

19. A committee of 3 is to be chosen from a group of 5 men and 6 women. What is the probability that all 3 are women?

20. In a single throw of 2 dice, determine the probability that they will total 6.

21. A bag contains 8 green marbles, 7 pink marbles, and 5 blue marbles. If 1 marble is drawn at random, what is the probability that the marble is not pink?

22. If a coin is tossed 4 times, what is the probability that all 4 tosses will be tails?

23. A box contains the numbers 1 through 9 inclusive. If 4 numbers are drawn consecutively, determine the probability that they are alternately odd, even, odd, even.

24. If 1 card is drawn at random from a deck of 52 cards, what is the probability that the card will not be a spade?

25. Three students are given a math problem to solve. The probability that the first student can solve the problem is $\frac{2}{3}$, that the second student can solve the problem is $\frac{3}{7}$, and that the third student can solve the problem is $\frac{3}{5}$. If all 3 students work on the problem, what is the probability that the problem will be solved?

Scoring the Diagnostic Test

The following section will assist you in scoring and analyzing your diagnostic test results. Use the answer key to score your results on the Analysis Sheet that follows. Read through the answer explanations on pages 309–317 to clarify the solutions to the problems.

Answer Key

Basic Statistics: Mean, Median, Mode, and Range

1. $26\frac{2}{3}$

2. 77

3. 18

4. 3 and 8

5. No mode

6. 93

Factorials

7. 5040

8. 1001

9. $n^3 - n$

Permutations and Combinations

10. 7920

11. 126

12. 720

13. 1225

14. 4536

Probability

15. $\dfrac{3}{65}$

16. $\dfrac{1}{5525}$

17. $\dfrac{20}{81}$

18. $\dfrac{41}{81}$

19. $\dfrac{4}{33}$

20. $\dfrac{5}{36}$

21. $\dfrac{13}{20}$

22. $\dfrac{1}{16}$

23. $\dfrac{5}{63}$

24. $\dfrac{3}{4}$

25. $\dfrac{97}{105}$

Charting and Analyzing Your Diagnostic Test Results

Record your diagnostic test results in the following chart and use these results as a guide for an effective data analysis review. Mark the problems that you missed and pay particular attention to those that were missed because of your "lack of knowledge." These are the areas you will want to focus on as you study data analysis topics.

Data Analysis Diagnostic Test Analysis Sheet

Topic	Total Possible	Number Correct	Number Incorrect		
			(A) Simple Mistake	(B) Misread Problem	(C) Lack of Knowledge
Mean, median, mode, and range	6				
Factorials	3				
Permutations and combinations	5				
Probability	11				
Total Possible Explanations for Incorrect Answers: Columns A, B, and C					
Total Number of Answers Correct and Incorrect	25	Add the total number of correct answers here: _____	Add columns A, B, and C: _____ Total number of incorrect answers		

Data Analysis Diagnostic Test Answers and Explanations

Basic Statistics: Mean, Median, Mode, and Range

1. $26\dfrac{2}{3}$

   The mean or average of 27, 30, 28, 22, 25, and 28 is

   $$(27 + 30 + 28 + 22 + 25 + 28) \div 6 = 160 \div 6$$
   $$= 26\frac{4}{6}$$
   $$= 26\frac{2}{3}$$

2. 77

Since there is an even number of items in the data, the median is the average of the two middle numbers. Arranging the numbers from smallest to largest (or largest to smallest) yields 53, 63, 71, 74, 80, 82, 83, and 85. The two middle numbers are 74 and 80, whose average is

$$(74+80) \div 2 = 154 \div 2$$
$$= 77, \text{ which is the median}$$

3. 18

The mode of 18, 19, 13, 17, 18, 16, and 20 is 18. It is the number that occurs most frequently in the given data.

4. 3 and 8

The mode of 8, 10, 3, 6, 8, 9, 7, and 3 is 3 and 8 since they both occur twice in the given data.

5. No mode

There is no mode for 16, 13, 20, 18, 11, 19, 15, 14, and 17. No number occurs more frequently than any of the other numbers in the given data.

6. 93

Let x = the sixth test score. For the average of the 6 test scores to equal 90:

$$(83+95+91+86+92+x) \div 6 = 90$$
$$\frac{447+x}{6} = 90$$
$$\frac{447+x}{6} \cdot 6 = 90 \cdot 6$$
$$447+x = 540$$
$$447+x-447 = 540-447$$
$$x = 93$$

Factorials

7. 5040

$$7! = 7 \cdot 6 \cdot 5 \cdot 4 \cdot 3 \cdot 2 \cdot 1 = 5040$$

8. 1001

$$\frac{14!}{10! \cdot 4!} = \frac{14 \cdot 13 \cdot 12 \cdot 11 \cdot \cancel{10!}}{\cancel{10!} \cdot 4!}$$

$$= \frac{\cancel{14} \cdot 13 \cdot \cancel{12} \cdot 11}{\cancel{4} \cdot \cancel{3} \cdot \cancel{2} \cdot 1}$$

$$= 7 \cdot 13 \cdot 11$$

$$= 1001$$

9. $n^3 - n$

$$\frac{(n+1)!}{(n-2)!} = \frac{(n+1)(n)(n-1)(n-2)!}{(n-2)!}$$

$$= (n+1)(n)(n-1)$$

$$= \left(n^2 + n\right)(n-1)$$

$$= n^3 - n$$

Permutations and Combinations

10. 7920

Since the order of the letters is important to consider, this is a permutation of 4 letters from a set of 11 letters. The number of different 4-letter groups is

$$_{11}P_4 = P(11,4) = \frac{11!}{(11-4)!} = \frac{11!}{7!}$$

$$= \frac{11 \cdot 10 \cdot 9 \cdot 8 \cdot \cancel{7!}}{\cancel{7!}}$$

$$= 11 \cdot 10 \cdot 9 \cdot 8$$

$$= 7920$$

11. **126**

Since the order of the 4 people chosen is not important, this is a combination of 4 people from a set of 9 people. The number of 4-person committees is

$$_9C_4 = C(9,4) = \frac{9!}{4!(9-4)!}$$

$$= \frac{9!}{4! \cdot 5!}$$

$$= \frac{9 \cdot 8 \cdot 7 \cdot 6 \cdot \cancel{5!}}{4! \cdot \cancel{5!}}$$

$$= \frac{9 \cdot \overset{2}{\cancel{8}} \cdot 7 \cdot \cancel{6}}{\cancel{4} \cdot \cancel{3} \cdot \cancel{2} \cdot 1}$$

$$= 9 \cdot 2 \cdot 7$$

$$= 126$$

12. **720**

Since the order of the people is important to consider, this is a permutation of 6 people from a group of 6 people. The number of different orders is

$$_6P_6 = P(6,6) = \frac{6!}{(6-6)!}$$

$$= \frac{6!}{0!}$$

$$= \frac{6 \cdot 5 \cdot 4 \cdot 3 \cdot 2 \cdot 1}{1}$$

$$= 720$$

13. **1225**

Each committee is formed by selecting 4 mathematicians out of 7 and 3 biologists out of 7 where the order is not important. The number of 7-person committees possible is

$$C(7,4) \cdot C(7,3) = \frac{7!}{4! \cdot 3!} \cdot \frac{7!}{3! \cdot 4!}$$

$$= \frac{7 \cdot \cancel{6} \cdot 5}{\cancel{3} \cdot \cancel{2} \cdot 1} \cdot \frac{7 \cdot \cancel{6} \cdot 5}{\cancel{3} \cdot \cancel{2} \cdot 1}$$

$$= 35 \cdot 35$$

$$= 1225$$

14. 4536

Since the first digit of a 4-digit number cannot be zero, there are 9 possible numbers for the thousands place. The remaining three place values will be selected from 9 possible numbers where the order is important, which is a permutation of 3 numbers from a group of 9 numbers. Hence, the number of 4-digit numbers possible is

$$9 \cdot P(9,3) = 9 \cdot \frac{9!}{(9-3)!}$$
$$= 9 \cdot \frac{9!}{6!}$$
$$= 9 \cdot \frac{9 \cdot 8 \cdot 7 \cdot \cancel{6!}}{\cancel{6!}}$$
$$= 9 \cdot 9 \cdot 8 \cdot 7$$
$$= 4536$$

Probability

15. $\dfrac{3}{65}$

The probability that the first letter drawn is a, b, c, d, e, or f is $\dfrac{6}{26}$, while the probability that the second letter is 1 of the remaining 5 is $\dfrac{5}{25}$. Hence, the probability P that the first 2 letters drawn are a, b, c, d, e, or f is

$$P = \frac{6}{26} \cdot \frac{5}{25}$$
$$= \frac{3}{13} \cdot \frac{1}{5}$$
$$P = \frac{3}{65}$$

16. $\dfrac{1}{5525}$

The probability that the first card drawn is an ace is $\dfrac{4}{52}$. The probability that the second card drawn is an ace is $\dfrac{3}{51}$, while the probability that the third card drawn is an ace is $\dfrac{2}{50}$. Hence, the probability P that all 3 cards drawn are aces is

$$P = \frac{4}{52} \cdot \frac{3}{51} \cdot \frac{2}{50}$$

$$= \frac{1}{13} \cdot \frac{1}{17} \cdot \frac{1}{25}.$$

$$P = \frac{1}{5525}$$

17. $\dfrac{20}{81}$

The probability that the marble drawn from the first bag is black is $\dfrac{4}{9}$. The probability that the marble drawn from the second bag is black is $\dfrac{5}{9}$. Hence, the probability P that the marbles are both black is $P = \dfrac{4}{9} \cdot \dfrac{5}{9} = \dfrac{20}{81}$.

18. $\dfrac{41}{81}$

The designed outcome of drawing 1 white marble and 1 black marble may occur in two different ways:

a. The marble drawn from the first bag is white, while the marble drawn from the second bag is black.

b. The marble drawn from the first bag is black, while the marble drawn from the second bag is white.

The probability P_1 that the marble drawn from the first bag is white and the marble drawn from the second bag is black is $P_1 = \dfrac{5}{9} \cdot \dfrac{5}{9} = \dfrac{25}{81}$.

The probability P_2 that the marble drawn from the first bag is black and the marble drawn from the second bag is white is $P_2 = \dfrac{4}{9} \cdot \dfrac{4}{9} = \dfrac{16}{81}$.

Hence, the probability P that 1 marble is white and 1 marble is black is

$$P = P_1 + P_2$$
$$= \frac{25}{81} + \frac{16}{81}$$
$$P = \frac{41}{81}$$

19. $\dfrac{4}{33}$

Since there is a total of 11 people of which 6 are women, the probability that the first person selected is a woman is $\dfrac{6}{11}$. The probability that the second person selected is a woman is $\dfrac{5}{10}$, while the probability that the third person selected is a woman is $\dfrac{4}{9}$. Hence, the probability P that all 3 people selected are women is

$$P = \frac{\cancel{6}^{2}}{11} \cdot \frac{\cancel{5}}{\cancel{10}_{2}} \cdot \frac{4}{\cancel{9}_{3}} = \frac{4}{33}$$

20. $\dfrac{5}{36}$

Since each die contains the numbers 1 through 6, there are $6 \cdot 6 = 36$ possible outcomes when 2 dice are thrown. There are 5 possible ways of throwing a total of 6: 1 and 5, 5 and 1, 2 and 4, 4 and 2, and 3 and 3. The probability P of the 2 dice having a total of 6 is $P = \dfrac{5}{36}$.

21. $\dfrac{13}{20}$

Since there is a total of 20 marbles, the probability that the marble drawn is pink is $\dfrac{7}{20}$. The probability P that the marble drawn is NOT pink is 1 minus the probability that the marble is pink: $P = 1 - \dfrac{7}{20} = \dfrac{13}{20}$.

22. $\dfrac{1}{16}$

Since there are only 2 possible outcomes, heads or tails, when a coin is tossed, the probability that a toss will result in tails is $\dfrac{1}{2}$. Hence, the probability P that all 4 tosses of a coin will be tails is $P = \dfrac{1}{2} \cdot \dfrac{1}{2} \cdot \dfrac{1}{2} \cdot \dfrac{1}{2} = \dfrac{1}{16}$.

23. $\dfrac{5}{63}$

For the numbers 1 through 9, there are 4 *even* numbers and 5 *odd* numbers. The probability that the first number is *odd* is $\dfrac{5}{9}$, and the probability that the second number is *even* is $\dfrac{4}{8}$, or $\dfrac{1}{2}$. The probability that the third number is *odd* is $\dfrac{4}{7}$, and the probability that the fourth number is *even* is $\dfrac{3}{6}$, or $\dfrac{1}{2}$. Hence, the probability P that the 4 numbers drawn are alternately odd, even, odd, even is $P = \dfrac{5}{9} \cdot \dfrac{1}{2} \cdot \dfrac{4}{7} \cdot \dfrac{1}{2} = \dfrac{20}{252} = \dfrac{5}{63}$.

24. $\dfrac{3}{4}$

Since there are 13 spades in a deck of 52 cards, the probability that 1 card selected from the deck will be a spade is $\dfrac{13}{52}$, or $\dfrac{1}{4}$. The probability P that the card drawn will NOT be a spade is 1 minus the probability that it is a spade: $P = 1 - \dfrac{1}{4} = \dfrac{3}{4}$.

25. $\dfrac{97}{105}$

The only way for the problem to not be solved is for all 3 students to be unable to solve the problem. The probability that the first student cannot solve the problem is $1 - \dfrac{2}{3} = \dfrac{1}{3}$. The probability that the second student cannot solve the problem is $1 - \dfrac{3}{7} = \dfrac{4}{7}$. The probability that the

third student cannot solve the problem is $1 - \dfrac{3}{5} = \dfrac{2}{5}$. The probability

that all 3 students will fail to solve the problem is $\dfrac{1}{3} \cdot \dfrac{4}{7} \cdot \dfrac{2}{5} = \dfrac{8}{105}$.

Hence, the probability P that the problem will be solved is 1 minus the

probability that it will not be solved: $P = 1 - \dfrac{8}{105} = \dfrac{97}{105}$.

Data Analysis Review

Data analysis questions draw upon your knowledge of descriptive statistics, standard deviation, factorials, combinations, permutations, and probability.

Descriptive Statistics

Descriptive statistics is the name given to the mathematical science of organizing and summarizing numerical data and its information. Why will you need to know descriptive statistics on the GRE? Most graduate programs require that you have some basic knowledge of statistics for research and experiments. Using data and information about the distribution of numbers helps to provide a clear picture about the data of real-life scenarios in many different academic disciplines, which is necessary to draw conclusions about this data. This section introduces the basic concepts of descriptive statistics to help you succeed with this type of quantitative problem. Topics include the fundamentals of frequency distribution and measures of central tendency (mean, median, mode, and range).

Frequency Distribution

Before the data you collect from a research project can be interpreted, it must be organized so that you can make sense of what you have collected. A **frequency distribution** table (chart) is used as a template to help you organize and summarize data from lowest to highest (intervals). Generally, there is a column on the left (the data values) and a column on the right (the frequency), which indicate how many of each data value are in the data set.

Here is an example of a frequency distribution table:

x	f
1	2
2	2
3	1
5	2
7	3

Note: Although frequency distribution tables are useful for gathering and organizing data, these tables do not provide you with a good visual picture of what the data actually means. This is why numerical data from a frequency table is transferred to a graphical display (bar graph, line graph, etc.). Graphical display types of questions, called *data interpretation,* commonly appear on the GRE and are discussed in Chapter 7.

Measures of Central Tendency

A **measure of central tendency** is any number that describes the distributed "center" of data in a frequency table from which all the other data falls. It indicates the "center of a distribution." The three basic measures of central tendency are *mean* (or arithmetic mean), *median*, and *mode*.

Mean

The **mean** for a set of data is found by adding the numbers in the set of data and then dividing by the total number of items in the set. The mean is also called the **average.** For any set of data, there is *one and only one mean.*

Median

The **median** for a set of data is the middle number in the set. Before the median can be determined, each number in the set of data should be written in order from smallest to largest, or from largest to smallest. For example, if there are five values in the data set, the median would be the third value after placing them in order. If the number of items in the data set is *even,* then the median is determined by finding the mean or average of the two middle numbers. For example, if there are six values in the data set, the two middle numbers after placing them in order would be the third and fourth values, and the median would be their mean or average. For any set of data, there is *one and only one median.*

Mode

The **mode** for a set of data is the number that occurs most frequently. One difference between the mode, mean, and median is that there may be *more than one mode or no mode* for any given set of data.

Range

The **range** for a set of data is simply the difference between the largest and the smallest numbers of the set. When a set of data values is listed from least to greatest, the median value is sometimes referred to as the *2nd quartile* or the *50th percentile* value. To the left of the median is a set of data values called the lower values and to the right of the median is a set of data values called the upper values. The median of the lower values is called the *1st quartile* or *25th percentile* value, and the median of the upper values is called the *3rd quartile* or the *75th percentile* value.

The difference between the 3rd quartile and the 1st quartile (or the 75th percentile and the 25th percentile) is called the *interquartile range*.

Standard Deviation

The **standard deviation** of a set of data is a measure of how far data values of a population are from the mean or average value of the population. A small standard deviation indicates that the data values tend to be very close to the mean value. A large standard deviation indicates that the data values are far from the mean value.

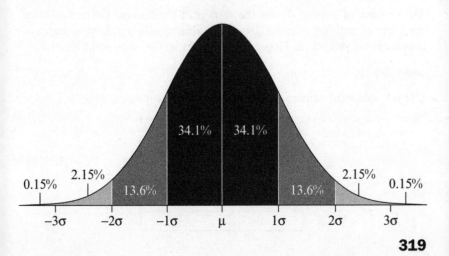

The preceding figure represents a set of data that has a normal distribution. In it, μ represents the mean value of the set of data. Each shaded band has a width of one standard deviation. For normally distributed data, you will find approximately 68 percent of all the data values are within one standard deviation from the mean. You will find approximately 95.5 percent of all the data values are within two standard deviations from the mean. At three standard deviations from the mean, approximately 99.7 percent of all the data values are found.

The basic method for calculating the standard deviation for a population is lengthy and time consuming. It involves six steps:

1. Find the mean or average value for the set of data.
2. Find the difference between the mean and each data value.
3. Square each of the differences.
4. Find the sum of the squares.
5. Divide the sum of the squares by the number of data values.
6. Find the square root of the quotient from step 5.

It should be noted that the method outlined here is for the entire population of data value and is often referred to as the **population standard deviation.** If the data values are a sample taken from a larger population of n values, then the method used to determine the standard deviation is changed slightly. In step 4, the sum of the squares would be divided by $n - 1$ instead of by n, and this would be called the **sample standard deviation.**

Variance

The **variance** of a set of data is the average of the squared differences from the mean of each value in the data. The variance is determined in step 5 of the preceding procedure. Now let's put it all together with some examples.

Examples

Use the following frequency distribution table to answer questions 1–4.

x	f
1	2
2	2
3	1
5	2
7	3

1. Find the mean.

   In order to make all the calculations, add three more columns with formulas to the table. Note that you do not need to memorize the formulas. These are for instructional purposes only. The "m" will be the mean value and the "f" is the *frequency*.

x	f	$(x)(f)$	$(x - m)^2$	$(x - m)^2(f)$
1	2			
2	2			
3	1			
5	2			
7	3			
Totals				

   Remember to *calculate the mean,* find the sum of all the data values and divide that by how many data values there are. By adding the values in the "f"column, you find how many data values there are. By multiplying each data value by its frequency, the "$(x)(f)$" column, then adding these totals together, you find a quick way to get the sum of all the data values.

x	f	$(x)(f)$	$(x - m)^2$	$(x - m)^2(f)$
1	2	2		
2	2	4		
3	1	3		
5	2	10		
7	3	21		
Totals	10	40		

   Therefore, $m = \dfrac{40}{10} = 4$. The mean has a value of 4.

2. Find the median.

   The median will be the average of the data values in the 5th and 6th positions. Based on the frequency table, the 1st and 2nd values are each 1 and the 3rd and 4th values are each 2. The 5th value is 3, and the 6th value is 5. The average of 3 and 5 is 4. The median value is 4. If the data values were all listed in order, it would look like this:

$$\underset{\text{1st}}{1},\underset{\text{2nd}}{1},\underset{\text{3rd}}{2},\underset{\text{4th}}{2},\underset{\text{5th}}{3}, \underset{\text{6th}}{5},\underset{\text{7th}}{5},\underset{\text{8th}}{7},\underset{\text{9th}}{7},\underset{\text{10th}}{7}$$

$$\uparrow$$
median

3. Find the mode.

Based on the frequency table, the value 7 occurs 3 times, which is more than any other value occurs. Therefore, the mode is the value 7.

4. Find the range.

Remember the range is the difference between the greatest value, 7, and the least value, 1. Since $7 - 1 = 6$, the range is 6.

5. A student has test scores of 85, 69, 88, 91, and 86 in math class. Find the mean test score.

The first step in finding the mean is to find the sum of the 5 test scores: $85 + 69 + 88 + 91 + 86 = 419$.

Since there are 5 test scores, the sum is divided by 5:

$$\frac{419}{5} = 83\frac{4}{5}, \text{ or } 83.8.$$

If the problem had asked for the answer to be rounded to the nearest whole number, the mean would be 84.

6. What score would the student in the previous example need to score on a sixth test to have an average score of 80?

The sum of 6 test scores required to have an average of 80 is $80 \times 6 = 480$. Since the first 5 scores have a sum of 419, the sixth test score must be $480 - 419 = 61$. The student would need a score of 61 on the sixth test.

7. Find the median for 8 given quiz scores: 8, 5, 4, 10, 7, 9, 9, 7.

The scores should first be arranged in numerical order: 4, 5, 7, 7, 8, 9, 9, 10 or 10, 9, 9, 8, 7, 7, 5, 4.

Since there is an even number of scores (8), the median is the average of the two middle scores.

$$\frac{7+8}{2} = \frac{15}{2} = 7\frac{1}{2}, \text{ or } 7.5$$

8. Find the mode of the quiz scores given in the previous example.

The mode refers to the score that occurs most frequently. Since there are two quiz scores of 7 and two quiz scores of 9, the mode is 7 and 9.

9. Find the mean, median, and mode of 3, 6, 6, 6, 9, 12, 12, 13, 14.

The mean is

$$(3+6+6+6+9+12+12+13+14) \div 9 =$$
$$81 \div 9 =$$
$$\text{mean} = 9$$

The median is the middle number in the set. In this set of 9 items, the median is the fifth number in the set of data: median = 9.

The mode is the number that occurs most frequently in the set of data: mode = 6.

10. Find the standard deviation for the following set of data: 5, 7, 8, 9, 10.

Step 1. Find the mean: $(5 + 7 + 8 + 9 + 10) \div 5 = 39 \div 5 = 7.8$.

Step 2. Calculate the difference between the mean and the data values:

$$5 - 7.8 = -2.8$$
$$7 - 7.8 = -0.8$$
$$8 - 7.8 = 0.2$$
$$9 - 7.8 = 1.2$$
$$10 - 7.8 = 2.2$$

Step 3. Square each of the differences:

$$(-2.8)^2 = 7.84$$
$$(-0.8)^2 = 0.64$$
$$(0.2)^2 = 0.04$$
$$(1.2)^2 = 1.44$$
$$(2.2)^2 = 4.84$$

Step 4. Find the sum of the squares: $7.84 + 0.64 + 0.04 + 1.44 + 4.84 = 14.8$.

Step 5. Divide by the number of data items (5): $14.8 \div 5 = 2.96$. This represents the variance of the data.

Step 6. Find the square root of the quotient from step 5: $\sqrt{2.96} \approx 1.72$. This is the standard deviation for the given set of data.

Counting Methods

The fundamental principle of counting states that if event 1 can be done in x different ways and event 2 can be done in y different ways, then the total number of outcomes of the events together is $x \cdot y$. Similarly, if event 1 can be done in x different ways, event 2 can be done in y different ways, and event 3 can be done in z different ways, then the total number of outcomes of the events together is $x \cdot y \cdot z$. In general, if there are n events that can be done in $x_1, x_2, x_3, ..., x_n$ different ways, then the total number of outcomes of the events is $x_1 \cdot x_2 \cdot x_3 ... x_n$.

Factorials, Combinations, and Permutations

Expressions of factorials, combinations, and permutations are often useful to determine the total number of outcomes possible for events.

Factorials

Factorials allow us to express the product of a set of decreasing natural numbers without having to write each factor. The symbol used for factorials is !; the general definition for $n!$, where n is a natural number, is as follows:

$$n! = n \cdot (n-1) \cdot (n-2) \cdot (n-3) \cdots 3 \cdot 2 \cdot 1.$$

By definition $0! = 1$.

Examples

1. $4! = 4 \cdot 3 \cdot 2 \cdot 1 = 24$

   $6! = 6 \cdot 5 \cdot 4 \cdot 3 \cdot 2 \cdot 1 = 720$

   $9! = 9 \cdot 8 \cdot 7 \cdot 6 \cdot 5 \cdot 4 \cdot 3 \cdot 2 \cdot 1 = 362,880$

2. Evaluate: $\dfrac{10!}{6!}$

$$\text{Since } 10! = 10 \cdot 9 \cdot 8 \cdot 7 \cdot 6!$$

$$\frac{10!}{6!} = \frac{10 \cdot 9 \cdot 8 \cdot 7 \cdot \cancel{6!}}{\cancel{6!}}$$

$$= 10 \cdot 9 \cdot 8 \cdot 7$$

$$\frac{10!}{6!} = 5040$$

3. Evaluate: $\dfrac{13!}{10! \cdot 3!}$

$$\text{Since } 13! = 13 \cdot 12 \cdot 11 \cdot 10!$$

$$\frac{13!}{10! \cdot 3!} = \frac{13 \cdot 12 \cdot 11 \cdot \cancel{10!}}{\cancel{10!} \cdot 3!}$$

$$= \frac{13 \cdot \overset{2}{\cancel{12}} \cdot 11}{\cancel{3} \cdot \cancel{2} \cdot 1}$$

$$\frac{13!}{10! \cdot 3!} = 286$$

4. Simplify: $\dfrac{(x+2)!}{(x-1)!}$

$$\text{Since } (x+2)! = (x+2)(x+1)(x)(x-1)!$$

$$\frac{(x+2)!}{(x-1)!} = \frac{(x+2)(x+1)(x)\cancel{(x-1)!}}{\cancel{(x-1)!}}$$

$$= (x+2)(x+1)(x)$$

$$\frac{(x+2)!}{(x-1)!} = x^3 + 3x^2 + 2x$$

Combinations

A selection of r objects from a set with a total of n objects without regard for the order of the selected objects is called a **combination**. The notation for the number of combinations of n objects taken r at a time is $_nC_r$ or $C(n, r)$.

The total number of ways to select r objects from a set of n objects without regard for the order of the selected objects is $_nC_r = C(n,r) = \dfrac{n!}{r!(n-r)!}$.

Examples

1. How many different groups of 5 students can be formed by choosing from a total of 11 students?

   Since the order of the students selected is not important, this is a combination of 5 students from a set of 11 students. The number of different groups possible is

   $$_{11}C_5 = C(11,5) = \frac{11!}{5!(11-5)!}$$

   $$= \frac{11!}{5! \cdot 6!}$$

   $$= \frac{11 \cdot 10 \cdot 9 \cdot 8 \cdot 7 \cdot \cancel{6!}}{5! \cdot \cancel{6!}}$$

   $$= \frac{11 \cdot \overset{2}{\cancel{10}} \cdot \overset{3}{\cancel{9}} \cdot \cancel{8} \cdot 7}{\cancel{5} \cdot \cancel{4} \cdot \cancel{3} \cdot \cancel{2} \cdot 1}$$

   $$= 462 \text{ groups}$$

   To illustrate that order is not important, note that a group consisting of students A, B, C, D, and E is the same as a group consisting of students B, E, A, D, and C.

2. How many different pairs of books may be selected from a shelf containing 15 books?

   This is a combination of 2 books from a set of 15 books. The number of different pairs possible is

   $$_{15}C_2 = C(15,2) = \frac{15!}{2!(15-2)!}$$

   $$= \frac{15!}{2! \cdot 13!}$$

   $$= \frac{15 \cdot 14 \cdot \cancel{13!}}{2! \cdot \cancel{13!}}$$

   $$= \frac{15 \cdot \overset{7}{\cancel{14}}}{\cancel{2} \cdot 1}$$

   $$= 105 \text{ pairs}$$

3. How many different 5-card poker hands are possible from a deck of 52 cards?

This is a combination of 5 cards from a set of 52 cards. The number of different 5-card hands is

$$_{52}C_5 = C(52,5) = \frac{52!}{5!(52-5)!}$$

$$= \frac{52!}{5! \cdot 47!}$$

$$= \frac{52 \cdot 51 \cdot 50 \cdot 49 \cdot 48 \cdot \cancel{47!}}{5! \cdot \cancel{47!}}$$

$$= \frac{\overset{26}{\cancel{52}} \cdot \overset{17}{\cancel{51}} \cdot \overset{10}{\cancel{50}} \cdot 49 \cdot \overset{12}{\cancel{48}}}{\cancel{5} \cdot \cancel{4} \cdot \cancel{3} \cdot \cancel{2} \cdot 1}$$

$$= 2{,}598{,}960 \text{ hands}$$

4. How many 5-person committees may be formed from a group of 6 males and 6 females if each committee must have 2 male and 3 female members?

This is a combination of 2 males from a group of 6 males and a combination of 3 females from a group of 6 females. The number of different groups of 2 males is

$$_6C_2 = C(6,2) = \frac{6!}{2!(6-2)!}$$

$$= \frac{6!}{2! \cdot 4!}$$

$$= \frac{6 \cdot 5 \cdot \cancel{4!}}{2! \cdot \cancel{4!}}$$

$$= \frac{6 \cdot 5}{2 \cdot 1}$$

$$= 15$$

The number of different groups of 3 females is

$$_6C_3 = C(6,3) = \frac{6!}{3!(6-3)!}$$

$$= \frac{6!}{3! \cdot 3!}$$

$$= \frac{6 \cdot 5 \cdot 4 \cdot \cancel{3!}}{3! \cdot \cancel{3!}}$$

$$= \frac{6 \cdot 5 \cdot 4}{3 \cdot 2 \cdot 1}$$

$$= 20$$

Hence, the number of 5-person committees composed of 2 males and 3 females is $_6C_2 \cdot {}_6C_3 = 15 \cdot 20 = 300$.

Permutations

A selection of r objects to be arranged in order from a set with a total of n objects is called a **permutation.** The primary difference between a combination and a permutation is that the order *is important* to consider in a permutation, but *not* in a combination. The notation for the number of permutations is $_nP_r$ or $P(n, r)$. The total number of ways to arrange r objects in order from a set of n objects is $_nP_r = P(n,r) = \dfrac{n!}{(n-r)!}$.

Examples

1. How many 4-letter groups can be formed using the letters in the word "importance"?

This is a permutation of 4 letters from a set of 10 letters where the order *is important*. The number of different 4-letter groups is

$$
\begin{aligned}
_{10}P_4 = P(10,4) &= \frac{10!}{(10-4)!} \\
&= \frac{10!}{6!} \\
&= \frac{10 \cdot 9 \cdot 8 \cdot 7 \cdot \cancel{6!}}{\cancel{6!}} \\
&= 5040 \text{ 4-letter groups}
\end{aligned}
$$

2. How many different first, second, and third place finishers are possible if there are 9 competitors in a race?

This is a permutation of 3 ordered finishers from a set of 9 competitors. The number of different finishers possible is

$$
\begin{aligned}
_9P_3 = P(9,3) &= \frac{9!}{(9-3)!} \\
&= \frac{9!}{6!} \\
&= \frac{9 \cdot 8 \cdot 7 \cdot \cancel{6!}}{\cancel{6!}} \\
&= 504 \text{ different finishers}
\end{aligned}
$$

3. Four offices—president, vice president, secretary, and treasurer—are to be selected from a 12-member committee. How many different ways can these offices be selected?

This is a permutation of 4 ordered offices to be selected from a set of 12 committee members. The number of different outcomes is

$$_{12}P_4 = P(12,4) = \frac{12!}{(12-4)!}$$
$$= \frac{12!}{8!}$$
$$= \frac{12 \cdot 11 \cdot 10 \cdot 9 \cdot \cancel{8!}}{\cancel{8!}}$$
$$= 11{,}880 \text{ outcomes}$$

4. How many numbers between 5000 and 9000 can be formed using the digits 0 through 9, if each digit may not be repeated once it is used?

The first place (thousands place) of the 4-digit number may be filled by only 1 of 4 numbers: 5, 6, 7, or 8. The remaining 9 numbers may be used to fill the other three place values, which is a permutation of 3 numbers from a set of 9 numbers. The total number of 4-digit numbers possible is

$$4 \cdot {}_9P_3 = 4 \cdot P(9,3) = 4 \cdot \frac{9!}{(9-3)!}$$
$$= 4 \cdot \frac{9!}{6!}$$
$$= 4 \cdot \frac{9 \cdot 8 \cdot 7 \cdot \cancel{6!}}{\cancel{6!}}$$
$$= 2016 \text{ four-digit numbers}$$

Probability

The term **probability** is used to indicate the likelihood that a particular outcome will occur. The probability is assigned a measure from 0 to 1, where 0 indicates that the outcome will never happen and 1 indicates that the outcome is sure to occur. As a formula, the probability P may be expressed as $P = \dfrac{\text{number of desired outcomes}}{\text{number of possible outcomes}}$.

If P is the probability that an event will occur, then the probability that the same event will not occur is $1 - P$.

Examples

1. A bag of marbles contains 9 red marbles, 6 blue marbles, 5 white marbles, and 4 green marbles. If a marble is drawn at random from the bag, what is the probability that the marble will be (a) red, (b), blue, (c) not white, and (d) not green?

a. The probability P that the marble is red is $P = \dfrac{9}{24} = \dfrac{3}{8}$. (Note that there are a total of 24 marbles in the bag.)

b. The probability P that the marble is blue is $P = \dfrac{6}{24} = \dfrac{1}{4}$.

c. Since the probability P that the marble is white is $P = \dfrac{5}{24}$, then the probability that it is not white is $1 - P = 1 - \dfrac{5}{24} = \dfrac{19}{24}$.

d. Since the probability P that the marble is green is $P = \dfrac{4}{24} = \dfrac{1}{6}$, then the probability that it is not green is $1 - P = 1 - \dfrac{1}{6} = \dfrac{5}{6}$.

2. In the previous example of 24 marbles in a bag, what is the probability that the first 2 marbles drawn will be red?

The probability that the first marble drawn is red is $\dfrac{9}{24} = \dfrac{3}{8}$. Since 8 of the remaining 23 marbles are red, the probability that the second marble drawn will be red is $\dfrac{8}{23}$. The probability P that the first 2 marbles drawn will be red is $P = \dfrac{3}{8} \cdot \dfrac{8}{23} = \dfrac{3}{23}$.

3. In the previous example of 24 marbles in a bag, what is the probability that if 2 marbles are drawn, 1 marble will be blue and 1 marble will be white?

The probability that the first marble drawn will be blue is $\dfrac{6}{24} = \dfrac{1}{4}$. Since 5 of the remaining 23 marbles are white, the probability that the second marble drawn is white is $\dfrac{5}{23}$. The probability that the first marble drawn will be blue and the second marble drawn will be white is $\dfrac{1}{4} \cdot \dfrac{5}{23} = \dfrac{5}{92}$.

Note that the probability is the same even if the order of selection is reversed, since the probability that the first marble drawn will be white is $\frac{5}{24}$, and the probability that the second marble drawn will be blue is $\frac{6}{23}$. The probability that the first marble drawn will be white and the second marble drawn will be blue is $\frac{5}{24} \cdot \frac{6}{23} = \frac{5}{92}$.

Hence, the probability P that 1 marble drawn will be blue and 1 marble drawn will be white is

$$P = \frac{5}{92} + \frac{5}{92}$$
$$= \frac{10}{92}$$
$$P = \frac{5}{46}$$

4. A student has 5 raffle tickets left from a total of 50 tickets sold. If there are 2 winning tickets, what is the probability that the student has exactly 1 winning ticket?

   The probability P_1 of having the first winning ticket, but not the second winning ticket, is $P_1 = \frac{\cancel{5}}{\cancel{50}} \cdot \frac{\overset{9}{\cancel{45}}}{49} = \frac{9}{98}$, and the probability P_2 of having the second winning ticket, but not the first winning ticket, is $P_2 = \frac{\overset{9}{\cancel{45}}}{\cancel{50}} \cdot \frac{\cancel{5}}{49} = \frac{9}{98}$.

   Hence, the probability P of having exactly 1 winning ticket is $P = \frac{9}{98} + \frac{9}{98} = \frac{18}{98} = \frac{9}{49}$.

5. A box contains 11 cards numbered 1 through 11. If 3 of the cards are drawn, 1 at a time, what is the probability that they will be alternatively odd, even, odd?

   Since there are 6 odd numbered cards and 5 even numbered cards, the probability that the first card drawn will be odd is $\frac{6}{11}$. The probability that the second card drawn will be even is $\frac{5}{10} = \frac{1}{2}$, and the probability that the third card drawn will be odd is $\frac{5}{9}$. The probability P that the 3 cards drawn are alternatively odd, even, odd is $P = \frac{\cancel{6}}{11} \cdot \frac{1}{\cancel{2}} \cdot \frac{5}{\cancel{9}} = \frac{5}{33}$.

6. In the previous example, what is the probability that the 3 cards drawn will be alternatively even, odd, even?

   The probability that the first card drawn will be even is $\frac{5}{11}$, that the second card drawn will be odd is $\frac{6}{10} = \frac{3}{5}$, and that the third card drawn will be even is $\frac{4}{9}$. The probability P that the 3 cards drawn will be alternatively even, odd, even is $P = \frac{\cancel{5}}{11} \cdot \frac{\cancel{3}}{\cancel{5}} \cdot \frac{4}{\cancel{9}} = \frac{4}{33}$.

7. In the previous example, what is the probability that the sum of the numbers on the first 2 cards drawn will be an odd number?

   For the sum of the numbers on the first 2 cards drawn to be odd, 1 of the numbers must be odd and the other number must be even. The probability that the first card drawn will be odd is $\frac{6}{11}$, and the probability that the second card drawn will be even is $\frac{5}{10} = \frac{1}{2}$. The probability P_1 that the first card drawn will be odd and the second card drawn will be even is $P_1 = \frac{\cancel{6}}{11} \cdot \frac{1}{\cancel{2}} = \frac{3}{11}$.

   The probability is the same if you consider the first card being drawn is even (a probability of $\frac{5}{11}$) and the second card drawn being odd (a probability of $\frac{6}{10} = \frac{3}{5}$). The probability P_2 that the first card drawn will be even and the second card drawn will be odd is $P_2 = \frac{\cancel{5}}{11} \cdot \frac{3}{\cancel{5}} = \frac{3}{11}$.

   Hence, the probability P that the sum of the numbers on the first 2 cards drawn will be odd is $P = P_1 + P_2 = \frac{3}{11} + \frac{3}{11} = \frac{6}{11}$.

Note that the probability of the sum of the numbers on the first 2 cards drawn will be even is $1 - P = 1 - \dfrac{6}{11} = \dfrac{5}{11}$.

8. If a number between 1 and 100 is drawn at random, what is the probability that the number will be divisible by 5?

For a number to be divisible by 5, its last digit must be 0 or 5. There are 9 numbers between 1 and 100 that end in 0 and 10 numbers that end in 5. There are a total of 98 numbers between 1 and 100. Hence, the probability P that a number chosen at random will be divisible by 5 is $P = \dfrac{9 + 10}{98} = \dfrac{19}{98}$.

Data Analysis Practice Questions

Now that you have reviewed data analysis topics and concepts, you can practice on your own. Questions appear in four categories by question type: quantitative comparison, multiple-choice (select one answer), multiple-choice (select one or more answers), and numeric entry (fill-in). These practice questions are grouped by question type to give you a chance to practice solving problems in the same format as the GRE. The answers and explanations that follow the questions will include strategies to help you understand how to solve the problems.

General Directions: For each question, indicate the best answer, using the directions given.

- All numbers used are real numbers.
- All figures are assumed to lie in a plane unless otherwise indicated.
- Geometric figures, such as lines, circles, triangles, and quadrilaterals, are not necessarily drawn to scale. That is, you should **not** assume that quantities, such as lengths and angle measurements, are as they appear in the figure. You should assume, however, that lines shown as straight are actually straight, points on a line are in the order shown, and more generally, all geometric objects are in the relative position shown. For questions with geometric figures, you should base your answer on geometric reasoning, not on estimating or comparing quantities by sight or by measurement.

- Coordinate systems, such as xy-planes and number lines, are drawn to scale; therefore, you can read, estimate, or compare quantities in such figures by sight or by measurement.

- Graphical data presentations, such as bar graphs, pie graphs, and line graphs, are drawn to scale; therefore, you can read, estimate, or compare data values by sight or by measurement.

Answer choices in this study guide have lettered choices A, B, C, D, E, etc., for clarity, but letters will not appear on the actual exam. On the actual computer version of the exam, you will be required to click on ovals or squares to select your answer.

HELPFUL HINT

○ oval—answer will be a single choice.

☐ square box—answer will be one or more choices.

Quantitative Comparison

Directions: For questions 1 to 7, compare Quantity A and Quantity B, using additional information centered above the two quantities if such information is given. Select one of the following four answer choices for each question:

Ⓐ   Quantity A is greater.
Ⓑ   Quantity B is greater.
Ⓒ   The two quantities are equal.
Ⓓ   The relationship cannot be determined from the information given.

	Quantity A	**Quantity B**
1.	the mean of	the median of
	8, 10, 7, 6, 5, and 10	8, 10, 7, 6, 5, and 10

	Quantity A	**Quantity B**
2.	the mode of	the median of
	18, 13, 15, 17, 19, 15, and 16	18, 13, 15, 17, 19, 15, and 16

	Quantity A	**Quantity B**
3.	$\dfrac{18!}{16!}$	$\dfrac{8!}{5!}$

Quantity A	**Quantity B**
4. the probability that a single throw of 2 dice will total 6	the probability that a single throw of 2 dice will total 8

Quantity A	**Quantity B**
5. a permutation of 7 different colors taken 4 at a time	a permutation of 7 different colors taken 3 at a time

Quantity A	**Quantity B**
6. a combination of 9 different letters taken 5 at a time	a combination of 9 different letters taken 4 at a time

Quantity A	**Quantity B**
7. the probability that a number chosen at random from the numbers 1 through 9 will be odd	the probability that a number chosen at random from the numbers 1 through 9 will be even

Multiple-Choice (Select One Answer)

Directions: Questions 8 to 14 require you to select one answer choice.

8. Evaluate: $\dfrac{15!}{3! \cdot 12!}$

Ⓐ 1

Ⓑ 7

Ⓒ 25

Ⓓ 455

Ⓔ 2730

9. How many different committees of 2 men and 1 woman can be formed from a group of 4 men and 5 women?

    Ⓐ 10
    Ⓑ 20
    Ⓒ 30
    Ⓓ 40
    Ⓔ 60

10. What is the probability of throwing a total of 7 with a single throw of 2 dice?

    Ⓐ $\dfrac{1}{12}$

    Ⓑ $\dfrac{1}{6}$

    Ⓒ $\dfrac{7}{36}$

    Ⓓ $\dfrac{1}{4}$

    Ⓔ $\dfrac{1}{2}$

11. Three marbles are drawn at random from a bag of 7 green, 5 blue, and 4 red marbles. What is the probability that all 3 marbles will be green?

    Ⓐ $\dfrac{105}{2048}$

    Ⓑ $\dfrac{1}{16}$

    Ⓒ $\dfrac{3}{16}$

    Ⓓ $\dfrac{1}{4}$

    Ⓔ $\dfrac{7}{16}$

12. How many different 3-digit numbers can be formed from the digits 3 through 8, if no digit is repeated in any number?

Ⓐ 512

Ⓑ 216

Ⓒ 125

Ⓓ 120

Ⓔ 60

13. Four cards are drawn from a deck of 52 cards. What is the probability that all 4 cards will be of the same suit?

Ⓐ $\dfrac{11}{4165}$

Ⓑ $\dfrac{1}{13}$

Ⓒ $\dfrac{44}{4165}$

Ⓓ $\dfrac{1}{4}$

Ⓔ $\dfrac{4}{13}$

14. The probability of Team X winning a baseball game against Team Y is $\dfrac{3}{5}$. What is the probability that Team X will win at least 1 game of a 3-game series?

Ⓐ $\dfrac{27}{125}$

Ⓑ $\dfrac{1}{3}$

Ⓒ $\dfrac{3}{5}$

Ⓓ $\dfrac{2}{3}$

Ⓔ $\dfrac{117}{125}$

Multiple-Choice (Select One or More Answers)

Directions: Questions 15 to 19 require you to select one or more answer choices.

15. A student has 5 test scores of 83, 79, 91, 88, and 83. Which of the following scores on the sixth test would give the student a mean greater than 85?

- A 84
- B 85
- C 86
- D 87
- E 88
- F 89

16. Which of the following is the mode of the scores 18, 11, 15, 13, 18, 19, 13, 17, and 11?

- A 11
- B 13
- C 15
- D 17
- E 18
- F 19

17. Which of the following would not change the median of the scores 8, 7, 9, 3, 4, 10, and 7?

- A 2
- B 4
- C 6
- D 8
- E 10

18. Which of the following totals for a single throw of 2 dice have a
probability of occurring that is greater than $\frac{1}{10}$?

- Ⓐ 3
- Ⓑ 4
- Ⓒ 5
- Ⓓ 8
- Ⓔ 9
- Ⓕ 10

19. Which of the following additional scores would make the median and
the mode equal for scores of 9, 5, 8, 6, 10, and 7?

- Ⓐ 5
- Ⓑ 6
- Ⓒ 7
- Ⓓ 8
- Ⓔ 9
- Ⓕ 10

Numeric Entry (Fill-in)

Directions: Questions 20 to 26 require you to solve the problem and write
your answer in a box or boxes.

- Write out your answer choice with numerals.
- Your answer may be an integer, a decimal, or a fraction, and it may
  be negative.
- If a question asks for a fraction, there will be two boxes—one for the
  numerator and one for the denominator.
- Equivalent forms of the correct answer, such as 4.5 and 4.50, are all
  correct. Fractions do not need to be reduced to lowest terms.
- Write out the exact answer unless the question asks you to round
  your answer.

20. Evaluate: $\dfrac{13!}{5! \cdot 8!}$

21. How many arrangements of the letters of the word "numeral" begin with a vowel and end with a consonant?

22. What is the probability of throwing a total of 3 or 8 in a single throw with 2 dice? Give the answer as a fraction.

23. What is the probability that a coin will turn up heads at least once in 5 tosses of the coin? Give the answer as a fraction.

24. How many different teams of 3 boys and 2 girls can be formed from a group of 7 boys and 6 girls?

25. In how many ways can a 10-member committee choose a president, a vice-president, a secretary, and a treasurer?

26. What is the probability of not obtaining a total of 10 in 3 throws with a pair of dice? Give the answer as a fraction.

Charting and Analyzing Your Practice Results

The first step in analyzing the practice exercises is to use the following chart to identify your strengths and areas that need further clarification. The answers and explanations following this chart will help you solve the practice problems, but you should look for trends in the types of errors (repeated errors). Look especially for low scores in *specific* topic areas. These are the areas that you may need to review again and again until the solutions become automatic.

Mark the problems that you missed and notice the topic and question type. Ask yourself, are you missing question(s) due to lack of knowledge of the topic/concept, or are you missing questions due to lack of knowledge of the question type?

Analysis/Tally Sheet

Topic	Total Possible	Number Correct	Number Incorrect (A) Simple Mistake	(B) Misread Problem	(C) Lack of Knowledge
Mean, median, mode, and range Questions 1, 2, 15, 16, 17, 19	6				
Factorials Questions 3, 8, 20	3				
Permutations and combinations Questions 5, 6, 9, 12, 21, 24, 25	7				
Probability Questions 4, 7, 10, 11, 13, 14, 18, 22, 23, 26	10				
Total Possible Explanations for Incorrect Answers: Columns A, B, and C					
Total Number of Answers Correct and Incorrect	26	Add the total number of correct answers here: _____	Add columns A, B, and C: _____ Total number of incorrect answers		

Answers and Explanations

Quantitative Comparison

1. **A.** The mean of 8, 10, 7, 6, 5, and 10 is

$$(8+10+7+6+5+10) \div 6$$
$$= 46 \div 6$$
$$= 7\frac{4}{6} = 7\frac{2}{3}$$

The median of 8, 10, 7, 6, 5, and 10 is the mean of the two middle numbers once they are placed in order of smallest to largest (or largest to smallest), like this: 5, 6, 7, 8, 10, and 10

$$(7+8) \div 2$$
$$= 15 \div 2$$
$$= 7\frac{1}{2}$$

Hence, Quantity A has the greater value.

2. **B.** The mode of 18, 13, 15, 17, 19, 15, and 16 is the number that occurs most frequently, which is 15.

The median of 18, 13, 15, 17, 19, 15, and 16 is the middle number once they are placed in order of smallest to largest (or largest to smallest), like this: 13, 15, 15, 16, 17, 18, and 19. The median is 16.

Hence, Quantity B has the greater value.

3. **B.**

$$\frac{18!}{16!} = \frac{18 \cdot 17 \cdot \cancel{16!}}{\cancel{16!}} = 18 \cdot 17 = 306$$

$$\frac{8!}{5!} = \frac{8 \cdot 7 \cdot 6 \cdot \cancel{5!}}{\cancel{5!}} = 8 \cdot 7 \cdot 6 = 336$$

Hence, Quantity B has the greater value.

4. **C.** Since each die contains the numbers 1 through 6, there are $6 \cdot 6 = 36$ possible outcomes when 2 dice are thrown. There are 5 possible ways of throwing a total of 6: 1 and 5, 5 and 1, 2 and 4, 4 and 2, and 3 and 3. Therefore, the probability of the 2 dice having a total of 6 is $\frac{5}{36}$.

There are 5 possible ways of throwing a total of 8: 2 and 6, 6 and 2, 3 and 5, 5 and 3, and 4 and 4. Therefore, the probability of the 2 dice having a total of 8 is $\frac{5}{36}$.

Hence, the two quantities are equal.

5. A. The number of outcomes from a permutation of 7 different colors taken 4 at a time is

$$\begin{aligned} P(7,4) &= \frac{7!}{(7-4)!} \\ &= \frac{7!}{3!} \\ &= \frac{7 \cdot 6 \cdot 5 \cdot 4 \cdot \cancel{3!}}{\cancel{3!}} \\ &= 7 \cdot 6 \cdot 5 \cdot 4 \\ P(7,4) &= 840 \end{aligned}$$

The number of outcomes from a permutation of 7 different colors taken 3 at a time is

$$\begin{aligned} P(7,3) &= \frac{7!}{(7-3)!} \\ &= \frac{7!}{4!} \\ &= \frac{7 \cdot 6 \cdot 5 \cdot \cancel{4!}}{\cancel{4!}} \\ &= 7 \cdot 6 \cdot 5 \\ P(7,3) &= 210 \end{aligned}$$

Hence, Quantity A has the greater value.

6. C. The number of outcomes from a combination of 9 different letters taken 5 at a time is $C(9,5) = \dfrac{9!}{5!(9-5)!} = \dfrac{9!}{5! \cdot 4!}$.

The number of outcomes from a combination of 9 different letters taken 4 at a time is $C(9,4) = \dfrac{9!}{4!(9-4)!} = \dfrac{9!}{4! \cdot 5!}$.

Hence, $C(9, 5) = C(9, 4)$ and the two quantities are equal.

7. **A.** Since there are 5 odd numbers in the numbers 1 through 9, the probability that a number chosen at random will be odd is $\frac{5}{9}$. Since there are 4 even numbers in the numbers 1 through 9, the probability that a number chosen at random will be even is $\frac{4}{9}$.

Hence, Quantity A has the greater value.

Multiple-Choice (Select One Answer)

8. **D.**

$$\frac{15!}{3! \cdot 12!} = \frac{15 \cdot 14 \cdot 13 \cdot \cancel{12!}}{3! \cdot \cancel{12!}}$$

$$= \frac{\overset{5}{\cancel{15}} \cdot \overset{7}{\cancel{14}} \cdot 13}{\cancel{3} \cdot \cancel{2} \cdot 1}$$

$$= 5 \cdot 7 \cdot 13$$

$$= 455$$

9. **C.** The number of committees of 2 men possible from a group of 4 men is

$$C(4,2) = \frac{4!}{2!(4-2)!}$$

$$= \frac{4 \cdot 3 \cdot \cancel{2!}}{2! \cdot \cancel{2!}}$$

$$= \frac{\overset{2}{\cancel{4}} \cdot 3}{\cancel{2} \cdot 1}$$

$$C(4,2) = 6$$

The number of committees of 1 woman possible from a group of 5 women is

$$C(5,1) = \frac{5!}{1!(5-1)!}$$

$$= \frac{5 \cdot \cancel{4!}}{1! \cdot \cancel{4!}}$$

$$C(5,1) = 5$$

Hence, the number of different committees of 2 men and 1 woman that can be formed is $C(4, 2) \cdot C(5, 1) = 6 \cdot 5 = 30$.

10. B. Since each die contains the numbers 1 through 6, there are $6 \cdot 6 = 36$ possible outcomes when 2 dice are thrown. There are 6 possible ways of throwing a total of 7: 1 and 6, 6 and 1, 2 and 5, 5 and 2, 3 and 4, and 4 and 3.

Therefore, the probability of the 2 dice having a total of 7 is $\dfrac{6}{36} = \dfrac{1}{6}$.

11. B. Since there are 7 green marbles out of a total of 16 marbles in the bag, the probability that the first marble drawn will be green is $\dfrac{7}{16}$.

The probability that the second marble drawn will be green is $\dfrac{6}{15} = \dfrac{2}{5}$, since there are 6 green marbles out of a total of 15 remaining marbles. Similarly, the probability that the third marble drawn will be green is $\dfrac{5}{14}$, since there are 5 green marbles out of a total of 14 remaining marbles.

Hence, the probability P that all 3 marbles will be green is

$$P = \frac{\overset{1}{\cancel{7}}}{16} \cdot \frac{\overset{1}{\cancel{2}}}{\underset{1}{\cancel{5}}} \cdot \frac{\overset{1}{\cancel{5}}}{\underset{2}{\cancel{14}}} = \frac{1}{16}.$$

12. D. Since the order of the digits is important, this is a permutation of 6 digits (3, 4, 5, 6, 7, and 8) taken 3 at a time.

$$P(6,3) = \frac{6!}{(6-3)!}$$
$$= \frac{6 \cdot 5 \cdot 4 \cdot \cancel{3!}}{\cancel{3!}}$$
$$= 6 \cdot 5 \cdot 4$$
$$P(6,3) = 120$$

13. C. Since the first card drawn determines the suit for the next 3 cards, there will be 12 remaining cards of that suit in the 51 cards that are left in the deck. The probability that the second card will be of the same suit as the first card is $\dfrac{12}{51} = \dfrac{4}{17}$. The probability that the third card will be of the same suit as the first 2 cards is $\frac{11}{50}$. The probability that the fourth card will be of the same suit as the first 3 cards is $\frac{10}{49}$. Therefore, the probability P that all 4 cards drawn will be of the same suit is $P = \frac{4}{17} \cdot \frac{11}{\cancel{50}^{5}} \cdot \frac{\cancel{10}}{49} = \frac{44}{4165}$.

14. **E.** Since the probability that Team X will win a game against Team Y is $\frac{3}{5}$, the probability that Team X will not win a game against Team Y is $1 - \frac{3}{5} = \frac{2}{5}$. The only way that Team X will not win at least 1 game of a 3-game series is for Team X to lose all 3 games. The probability of Team X losing game 1, game 2, and game 3 is $\frac{2}{5} \cdot \frac{2}{5} \cdot \frac{2}{5} = \frac{8}{125}$. Hence, the probability P that Team X will win at least 1 game of a 3-game series is

$$P = 1 - (\text{the probability that Team X will lose all 3 games})$$

$$= 1 - \frac{8}{125}$$

$$P = \frac{117}{125}$$

Multiple-Choice (Select One or More Answers)

15. **D, E, and F.** Let $x =$ the sixth test score.

For the average of the 6 test scores to be greater than 85,

$$(83 + 79 + 91 + 88 + 83 + x) \div 6 > 85$$

$$\frac{424 + x}{6} > 85$$

$$\frac{424 + x}{6} \cdot 6 > 85 \cdot 6$$

$$424 + x > 510$$

$$424 + x - 424 > 510 - 424$$

$$x > 86$$

Hence, the sixth test score could be 87, 88, or 89.

16. A, B, and E. Since the mode of a given set of data is the number that occurs most frequently, the mode of 18, 11, 15, 13, 18, 19, 13, 17, and 11 is 11, 13, and 18 since each of these scores occur twice in the given data.

17. A, B, and C. The median of 8, 7, 9, 3, 4, 10, and 7 is the middle number when ordered smallest to largest (or largest to smallest): 3, 4, 7, 7, 8, 9, 10. The median is 7. If there had been another score given, the median would be the average of the two middle numbers since there would be an even number in the given data.

For 2, 3, 4, 7, 7, 8, 9, 10, the median is $\dfrac{7+7}{2} = \dfrac{14}{2} = 7$.

For 3, 4, 4, 7, 7, 8, 9, 10, the median is $\dfrac{7+7}{2} = \dfrac{14}{2} = 7$.

For 3, 4, 6, 7, 7, 8, 9, 10, the median is $\dfrac{7+7}{2} = \dfrac{14}{2} = 7$.

For 3, 4, 7, 7, 8, 8, 9, 10, the median is $\dfrac{7+8}{2} = \dfrac{15}{2} = 7\dfrac{1}{2}$.

For 3, 4, 7, 7, 8, 9, 10, 10, the median is $\dfrac{7+8}{2} = \dfrac{15}{2} = 7\dfrac{1}{2}$.

Hence, additional test scores of 2, 4, and 6 will not change the median of the data.

18. C, D, and E. Since each die contains the numbers 1 through 6, there are $6 \cdot 6 = 36$ possible outcomes when 2 dice are thrown.

There are only 2 possible ways of totaling 3 (1 and 2, 2 and 1) for a probability of $\dfrac{2}{36} = \dfrac{1}{18} < \dfrac{1}{10}$.

There are 3 possible ways of totaling 4 (1 and 3, 3 and 1, 2 and 2) for a probability of $\dfrac{3}{36} = \dfrac{1}{12} < \dfrac{1}{10}$.

There are 4 possible ways of totaling 5 (1 and 4, 4 and 1, 2 and 3, 3 and 2) for a probability of $\dfrac{4}{36} = \dfrac{1}{9} > \dfrac{1}{10}$.

There are 5 possible ways of totaling 8 (2 and 6, 6 and 2, 3 and 5, 5 and 3, 4 and 4) for a probability of $\frac{5}{36} > \frac{1}{10}$.

There are 4 possible ways of totaling 9 (3 and 6, 6 and 3, 4 and 5, 5 and 4) for a probability of $\frac{4}{36} = \frac{1}{9} > \frac{1}{10}$.

There are 3 possible ways of totaling 10 (4 and 6, 6 and 4, 5 and 5) for a probability of $\frac{3}{36} = \frac{1}{12} < \frac{1}{10}$.

19. **C and D.** Put the scores in order from smallest to largest (or largest to smallest) to test each answer choice.

Score of $5 \to 5, 5, 6, 7, 8, 9, 10$. The median = 7 and the mode = 5.

Score of $6 \to 5, 6, 6, 7, 8, 9, 10$. The median = 7 and the mode = 6.

Score of $\underline{7} \to 5, 6, 7, 7, 8, 9, 10$. The median = $\underline{7}$ and the mode = $\underline{7}$.

Score of $\underline{8} \to 5, 6, 7, 8, 8, 9, 10$. The median = $\underline{8}$ and the mode = $\underline{8}$.

Score of $9 \to 5, 6, 7, 8, 9, 9, 10$. The median = 8 and the mode = 9.

Score of $10 \to 5, 6, 7, 8, 9, 10, 10$. The median = 8 and the mode = 10.

Numeric Entry (Fill-in)

20. **1287**

$$\frac{13!}{5! \cdot 8!} = \frac{13 \cdot 12 \cdot 11 \cdot 10 \cdot 9 \cdot \cancel{8!}}{5! \cdot \cancel{8!}}$$

$$= \frac{13 \cdot \cancel{12} \cdot 11 \cdot \cancel{10} \cdot 9}{\cancel{5} \cdot \cancel{4} \cdot \cancel{3} \cdot \cancel{2} \cdot 1}$$

$$= 13 \cdot 11 \cdot 9$$

$$= 1287$$

21. 1440

Since there are 3 vowels and 4 consonants in the word "numeral," the first letter of any arrangement has 3 possible choices and the last letter has 4 possible choices. Since the order is important for the letters in the five middle positions of any arrangement, this is a permutation of 5 letters taken 5 at a time, or $P(5, 5)$. Therefore, the total number of arrangements under the given conditions is

$$3 \cdot P(5,5) \cdot 4 = 3 \cdot \frac{5!}{(5-5)!} \cdot 4$$
$$= 3 \cdot \frac{5!}{0!} \cdot 4$$
$$= 3 \cdot (5 \cdot 4 \cdot 3 \cdot 2 \cdot 1) \cdot 4$$
$$= 1440$$

22. $\dfrac{7}{36}$

Since each die contains the numbers 1 through 6, there are $6 \cdot 6 = 36$ possible outcomes when 2 dice are thrown. There are only 2 possible ways of totaling 3 (1 and 2, 2 and 1) for a probability of $\dfrac{2}{36}$. There are 5 possible ways of totaling 8 (2 and 6, 6 and 2, 3 and 5, 5 and 3, 4 and 4) for a probability of $\dfrac{5}{36}$.

Hence, the probability P of throwing a total of 3 or 8 in a single throw with 2 dice is $P = \dfrac{2}{36} + \dfrac{5}{36} = \dfrac{7}{36}$.

23. $\dfrac{31}{32}$

Since a coin toss has only 2 possibilities, heads or tails, the probability is the same for either outcome: $\dfrac{1}{2}$. The only way that 5 tosses of a coin would not turn up heads at least once is for all 5 tosses to be tails. The probability that all 5 tosses are tails is $\dfrac{1}{2} \cdot \dfrac{1}{2} \cdot \dfrac{1}{2} \cdot \dfrac{1}{2} \cdot \dfrac{1}{2} = \dfrac{1}{32}$.

Hence, the probability P that at least 1 of the 5 tosses of a coin will turn up heads is

$$P = 1 - (\text{the probability of all tails})$$
$$= 1 - \frac{1}{32}$$
$$P = \frac{31}{32}$$

24. 525

The number of teams of 3 boys possible from a group of 7 boys is

$$C(7,3) = \frac{7!}{3!(7-3)!}$$
$$= \frac{7 \cdot 6 \cdot 5 \cdot \cancel{4!}}{3! \cdot \cancel{4!}}$$
$$= \frac{7 \cdot \cancel{6} \cdot 5}{\cancel{3} \cdot \cancel{2} \cdot 1}$$
$$= 7 \cdot 5$$
$$C(7,3) = 35$$

The number of teams of 2 girls possible from a group of 6 girls is

$$C(6,2) = \frac{6!}{2!(6-2)!}$$
$$= \frac{6 \cdot 5 \cdot \cancel{4!}}{2! \cdot \cancel{4!}}$$
$$= \frac{\overset{3}{\cancel{6}} \cdot 5}{\cancel{2} \cdot 1}$$
$$= 3 \cdot 5$$
$$C(6,2) = 15$$

Hence, the number of different teams of 3 boys and 2 girls is $C(7, 3) \cdot C(6, 2) = 35 \cdot 15 = 525$.

25. **5040**

Since the indicated offices to be filled make the order important, this is a permutation of 10 people taken 4 at a time. The total number of outcomes is

$$P(10,4) = \frac{10!}{(10-4)!}$$

$$= \frac{10 \cdot 9 \cdot 8 \cdot 7 \cdot \cancel{6!}}{\cancel{6!}}$$

$$= 10 \cdot 9 \cdot 8 \cdot 7$$

$$P(10,4) = 5040$$

26. $\dfrac{1331}{1728}$

Since each die contains the numbers 1 through 6, there are $6 \cdot 6 = 36$ possible outcomes when 2 dice are thrown. There are 3 possible ways of totaling 10 (4 and 6, 6 and 4, 5 and 5) for a probability of $\dfrac{3}{36} = \dfrac{1}{12}$.

The probability that a total other than 10 occurs is $1 - \dfrac{1}{12} = \dfrac{11}{12}$. The only way that 3 throws with a pair of dice would not have at least one 10 is for all 3 throws to total some number other than 10. The probability P of this occurring is $P = \dfrac{11}{12} \cdot \dfrac{11}{12} \cdot \dfrac{11}{12} = \dfrac{1331}{1728}$.

Chapter 7

Data Interpretation

Data interpretation math questions are based on data provided in graphs, charts, and tables. To answer questions, you must accurately read and draw conclusions about visual graphic illustrations before performing calculations. A solid understanding of arithmetic and the ability to make sound decisions by extrapolating, interpreting, and calculating numerical data will help you solve these types of problems. Multiple questions may refer to the same graphic illustration, and some questions have multiple graphs that require you to recognize how each graph relates to one another.

To start your review of data interpretation questions, take the diagnostic test that follows and then study each of the major data interpretation topics covered on the following checklist. Chart your progress as you review each topic. Use the list to check off topics as you review them. As you evaluate your understanding of each topic area, pinpoint areas that require further study by placing a check mark next to the topic. Continue to measure your progress, and refer to this list as often as necessary.

To reinforce what you have learned, work the practice questions at the end of this chapter (answer explanations are provided). The practice questions are arranged by question type to help you practice solving data interpretation problems that are specific to the GRE exam.

Data Interpretation Topics You Should Know

Topic	Study Pages	Worked Examples	Further Study Required
Circle or pie graphs	pp. 364–366		
Bar graphs	pp. 366–367		
Line graphs	pp. 367–368		
Charts and tables	pp. 368–369		
Venn diagrams	pp. 369–371		

The following diagnostic test is designed to help you identify specific data interpretation topics that require further concentration. After you take the diagnostic test, analyze your test results and develop a step-by-step action plan to pinpoint topics to study.

Data Interpretation Diagnostic Test

25 Questions

Directions: Solve each problem in this section by using the information given and your own mathematical calculations.

Questions 1–5 refer to the following graph.

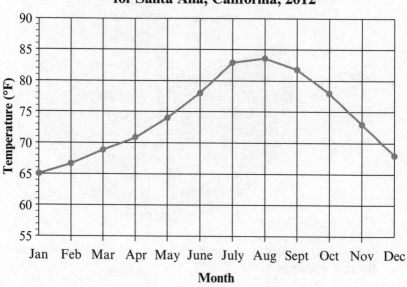

Average Monthly High Temperature (°F) for Santa Ana, California, 2012

1. Which month had the greatest increase in average high temperature compared to the previous month?

2. What is the difference, in degrees, between the highest average high temperature and the lowest average high temperature?

3. What is the ratio of the number of months with decreasing average high temperatures to the number of months with increasing average high temperatures in 2012?

4. Which two months had the same average high temperatures in 2012?

5. What was the approximate percent decrease in the average high temperature from August to December? Round the answer to the nearest percent.

Questions 6–10 refer to the following graph.

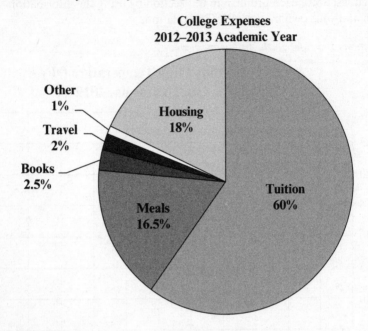

**College Expenses
2012–2013 Academic Year**

6. If the total expenses for the academic year were $30,000, what was the cost of tuition?

7. If the total expenses for the academic year were $30,000, how much more was spent on housing than on meals?

8. What is the ratio of the amount spent on housing to the amount spent on tuition?

9. If the total expenses for the academic year were $30,000, how much was spent on books?

10. If the total expenses for the academic year were $30,000, how much more was spent on tuition than on all other additional expenses?

Questions 11–15 refer to the following table.

Male and Female Life Expectancy (in Years)

Country	Male	Female
Austria	76.9	82.6
Canada	78.3	82.9
Finland	76.1	82.4
Greece	77.1	81.9
Israel	78.5	82.8
New Zealand	78.2	82.2
Norway	77.8	82.5
Sweden	78.7	83.0
United States	75.5	83.3

11. Which country has the greatest disparity between female and male life expectancies?

12. Which two countries have the same disparity between female and male life expectancies?

13. What is the difference between the highest female life expectancy and the lowest male life expectancy among the countries in the table?

14. What is the approximate percent decrease from the female life expectancy to the male life expectancy in New Zealand? Round your answer to the nearest whole percent.

15. What is the difference between the highest male life expectancy and the lowest female life expectancy among the countries in the table?

Questions 16–20 refer to the following graph.

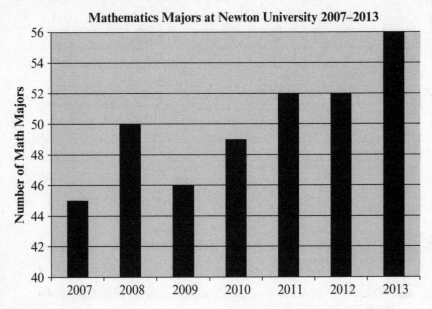

Mathematics Majors at Newton University 2007–2013

16. What is the only year in which there was a decrease in the number of mathematics majors compared to the previous year?

17. What is the approximate percent increase from the year with the lowest number of math majors to the year with the highest number of math majors? Round your answer to the nearest percent.

18. What is the average number of math majors at Newton University for the time period of the graph?

19. In what year did the greatest increase in the number of math majors occur?

20. If the number of math majors at Newton University is expected to increase by 12 percent in 2014, how many additional math majors will that be? Round your answer to the nearest whole number.

Questions 21–25 refer to the following diagram.

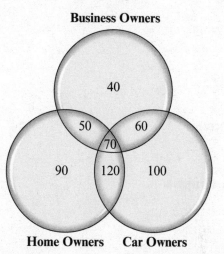

Business Owners

40

50   60

70

90   120   100

Home Owners   **Car Owners**

21. If the data above was collected from 600 people, how many of the people did not own a home, car, or business?

22. How many people surveyed own a home and a car, but do not own a business?

23. What percent of the 600 people surveyed are home owners?

24. How many of the people surveyed own exactly two of the indicated categories?

25. How many of the people surveyed own at least two of the indicated categories?

Scoring the Diagnostic Test

The following section will assist you in scoring and analyzing your diagnostic test results. Use the answer key to score your results on the Analysis Sheet that follows. Read through the answer explanations on pages 360–363 to clarify the solutions to the problems.

Answer Key

Line Graphs

1. July
2. 19°
3. $\frac{4}{7}$
4. June and October
5. 19%

Circle or Pie Graphs

6. $18,000
7. $450
8. $\frac{3}{10}$
9. $750
10. $6,000

Charts and Tables

11. United States
12. Israel and Sweden
13. 7.8 years
14. 5%
15. 3.2 years

Bar Graphs

16. 2009
17. 24%
18. 50
19. 2008
20. 7

Venn Diagrams

21. 70

22. 120

23. 55%

24. 230

25. 300

Charting and Analyzing Your Diagnostic Test Results

Record your diagnostic test results in the following chart and use these results as a guide for an effective data interpretation review. Mark the problems that you missed, paying particular attention to those that were missed because of a "lack of knowledge." These are the areas you will want to focus on as you study data interpretation topics.

Data Interpretation Diagnostic Test Analysis Sheet

Topic	Total Possible	Number Correct	Number Incorrect		
			(A) Simple Mistake	(B) Misread Problem	(C) Lack of Knowledge
Line graphs	5				
Circle or pie graphs	5				
Charts and tables	5				
Bar graphs	5				
Venn diagrams	5				
Total Possible Explanations for Incorrect Answers: Columns A, B, and C					
Total Number of Answers Correct and Incorrect	25	Add the total number of correct answers here: _____	Add columns A, B, and C: _____ Total number of incorrect answers		

Data Interpretation Diagnostic Test Answers and Explanations

Line Graphs

1. July

July's average high temperature of 83° represents a 5° increase over June's average high temperature of 78°.

2. 19°

The highest average high temperature is 84° in August, and the lowest average high temperature is 65° in January. The difference between the two is 84° − 65° = 19°.

3. $\dfrac{4}{7}$

There are 4 months with decreasing average high temperature (September, October, November, and December) compared to 7 months with increasing average high temperatures (February, March, April, May, June, July, and August) for a ratio of $\dfrac{4}{7}$.

Note: Data is not provided for December 2011, so you cannot determine if the January 2012 average monthly high temperature of 65° was an increase or a decrease from the prior month.

4. June and October

June and October each had the same average high temperature in 2012 of 78°.

5. 19%

$$\text{percent decrease} = \frac{\text{decrease amount}}{\text{original amount}}$$

The average high temperature dropped from 84° in August to 68° in December for a decrease of 16°.

$$\text{percent decrease} = \frac{16}{84} \approx 0.190 \approx 19\%$$

Circle or Pie Graphs

6. $18,000

Since tuition accounted for 60% of college expenses, 60% of $30,000 = (0.6)(30,000) = $18,000.

7. $450

Housing accounted for 18% of college expenses: 18% of $30,000 = (0.18)(30,000) = $5,400.

Meals accounted for 16.5% of college expenses: 16.5% of $30,000 = (0.165)(30,000) = $4,950.

The difference is $5,400 – $4,950 = $450.

8. $\dfrac{3}{10}$

Since housing accounted for 18% of college expenses and tuition accounted for 60% of college expenses, the ratio of the amount spent on housing to the amount spent on tuition is $\dfrac{18}{60} = \dfrac{3}{10}$.

9. $750

Books accounted for 2.5% of college expenses: 2.5% of $30,000 = (0.025)(30,000) = $750.

10. $6,000

Tuition accounted for 60% of college expenses: 60% of $30,000 = (0.6)(30,000) = $18,000.

The other expenses accounted for 40% of college expenses: 40% of $30,000 = (0.4)(30,000) = $12,000.

The difference is $18,000 – $12,000 = $6,000.

Charts and Tables

11. United States

The difference between the female life expectancy and the male life expectancy in the United States is 83.3 – 75.5 = 7.8 years, which exceeds all other disparities in the table.

12. Israel and Sweden

The difference between the female and male life expectancy in Israel is 82.8 – 78.5 = 4.3 years. The difference between the female and male life expectancy in Sweden is 83.0 – 78.7 = 4.3 years.

13. 7.8 years

The highest female life expectancy is 83.3 years in the United States, while the lowest male life expectancy is 75.5 years, also in the United States. The difference is 83.3 – 75.5 = 7.8 years.

14. **5%**

$$\text{percent decrease} = \frac{\text{decrease amount}}{\text{original amount}}$$

The female life expectancy in New Zealand is 82.2 years, while the male life expectancy is 78.2 years, or a decrease of 4.0 years.

$$\text{percent decrease} = \frac{4.0}{82.2} \approx 0.048 \approx 5\%$$

15. **3.2 years**

The highest male life expectancy is 78.7 years in Sweden, while the lowest female life expectancy is 81.9 years in Greece. The difference is $81.9 - 78.9 = 3.2$ years.

Bar Graphs

16. **2009**

The number of mathematics majors dropped from 50 in 2008 to 46 in 2009.

17. **24%**

$$\text{percent increase} = \frac{\text{increase amount}}{\text{original amount}}$$

The lowest number of mathematics majors was 45 in 2007, while the highest number of mathematics majors was 56 in 2013, or an increase of 11 mathematics majors.

$$\text{percent increase} = \frac{11}{45} \approx 0.244 \approx 24\%$$

18. **50**

Since the graph covers the number of math majors over a 7-year period, the average is

$$\text{(sum of the number of math majors)} \div 7$$
$$= (45 + 50 + 46 + 49 + 52 + 52 + 56) \div 7$$
$$= 350 \div 7$$
$$= 50$$

19. **2008**

The number of mathematics majors increased from 45 in 2007 to 50 in 2008—an increase of 5 mathematics majors, which exceeds all other increases on the graph.

20. **7**

Since there were 56 mathematics majors at Newton University in 2013, an increase of 12% in 2014 is 12% of $56 = (0.12)(56) = 6.72 \approx 7$.

Venn Diagrams

21. **70**

The sum of all the people given in the diagram is $90 + 120 + 70 + 50 + 100 + 60 + 40 = 530$.

If the data was collected from 600 people, then the number who did not own a home, car, or business is $600 - 530 = 70$.

22. **120**

The number of people surveyed who own a home and a car, but do not own a business, would be found where the home and car circles overlap, which is 120; this excludes the region where all three circles overlap, which is 70.

23. **55%**

The total number of people surveyed who own a home is $90 + 120 + 70 + 50 = 330$.

The percent of the 600 people surveyed who own a home is

$$\frac{330}{600} = 0.55 = 55\%.$$

24. **230**

The number of people surveyed who own exactly two of the indicated categories would be found where each pair of circles overlap, excluding the region where all three circles overlap, or $120 + 60 + 50 = 230$.

25. **300**

The number of people surveyed who own at least two of the indicated categories would be found where each pair of circles overlap, including the region where all three circles overlap, or $120 + 60 + 50 + 70 = 300$.

Data Interpretation Review

Data interpretation questions draw upon your knowledge of descriptive arithmetic, analytical reasoning, and graph interpretation. In qualitative research and analysis, visual illustrations of charts, graphs, and tables are commonly used to evaluate and report the value of the collected and measured data. Information that is being measured are called **variables,** and in most graphs variables are plotted on vertical and horizontal axes. These visual graphs help to provide a clear picture about the data compiled in order to show patterns and trends and draw conclusions.

Your familiarity with a wide range of the following graphic illustrations will help you with these questions:

- *Circle or pie graphs*—Show comparisons of data as percentages of a whole.
- *Bar graphs*—Show comparisons among items in a data set.
- *Line graphs*—Show change in data over time.
- *Charts and tables*—Show data in columns and rows similar to a spreadsheet.
- *Venn diagrams*—Show where individual data points fall in relation to a pair of parameters.

Circle or Pie Graphs

A **circle graph,** also referred to as a **pie graph** or **pie chart,** is used to show relative proportions (fractions) of a whole circle. Circle graphs are a good visual representation of percentages. For example, a circle graph shows the relationship between a whole circle (100%) and portions (slices) of a circle called **sectors.** The size of each sector compared to the whole circle represents the ratio of the individual categories to the whole circle.

As you interpret a circle graph, always read the following:

- *Title*—The title provides an overview of the graph.
- *Sector categories*—Each sector (slice) category provides information about the whole picture.
- *Sector values*—The visual illustration of each sector quickly distinguishes variations in data (largest and smallest numerical values).

Examples

Questions 1–3 refer to the following circle graph.

The graph shows the grade distribution of 350 students enrolled in freshman mathematics at a state university. A "W" indicates the students who withdrew from the class and therefore did not receive a letter grade.

**Grade Distribution of
350 Students Enrolled in
Freshman Mathematics**

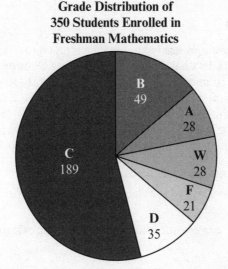

1. What percentage of the students enrolled in freshman mathematics received a grade of C?

   Per the graph, 189 of the 350 students received a grade of C:
   $\frac{189}{350} = 0.54 = 54\%$.

2. What is the ratio of students who received a grade of B to the total number of students who completed the course?

   Since 28 students withdrew from the class and did not receive a letter grade, $350 - 28 = 322$ students completed the course, of which 49 earned a grade of B. The ratio is $\frac{49}{322} = \frac{7}{46}$.

3. If a grade of C or better is required to take the next level mathematics course, what percent of the students qualify?

The number of students who received a grade of C or better is $28 + 49 + 189 = 266$.

Since $\dfrac{266}{350} = 0.76 = 76\%$, 76% of the students qualify to take the next level mathematics course.

Bar Graphs

A **bar graph** is commonly used as a visual illustration to quickly compare data or frequencies. In a bar graph, numerical data is converted into separate rectangular bars (columns) that are used to represent the relationship between the different data categories. The bars can be either vertical or horizontal and can appear as single bars, a group of bars, or stacked bars. The bars should be labeled to indicate the differences between the various categories. As you interpret a bar graph, always read the following:

- *Title*—The title provides an overview of the graph.
- *Axes labels*—The two axes labels provide information about the data to be compared.
- *Bars*—The bars provide information about the categories to be compared.

Examples

Questions 1–2 refer to the following bar graph.

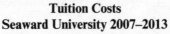

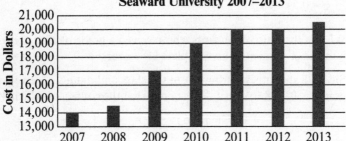

1. In which year did the largest increase in tuition occur?

The largest tuition increase occurred in 2009, which was $17,000 – $14,500 = $2,500.

2. In which year was there no change in tuition compared to the previous year?

The tuition for both 2011 and 2012 was $20,000. Therefore, there was not a change in tuition in 2012.

Line Graphs

A **line graph** represents data information as points on a two-dimensional coordinate system. This type of graph provides a good visual picture of changes or trends in data values and can be valuable in hypothesizing predictions over time.

For example, the points that are connected to show a numerical trend may show the slope of a line with *increasing* or *decreasing* data. Dramatic changes are indicated by the steepness of the segments connecting one data item to the next data item. The larger the absolute value of the slope, the greater the change will be from one item to another, either up or down.

As you interpret a line graph, always read the following:

- *Title*—The title provides an overview of the graph.
- *Axes labels*—The two axes labels provide information about the data that is plotted along the axes.
- *Lines*—Look for visual dramatic changes in the data values.

Examples

Questions 1–2 refer to the following line graph.

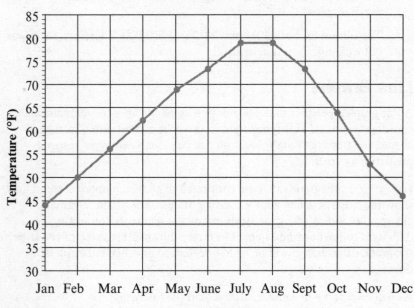

**Average Monthly High Temperature (°F)
for Portland, Oregon, 2012**

1. For which two months did the average high temperature remain unchanged?

   From the graph, there is no change in the average high temperature in July and August. Note that the graph is horizontal between July and August.

2. Between what months is the average high temperature always increasing?

   From the graph, the average high temperature is increasing from January to July. Note that the graph is moving up and to the right from January to July.

Charts and Tables

A **chart** or **table** is often used to organize lists of data in a more readable format. Charts often help to effectively view multiple values of data simultaneously, making it easier to compare and compute averages or ranges. Headings are used to identify the relationship between the given information.

Examples

Questions 1–2 refer to the following table.

Male and Female Life Expectancy Worldwide (in Years)

Country	Male	Female
Australia	78.9	83.6
Canada	78.3	82.9
Germany	76.5	82.1
Japan	79.0	86.1
United States	75.5	83.3
United Kingdom	77.2	81.6

1. Which of the countries listed has the greatest difference between life expectancy for females compared to males?

   The greatest difference between life expectancy between females and males occurs in the United States, which is 83.3 – 75.5 = 7.8 years.

   The next closest is Japan, which is 86.1 – 79.0 = 7.1 years.

2. What is the difference between the country with the highest female life expectancy and the country with the lowest female life expectancy?

   Japan has the highest female life expectancy of 86.1 years, while the United Kingdom has the lowest of 81.6 years. The difference is 86.1 – 81.6 = 4.5 years.

Venn Diagrams

A **Venn diagram** is a useful method to visually represent two or more sets and to illustrate whether or not the sets have any elements in common. Sets are generally represented as circles or ovals, but other geometric figures can be used. Sets that have elements in common will overlap, while sets that have no elements in common are shown disjointed from each other. When a number is positioned in an area of overlapping regions, that is how many objects, or the percent of objects, share the characteristics of the overlapping regions.

Examples

Questions 1–3 refer to the following Venn diagram.

**Tech University Mathematics Majors
Enrolled in Calculus, Physics, and Statistics**

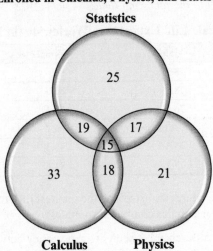

Statistics

Calculus   Physics

1. How many mathematics majors are enrolled in calculus and statistics, but not in physics?

   The number of students enrolled in calculus and statistics, but not physics, is found in the overlapping area of calculus and statistics, but outside the physics circle. This would yield an answer of 19 students.

2. What percent of mathematics majors are enrolled in calculus? Give the answer to the nearest whole percent.

   The number of mathematics majors enrolled in calculus is
   $33 + 18 + 15 + 19 = 85$.

   The total number of mathematics majors is
   $33 + 18 + 15 + 19 + 21 + 17 + 25 = 148$.

   The percentage of mathematics majors that are enrolled in calculus is
   $\dfrac{85}{148} \approx 0.574 \approx 57.4\% \approx 57\%$ to the nearest whole percent.

3. How many mathematics majors are enrolled in at least two of the given courses?

The total number of mathematics majors enrolled in at least two of the given courses is found where any of the circles overlap: $19 + 18 + 17 + 15 = 69$.

Data Interpretation Practice Questions

Now that you have reviewed data interpretation topics and concepts, you can practice on your own. Questions appear in four categories by question type: quantitative comparison, multiple-choice (select one answer), multiple-choice (select one or more answers), and numeric entry (fill-in). These practice questions are grouped by question type to give you a chance to practice solving problems in the same format as the GRE. The answers and explanations that follow the questions will include strategies to help you understand how to solve the problems.

General Directions: For each question, indicate the best answer, using the directions given.

- All numbers used are real numbers.

- All figures are assumed to lie in a plane unless otherwise indicated.

- Geometric figures, such as lines, circles, triangles, and quadrilaterals, are not necessarily drawn to scale. That is, you should **not** assume that quantities, such as lengths and angle measurements, are as they appear in the figure. You should assume, however, that lines shown as straight are actually straight, points on a line are in the order shown, and more generally, all geometric objects are in the relative position shown. For questions with geometric figures, you should base your answer on geometric reasoning, not on estimating or comparing quantities by sight or by measurement.

- Coordinate systems, such as xy-planes and number lines, are drawn to scale; therefore, you can read, estimate, or compare quantities in such figures by sight or by measurement.

- Graphical data presentations, such as bar graphs, circle graphs, and line graphs, are drawn to scale; therefore, you can read, estimate, or compare data values by sight or by measurement.

Answer choices in this study guide have lettered choices A, B, C, D, E, etc., for clarity, but letters will not appear on the actual exam. On the actual computer version of the exam, you will be required to click on ovals or squares to select your answer.

HELPFUL HINT

○ oval—answer will be a single choice.

☐ square box—answer will be one or more choices.

Quantitative Comparison

Directions: For questions 1 to 6, compare Quantity A and Quantity B, using additional information centered above the two quantities if such information is given. Select one of the following four answer choices for each question:

Ⓐ   Quantity A is greater.

Ⓑ   Quantity B is greater.

Ⓒ   The two quantities are equal.

Ⓓ   The relationship cannot be determined from the information given.

Questions 1–3 refer to the following circle graph.

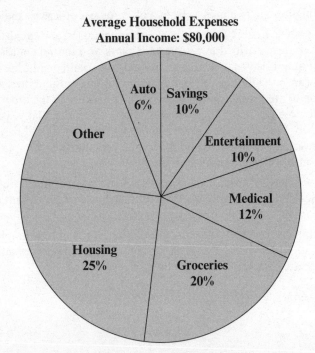

Average Household Expenses
Annual Income: $80,000

Auto 6%

Savings 10%

Other

Entertainment 10%

Medical 12%

Housing 25%

Groceries 20%

	Quantity A	Quantity B
1.	entertainment and auto expenses	other expenses

	Quantity A	Quantity B
2.	average monthly amount spent on housing	$1,600

	Quantity A	Quantity B
3.	ratio of the percent spent on medical expenses to the percent spent on housing	ratio of the percent spent on entertainment to the percent spent on groceries

Questions 4–6 refer to the following table.

Male and Female Life Expectancy—European Countries (in Years)

Country	Male	Female
Austria	76.9	82.6
France	77.1	84.1
Germany	76.5	82.1
Italy	77.5	83.5
Spain	77.7	84.2
Switzerland	79.0	84.2

	Quantity A	Quantity B
4.	the difference between female life expectancy in Austria and France	the difference between male life expectancy in Germany and Spain

	Quantity A	Quantity B
5.	the percent of male life expectancy to female life expectancy in Italy	the percent of male life expectancy to female life expectancy in Germany

	Quantity A	**Quantity B**
6.	the difference between the highest and lowest female life expectancy	the difference between the highest and lowest male life expectancy

Multiple-Choice (Select One Answer)

Directions: Questions 7 to 13 require you to select one answer choice.

Questions 7–10 refer to the following line graph.

Average Monthly Low Temperature (°F) for Portland, Oregon, 2012

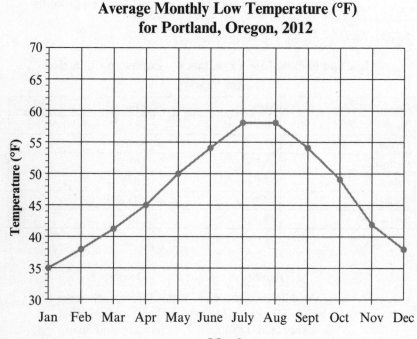

7. Which month had the greatest difference in average low temperature from the previous month?

    Ⓐ   May

    Ⓑ   September

    Ⓒ   July

    Ⓓ   November

    Ⓔ   December

8. What was the approximate percent increase in the average low temperature from April to May?

    Ⓐ   5

    Ⓑ   10

    Ⓒ   11

    Ⓓ   12

    Ⓔ   13

9. For what month was there no change in the average low temperature compared to the previous month?

    Ⓐ   February

    Ⓑ   March

    Ⓒ   July

    Ⓓ   August

    Ⓔ   December

10. What is the ratio of the number of months with increasing average low temperatures to the number of months with decreasing average low temperatures?

    Ⓐ $\dfrac{6}{5}$

    Ⓑ $\dfrac{7}{5}$

    Ⓒ $\dfrac{3}{2}$

    Ⓓ $\dfrac{7}{4}$

    Ⓔ $\dfrac{2}{1}$

Questions 11–13 refer to the following circle graph.

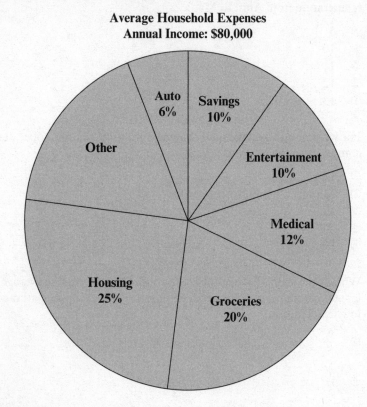

**Average Household Expenses
Annual Income: $80,000**

11. What is the annual amount spent in dollars on the *other* category?

   Ⓐ 10,400
   Ⓑ 12,000
   Ⓒ 13,600
   Ⓓ 16,000
   Ⓔ 17,000

12. How much more is spent in dollars annually on *medical* than on *entertainment*?

   Ⓐ 1,600
   Ⓑ 2,000
   Ⓒ 3,600
   Ⓓ 4,800
   Ⓔ 9,600

13. If an additional $1,600 was added to *savings,* what percent of the annual income would then be going toward *savings*?

    Ⓐ   2

    Ⓑ   6

    Ⓒ   10

    Ⓓ   12

    Ⓔ   16

Multiple-Choice (Select One or More Answers)

Directions: Questions 14 to 18 require you to select one or more answer choices.

Questions 14–18 refer to the following bar graph.

Mario's Used Car Sales January–June 2013

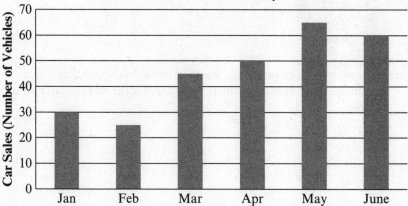

14. For which months did used car sales increase when compared to the previous month?

    Ⓐ   January

    Ⓑ   February

    Ⓒ   March

    Ⓓ   April

    Ⓔ   May

15. For which months were used car sales larger than the average sales for the six-month period?

- Ⓐ January
- Ⓑ February
- Ⓒ March
- Ⓓ April
- Ⓔ May
- Ⓕ June

16. During which months did used car sales increase more than 25% compared to the previous month?

- Ⓐ January
- Ⓑ February
- Ⓒ March
- Ⓓ April
- Ⓔ May
- Ⓕ June

17. For the month of July 2013, which of the following used car sales would yield an average of 50 or more cars for the seven-month time period?

- Ⓐ 90
- Ⓑ 80
- Ⓒ 70
- Ⓓ 60
- Ⓔ 50
- Ⓕ 40

18. Historically, if July's used car sales are at least 20% higher than June's used car sales for the same year, which of the following could be expected for the July 2013 sales?

- Ⓐ 65
- Ⓑ 70
- Ⓒ 75
- Ⓓ 80
- Ⓔ 85
- Ⓕ 90

Numeric Entry (Fill-in)

Directions: Questions 19 to 24 require you to solve the problem and write your answer in a box or boxes.

- Write out your answer choice with numerals.
- Your answer may be an integer, a decimal, or a fraction, and it may be negative.
- If a question asks for a fraction, there will be two boxes—one for the numerator and one for the denominator.
- Equivalent forms of the correct answer, such as 4.5 and 4.50, are all correct. Fractions do not need to be reduced to lowest terms.
- Write out the exact answer unless the question asks you to round your answer.

Questions 19–24 refer to the following diagram.

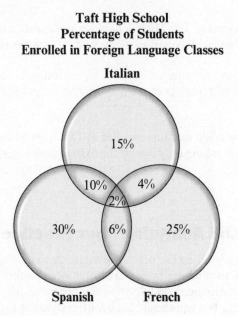

Taft High School
Percentage of Students
Enrolled in Foreign Language Classes

19. What percent of all students at Taft High School are NOT enrolled in one of the foreign language classes?

20. If there are 1,200 students enrolled at Taft High School, how many students are taking two or more of the foreign languages?

21. If there are 1,200 students enrolled at Taft High School, how many students are taking Spanish but are not taking Italian?

22. If there are 1,200 students enrolled at Taft High School, how many students are taking exactly two foreign languages?

23. If 110 students at Taft High School are not enrolled in any of the three foreign languages, how many students are enrolled at Taft High School?

24. If there are 1,500 students enrolled at Taft High School, how many students are taking only one of the foreign languages?

Charting and Analyzing Your Practice Results

The first step in analyzing the practice exercises is to use the following chart to identify your strengths and areas that need further clarification. The answers and explanations following this chart will help you solve the practice problems, but you should look for trends in the types of errors (repeated errors). Look especially for low scores in *specific* topic areas. These are the areas that you may need to review again and again until the solutions become automatic.

Mark the problems that you missed and notice the topic and question type. Ask yourself, are you missing question(s) due to lack of knowledge of the topic/concept, or are you missing questions due to lack of knowledge of the question type?

Analysis/Tally Sheet

Topic	Total Possible	Number Correct	Number Incorrect		
			(A) Simple Mistake	(B) Misread Problem	(C) Lack of Knowledge
Circle or pie graphs Questions 1, 2, 3, 11, 12, 13	6				
Bar graphs Questions 14, 15, 16, 17, 18	5				
Line graphs Questions 7, 8, 9, 10	4				
Tables and charts Questions 4, 5, 6	3				
Venn diagrams Questions 19, 20, 21, 22, 23, 24	6				
Total Possible Explanations for Incorrect Answers: Columns A, B, and C					
Total Number of Answers Correct and Incorrect	24	Add the total number of correct answers here: _____	Add columns A, B, and C: _____ Total number of incorrect answers		

Answers and Explanations

Quantitative Comparison

1. B. The percentage spent on *entertainment* and *auto* is $10 + 6 = 16\%$. The total percentage for all of the indicated categories except *other* is $25 + 20 + 12 + 10 + 10 + 6 = 83\%$. Therefore, the percentage for the *other* category is $100 - 83 = 17\%$.

Hence, Quantity B has the greater value.

2. A. The average annual amount spent on *housing* is 25% of $\$80,000 = (0.25)(80,000) = \$20,000$.

The average monthly amount spent on *housing* is $\$20,000 \div 12 = \$1,666.67$.

Hence, Quantity A has the greater value.

3. B. The ratio of the percent spent on *medical* compared to the percent spent on *housing* is $\dfrac{12\%}{25\%} = \dfrac{12}{25} = 0.48$.

The ratio of the percent spent on *entertainment* to the percent spent on *groceries* is $\dfrac{10\%}{20\%} = \dfrac{10}{20} = \dfrac{1}{2} = 0.5$.

Hence, Quantity B has the greater value.

4. A. The difference between female life expectancy in Austria and France is $84.1 - 82.6 = 1.5$ years.

The difference between male life expectancy in Germany and Spain is $77.7 - 76.5 = 1.2$ years.

Hence, Quantity A has the greater value.

5. B. The percent of male life expectancy to female life expectancy in Italy is $\dfrac{77.5}{83.5} \approx 0.9281 \approx 92.8\%$.

The percent of male life expectancy to female life expectancy in Germany is $\dfrac{76.5}{82.1} \approx 0.9317 \approx 93.2\%$.

Hence, Quantity B has the greater value.

6. B. The difference between the highest and lowest female life expectancy is $84.2 - 82.1 = 2.1$ years.

The difference between the highest and lowest male life expectancy is $79.0 - 76.5 = 2.5$ years.

Hence, Quantity B has the greater value.

Multiple-Choice (Select One Answer)

7. D. The greatest difference in the average low temperature occurs from October to November: $49° - 42° = 7°$.

Note that this is the steepest part of the line graph, which would indicate the greatest change in average temperature.

8. C. The approximate percent increase in average low temperature from April to May is $\dfrac{\text{increase amount}}{\text{original amount}} = \dfrac{50 - 45}{45} = \dfrac{5}{45} = \dfrac{1}{9} \approx 0.11 \approx 11\%$.

9. D. There was no change in the average low temperature from July to August, which both recorded temperatures of $58°$. Note that the graph is horizontal between these two months, which would indicate that there was no change in the average low temperature.

10. C. There are 6 months with increasing average low temperatures (February, March, April, May, June, and July) and 4 months with decreasing average low temperatures (September, October, November, and December).

Hence, the ratio of the number of months with increasing average low temperatures to the number of months with decreasing average low temperatures is $\dfrac{6}{4} = \dfrac{3}{2}$.

11. C. The total percentage for all of the indicated categories except *other* is $25 + 20 + 12 + 10 + 10 + 6 = 83\%$. Therefore, the percentage for the *other* category is $100 - 83 = 17\%$.

The annual amount spent on the *other* category is 17% of $80,000 = (0.17)(80,000) = \$13,600$.

12. A. The annual amount spent on *medical* is 12% of $80,000 = (0.12)(80,000) = \$9,600$.

The annual amount spent on *entertainment* is 10% of $80,000 = (0.10)(80,000) = \$8,000$.

383

Therefore, the difference between the two amounts is $9,600 – $8,000 = $1,600.

13. D. On the circle graph, the annual amount saved is 10% of $80,000 = (0.10)(80,000) = $8,000.

If an additional $1,600 is added to *savings,* the new annual amount saved is $8,000 + $1,600 = $9,600.

The new percentage for the *savings* category is
$\dfrac{\$9,600}{\$80,000} = \dfrac{3}{25} = 0.12 = 12\%.$

Multiple-Choice (Select One or More Answers)

14. C, D, E. The bar graph indicates that the sales increased from February to March, from March to April, and from April to May. Therefore, compared to the previous month, sales increased in March, April, and May.

15. D, E, F. The average used car sales for the six-month period is

$$(30 + 25 + 45 + 50 + 65 + 60) \div 6$$
$$= 275 \div 6$$
$$= 45\frac{5}{6}$$

The average used car sales in April, May, and June were larger than the average of $45\frac{5}{6}$.

16. C, E. Used car sales increased in March, April, and May. However, notice that only during the months of March and May did used car sales increase more than 25% when compared to the previous month.

The percent increase from February to March was
$\dfrac{\text{increase amount}}{\text{original amount}} = \dfrac{45 - 25}{25} = \dfrac{20}{25} = \dfrac{4}{5} = 0.8 = 80\%.$

The percent increase from March to April was
$\dfrac{\text{increase amount}}{\text{original amount}} = \dfrac{50 - 45}{45} = \dfrac{5}{45} = \dfrac{1}{9} \approx 0.11 \approx 11\%.$

The percent increase from April to May was

$$\frac{\text{increase amount}}{\text{original amount}} = \frac{65 - 50}{50} = \frac{15}{50} = \frac{3}{10} = 0.3 = 30\%.$$

17. **A, B.** The average for the seven-month period is the sum of the used car sales divided by 7. For the average to be 50 or more, the sum of the used car sales for the seven-month period must be greater than or equal to $50 \cdot 7 = 350$.

For 90 cars sold in July:

$30 + 25 + 45 + 50 + 65 + 60 + 90 = 365 > 350$

For 80 cars sold in July:

$30 + 25 + 45 + 50 + 65 + 60 + 80 = 355 > 350$

For 70 cars sold in July:

$30 + 25 + 45 + 50 + 65 + 60 + 70 = 345 < 350$

For 60 cars sold in July:

$30 + 25 + 45 + 50 + 65 + 60 + 60 = 335 < 350$

For 50 cars sold in July:

$30 + 25 + 45 + 50 + 65 + 60 + 50 = 325 < 350$

For 40 cars sold in July:

$30 + 25 + 45 + 50 + 65 + 60 + 40 = 315 < 350$

18. **C, D, E, F.** Since 60 used cars were sold in June, an expected 20% or higher increase for July would be at least 20% of $60 = (0.20)(60) = 12$ cars.

Hence, the used car sales for July could be $60 + 12 = 72$ or more cars.

Numeric Entry (Fill-in)

19. **8**

The percentage of students at Taft High School enrolled in at least one of the foreign languages is $30 + 25 + 15 + 10 + 6 + 4 + 2 = 92\%$.

Therefore, the percentage of students at Taft High School who are not enrolled in one of the foreign languages is $100 - 92 = 8\%$.

20. 264

The percentage of students at Taft High School who are taking two or more of the foreign languages is $10 + 6 + 4 + 2 = 22\%$.

If there are 1,200 students enrolled at Taft High School, then 22% of $1,200 = (0.22)(1,200) = 264$ students are enrolled in two or more of the foreign languages.

21. 432

The percentage of students taking Spanish, but not taking Italian is $30 + 6 = 36\%$.

If there are 1,200 students enrolled at Taft High School, then 36% of $1,200 = (0.36)(1,200) = 432$ students are enrolled in Spanish but not Italian.

22. 240

The percentage of students taking exactly two of the foreign languages is $10 + 6 + 4 = 20\%$.

If there are 1,200 students enrolled at Taft High School, then 20% of $1,200 = (0.20)(1,200) = 240$ students are enrolled in exactly two of the foreign languages.

23. 1375

It was determined in question 19 above that 8% of the students at Taft High School are not enrolled in any of the foreign languages. If 110 students are not enrolled in any of the foreign languages, then

$$8\% \text{ of } x \text{ is } 110$$
$$(0.08)(x) = 110$$
$$x = 110 \div 0.08$$
$$x = 1375$$

Hence, there would be 1,375 students enrolled at Taft High School.

24. 1050

The percentage of students taking only one of the foreign languages is $30 + 25 + 15 = 70\%$.

If there are 1,500 students enrolled at Taft High School, then 70% of $1,500 = (0.70)(1,500) = 1,050$ students are taking only one of the three foreign languages.

FULL-LENGTH PRACTICE TESTS

Chapter 8

Practice Test 1

This chapter contains one full-length Quantitative Reasoning test designed to give you extra practice and insight. Although this practice test does not adapt by section (as the computer adaptive test does) based upon your previous sections' correct or incorrect answers, you will gain valuable test-taking skills and insight into your strengths and weaknesses. The practice test is followed by answers, analysis, and answer explanations.

The format, level of difficulty, question structure, and number of questions are similar to those on the actual Quantitative Reasoning section of the GRE General Test. The actual GRE is copyrighted and may not be duplicated; these questions are not taken directly from actual tests.

When taking this practice test, try to simulate the test conditions. Remember the total testing time when you take the computer-based GRE is about 3 hours and 45 minutes, but only 70 minutes are allowed for the Quantitative Reasoning questions. Budget your time effectively. If you need a break, stop the clock and take a 10-minute break after the first 20 questions. Try to spend no more than 1½ minutes on each question.

Section 1: Quantitative Reasoning (20 questions)

Section 2: Quantitative Reasoning (20 questions)

General Directions: For each question, indicate the best answer, using the directions given.

- All numbers used are real numbers.

- All figures are assumed to lie in a plane unless otherwise indicated.

- Geometric figures, such as lines, circles, triangles, and quadrilaterals, are not necessarily drawn to scale. That is, you should **not** assume that quantities, such as lengths and angle measurements, are as they appear in the figure. You should assume, however, that lines shown as straight are actually straight, points on a line are in the order shown, and more generally, all geometric objects are in the relative position shown. For questions with geometric figures, you should base your answer on geometric reasoning, not on estimating or comparing quantities by sight or by measurement.

- Coordinate systems, such as *xy*-planes and number lines, are drawn to scale; therefore, you can read, estimate, or compare quantities in such figures by sight or by measurement.

- Graphical data presentations, such as bar graphs, pie graphs, and line graphs, are drawn to scale; therefore, you can read, estimate, or compare data values by sight or by measurement.

Answer choices in this study guide have lettered choices A, B, C, D, E, etc., for clarity, but letters will not appear on the actual exam. On the actual computer version of the exam, you will be required to click on ovals or squares to select your answer.

HELPFUL HINT

○ oval—answer will be a single choice.

☐ square box—answer will be one or more choices.

Section 1: Quantitative Reasoning

Time: 35 minutes

20 questions

Directions: For questions 1 to 7, compare Quantity A and Quantity B, using additional information centered above the two quantities if such information is given. Select one of the following four answer choices for each question:

   Ⓐ   Quantity A is greater.

   Ⓑ   Quantity B is greater.

   Ⓒ   The two quantities are equal.

   Ⓓ   The relationship cannot be determined from the information given.

	Quantity A	**Quantity B**
1.	the area of a right triangle with a hypotenuse of 13 and a leg of 5	the area of a right triangle with a hypotenuse of 13 and a leg of 12

$$a^3b^4 > 0$$
$$a^4b^3 < 0$$

	Quantity A	**Quantity B**
2.	a	b

	Quantity A	**Quantity B**
3.	the slope of $\overrightarrow{AB}$	the slope of $\overrightarrow{AC}$

	Quantity A	**Quantity B**
4.	the number of prime numbers between 1 and 30	the number of perfect squares between 0 and 100

	Quantity A	**Quantity B**
5.	the number of different 4-person committees that can be formed from a group of 9 people	the number of different 5-person committees that can be formed from a group of 9 people

	Quantity A	**Quantity B** ✓
6.	the probability of randomly selecting an even number from the numbers 1 through 19	the probability of randomly selecting an odd number from the numbers 1 through 19

	Quantity A	**Quantity B**
7.	the x-intercept of a line whose equation is $5x + 4y + 20 = 0$	the y-intercept of a line whose equation is $5x + 4y + 20 = 0$

Directions: Questions 8 to 20 have several different formats. Unless otherwise directed, select a single answer choice. For **Numeric Entry** questions, follow the instructions below.

Write out your answer in the answer box(es) below the question.

- Your answer may be an integer, a decimal, or a fraction, and it may be negative.
- If a question asks for a fraction, there will be two boxes, one for the numerator and one for the denominator.
- Equivalent forms of the correct answer, such as 2.5 and 2.50, are all correct. Fractions do not need to be reduced (simplified) to lowest terms.
- Write out the exact answer unless the question asks you to round your answer.

8. If the average (arithmetic mean) of z, $2z$, $3z$, and $4z$ is 20, what is the value of z?

- ✓ Ⓐ 2
- Ⓑ 4
- Ⓒ 6
- Ⓓ 8
- Ⓔ 10

9. A bag contains 8 red marbles, 7 green marbles, and 6 blue marbles. If 1 marble is randomly selected, what is the probability that the marble is NOT green? Give the answer as a fraction.

10. If $(3x + 4)(3x - 4) = 20$, what is the value of $3x^2$?

    Ⓐ   4

    ✓Ⓑ   12

    Ⓒ   16

    Ⓓ   36

    Ⓔ   It cannot be determined from the information given.

11. A conference room has 25 tables that can seat a total of 220 people. Some of the tables seat 10 people and others seat 8 people. How many tables seat 8 people?

    Ⓐ   5

    Ⓑ   10

    Ⓒ   12

    Ⓓ   15

    Ⓔ   20

12. If two sides of a triangle have lengths 7 and 15, which of the following could be the length of the third side? Indicate *all* that apply.

    Ⓐ   7

    Ⓑ   8

    Ⓒ   15

    Ⓓ   16

    Ⓔ   21

    Ⓕ   22

13. What is the measure in degrees of each angle of a regular polygon with 20 sides?

    Ⓐ   140

    Ⓑ   144

    Ⓒ   152

    Ⓓ   160

    Ⓔ   162

14. The first term of a sequence is −1, and each subsequent term is the product of −3 and the preceding term. What is the seventh term of the sequence?

  Ⓐ −2187

 ✓Ⓑ −729

  Ⓒ −243

  Ⓓ 243

  Ⓔ 729

15. The ratio of $\dfrac{5}{9}$ to $\dfrac{9}{11}$ is equivalent to what other ratio? Give the answer as a fraction.

16. If $x^2 - 8 = 8$ and $y^2 - 25 = 0$, which of the following could be equal to $x + y$? Indicate *all* that apply.

 Ⓐ −9

 Ⓑ −5

 Ⓒ −1

 Ⓓ 1

 Ⓔ 5

 Ⓕ 9 ✓

17. What is the probability of throwing a total of 8 with a single throw of a pair of dice?

  Ⓐ $\dfrac{1}{18}$

  Ⓑ $\dfrac{1}{12}$

  Ⓒ $\dfrac{1}{9}$

  Ⓓ $\dfrac{5}{36}$

  Ⓔ $\dfrac{1}{6}$ ✓

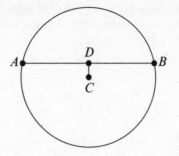

18. If C is the center of the circle above with $CD = 5$ and $AB = 24$, what is the radius of the circle?

   Ⓐ   12
   Ⓑ   13
   Ⓒ   17
   Ⓓ   19
   Ⓔ   It cannot be determined from the information given.

19. In a parallelogram $WXYZ$, $\angle X$ is 28° larger than $\angle Y$. What is the degree measure of $\angle Z$?

   Ⓐ   62
   Ⓑ   76
   Ⓒ   104
   Ⓓ   152
   Ⓔ   It cannot be determined from the information given.

20. If $5x(5x - 4)(3x + 4)(x + 1)(x - 3) = 0$, what is the smallest value of x? Give the answer as a fraction.

Section 2: Quantitative Reasoning

Directions: For questions 1 to 7, compare Quantity A and Quantity B, using additional information centered above the two quantities if such information is given. Select one of the following four answer choices for each question:

- Ⓐ   Quantity A is greater.
- Ⓑ   Quantity B is greater.
- Ⓒ   The two quantities are equal.
- Ⓓ   The relationship cannot be determined from the information given.

	Quantity A	**Quantity B**
1.	the height of a triangle with an area of 81 and a base of 18	the height of a trapezoid with an area of 80 and bases of 6 and 10

$$x^2 - y^2 = 40$$

	Quantity A	**Quantity B**
2.	x	y

	Quantity A	**Quantity B**
3.	the probability that 3 flips of a coin will result in 2 heads and 1 tail	the probability that 3 flips of a coin will result in at least 2 tails

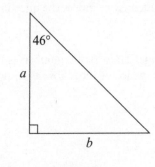

	Quantity A	**Quantity B**
4.	1	$\dfrac{a}{b}$

	Quantity A	**Quantity B**
5.	the number of feet in 48 yards	the number of pints in 18 gallons

	Quantity A	**Quantity B**
6.	the number of prime numbers that are factors of 210	the number of perfect cubes between 1 and 100

x is an integer greater than 0

	Quantity A	**Quantity B**
7.	2^{x+2}	3^x

Directions: Questions 8 to 20 have several different formats. Unless otherwise directed, select a single answer choice. For **Numeric Entry** questions, follow the instructions below.

Write out your answer in the answer box(es) below the question.

- Your answer may be an integer, a decimal, or a fraction, and it may be negative.
- If a question asks for a fraction, there will be two boxes, one for the numerator and one for the denominator.
- Equivalent forms of the correct answer, such as 2.5 and 2.50, are all correct. Fractions do not need to be reduced (simplified) to lowest terms.
- Write out the exact answer unless the question asks you to round your answer.

8. If the average (arithmetic mean) of 3 numbers is 15 and two of the numbers are x and y, which of the following could be an expression for the third number?

Ⓐ $15 - x + y$

Ⓑ $15 - x - y$

Ⓒ $45 - x + y$

Ⓓ $45 - x - y$

Ⓔ $x + y$

9. If a number n is 9 times the value of a number m and the value of m is increased by 5, then the value of n is increased by how much?

   Ⓐ   4

   Ⓑ   5

   Ⓒ   9

   Ⓓ   14

   Ⓔ   45

10. Which of the following lines have a slope greater than 1? Indicate *all* that apply.

   Ⓐ $x = 5$

   Ⓑ $y = 3$

   Ⓒ $2x - y = 9$

   Ⓓ $3x + 4y = 12$

   Ⓔ $5x - 3y = 15$

   Ⓕ $2x - 7y = 20$

11. If Δ is defined as $x \Delta y = x^{-y} + y^{-x}$, what is the value of $2 \Delta 3$? Give the answer as a fraction.

12. If a and b are positive integers such that $a + b = 7$, which of the following are possible values of $3a + 5b$? Indicate *all* that apply.

   Ⓐ   29

   Ⓑ   28

   Ⓒ   27

   Ⓓ   26

   Ⓔ   25

   Ⓕ   24

Questions 13 and 14 refer to the following information.

The following bar graph shows the distribution for 16 different income brackets in Los Angeles. Each bar represents the percentage of the Los Angeles population whose yearly income falls within that range.

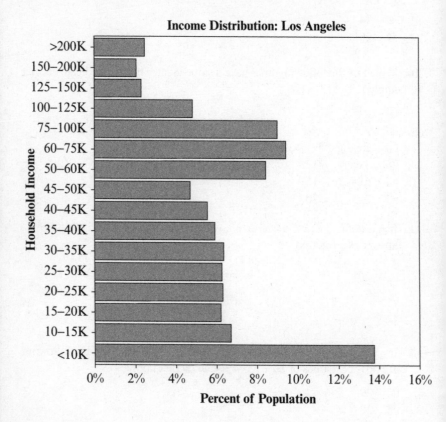

Income Distribution: Los Angeles

13. All of the people at the top of the lowest half of Los Angeles' population (the lowest 50%) earn approximately how much money per year?

   Ⓐ $35,000

   Ⓑ $40,000

   Ⓒ $45,000

   Ⓓ $50,000

   Ⓔ $100,000

14. Approximately what fraction of the total population of Los Angeles earns between $45,000 and $100,000 per year? Give the answer as a fraction.

15. If a right triangle has two sides with lengths of 16 and 20, which of the following could be the area of the triangle? Indicate *all* that apply.

   A   320

   B   192

   C   160

   D   96

   E   80

16. How many different committees of 2 men and 2 women can be formed from a group of 5 men and 6 women?

   Ⓐ   30

   Ⓑ   60

   ©   120

   Ⓓ   150

   Ⓔ   600

17. What is the greatest of 6 consecutive integers if the sum of the integers is 375?

18. How many square yards of carpet would be needed to cover a rectangular conference room that is 100 feet by 180 feet?

   Ⓐ $222\frac{2}{9}$

   Ⓑ   280

   ©   2,000

   Ⓓ   6,000

   Ⓔ   18,000

19. Which of the following would NOT change the value of the median of a set of 15 different numbers?

   Ⓐ   Decrease the largest number only.

   Ⓑ   Decrease the smallest number only.

   Ⓒ   Take half of each number.

   Ⓓ   Decrease each number by 1.

   Ⓔ   Double each number.

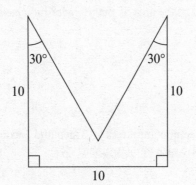

20. What is the perimeter of the figure above?

   Ⓐ   60

   Ⓑ   50

   Ⓒ   48

   Ⓓ   46

   Ⓔ   40

Answer Key

Section 1

1. C
2. A
3. B
4. A
5. C
6. B
7. A
8. D
9. $\frac{14}{21}$, or $\frac{2}{3}$
10. B
11. D
12. C, D, E
13. E
14. B
15. $\frac{55}{81}$
16. A, C, D, F
17. D
18. B
19. C
20. $\frac{-4}{3}$

Section 2

1. B
2. D
3. B
4. A
5. C
6. A
7. D
8. D
9. E
10. C, E
11. $\frac{17}{72}$
12. A, C, E
13. B
14. $\frac{1}{3}$
15. C, D
16. D
17. 65
18. C
19. B
20. B

Charting and Analyzing Your Test Results

The first step in analyzing your results is to chart your answers. Use the answer key and chart to identify your strengths and areas of improvement. The answers and explanations following this chart will help you solve the practice problems, but you should re-evaluate your results as you look for the following:

- Trends
- Types of errors (frequently repeated errors)
- Low scores in results of *specific* topic areas

This re-examination and analysis is a tremendous asset to help you maximize your best possible score. The answers and explanations following this chart will provide you with clarification to help you solve these types of questions in the future.

Analysis/Tally Sheet

			Number Incorrect		
Content Style Topic	**Total Possible**	**Number Correct**	**(A) Simple Mistake**	**(B) Misread Problem**	**(C) Lack of Knowledge**
Arithmetic Section 1 – Questions 2, 4, 15 Section 2 – Questions 6, 12	5				
Algebra Section 1 – Questions 3, 7, 10, 14, 16, 20 Section 2 – Questions 2, 7, 10, 11, 17	11				
Geometry Section 1 – Questions 1, 12, 13, 18, 19 Section 2 – Questions 1, 4, 15, 18, 20	10				

(continued)

Analysis/Tally Sheet (*continued*)

Content Style Topic	Total Possible	Number Correct	Number Incorrect		
			(A) Simple Mistake	(B) Misread Problem	(C) Lack of Knowledge
Data Analysis Section 1 – Questions 5, 6, 8, 9, 17 Section 2 – Questions 3, 8, 16, 19	9				
Word Problems Section 1 – Question 11 Section 2 – Questions 5, 9	3				
Data Interpretation Section 2 – Questions 13, 14	2				
Total Possible Explanations for Incorrect Answers: Columns A, B, and C					
Total Number of Answers Correct and Incorrect	40	Add the total number of correct answers here: ___	Add columns A, B, and C: _____ Total number of incorrect answers		

Answers and Explanations

Section 1

1. **C.** Use the Pythagorean theorem to find the missing leg of the first right triangle.

$$a^2 + b^2 = c^2$$
$$5^2 + b^2 = 13^2$$
$$25 + b^2 = 169$$
$$b^2 = 169 - 25 = 144$$
$$b = \sqrt{144} = 12$$

The area A of the first triangle is $A = \frac{1}{2}bh = \frac{1}{2}(12)(5) = 30$.

Similarly, the Pythagorean theorem can be used to find the missing leg of the second triangle.

$$a^2 + b^2 = c^2$$
$$12^2 + b^2 = 13^2$$
$$144 + b^2 = 169$$
$$b^2 = 169 - 144 = 25$$
$$b = \sqrt{25} = 5$$

The area A of the second triangle is $A = \frac{1}{2}bh = \frac{1}{2}(5)(12) = 30$.

Hence, the two quantities are equal.

2. **A.** If $a^3b^4 > 0$, $a^3 > 0$ and $b^4 > 0$. This requires that $a > 0$, but b could be positive or negative and no relationship between a and b can be determined.

If $a^4b^3 < 0$, $a^4 > 0$ and $b^3 < 0$. This requires that $b < 0$, but a could be positive or negative and no relationship between a and b can be determined.

Taking the two statements together requires that $a > 0$ and $b < 0$. Therefore, Quantity A has the greater value.

3. **B.** Since both lines slant up to the right, their slopes are positive. Both lines also pass through the same point A, but $\overline{AC}$ is steeper than $\overline{AB}$ and, therefore, will have the larger slope. Hence, Quantity B has the greater value.

4. A. There are 10 prime numbers between 1 and 30: 2, 3, 5, 7, 11, 13, 17, 19, 23, and 29.

There are 9 perfect squares between 0 and 100: 1, 4, 9, 16, 25, 36, 49, 64, and 81.

Hence, Quantity A has the greater value.

5. C. The number of 4-person committees that can be formed from a group of 9 people is a combination of 9 objects taken 4 at a time.

$$
\begin{aligned}
C(9,4) &= \frac{9!}{4!(9-4)!} \\
&= \frac{9!}{4! \cdot 5!} \\
&= \frac{9 \cdot 8 \cdot 7 \cdot 6 \cdot \cancel{5!}}{4! \cdot \cancel{5!}} \\
&= \frac{9 \cdot 8 \cdot 7 \cdot 6}{4 \cdot 3 \cdot 2 \cdot 1} \\
&= 126 \text{ committees}
\end{aligned}
$$

The number of 5-person committees that can be formed from a group of 9 people is a combination of 9 objects taken 5 at a time.

$$
\begin{aligned}
C(9,5) &= \frac{9!}{5!(9-5)!} \\
&= \frac{9!}{5! \cdot 4!} \\
&= \frac{9 \cdot 8 \cdot 7 \cdot 6 \cdot \cancel{5!}}{\cancel{5!} \cdot 4!} \\
&= \frac{9 \cdot 8 \cdot 7 \cdot 6}{4 \cdot 3 \cdot 2 \cdot 1} \\
&= 126 \text{ committees}
\end{aligned}
$$

Hence, the two quantities are equal.

6. B. Since there are 9 even numbers in the set of 19 numbers 1 through 19, the probability of selecting an even number is $\frac{9}{19}$.

Since there are 10 odd numbers in the set of 19 numbers 1 through 19, the probability of selecting an odd number is $\frac{10}{19}$. Therefore, Quantity B has the greater value.

7. A. The x-intercept of a line is the x value at the point $(x, 0)$ on the line where the graph crosses the x-axis.

For the line $5x + 4y + 20 = 0$,

$$5x + 4(0) + 20 = 0$$
$$5x + 20 = 0$$
$$5x + 20 - 20 = 0 - 20$$
$$5x = -20$$
$$x = -4$$

The y-intercept of a line is the y value at the point $(0, y)$ on the line where the graph crosses the y-axis.

For the line $5x + 4y + 20 = 0$,

$$5(0) + 4y + 20 = 0$$
$$4y + 20 - 20 = 0 - 20$$
$$4y = -20$$
$$y = -5$$

Hence, Quantity A has the greater value.

8. D. Since the average of z, $2z$, $3z$, and $4z$ is 20,

$$\frac{z + 2z + 3z + 4z}{4} = 20$$
$$\frac{10z}{4} = 20$$
$$\frac{10z}{4} \cdot 4 = 20 \cdot 4$$
$$10z = 80$$
$$z = 8$$

9. $\dfrac{14}{21}$, or $\dfrac{2}{3}$

The bag contains 21 marbles with 14 of the marbles not green (8 red and 6 blue). The probability that the marble selected is *not* green is $\dfrac{14}{21} = \dfrac{2}{3}$.

Another method that could be used is to determine the probability that the marble selected *is* green is $\dfrac{7}{21} = \dfrac{1}{3}$.

The probability that it will not be green is

$$1 - (\text{the probability it is green})$$

$$= 1 - \frac{1}{3}$$

$$= \frac{2}{3}$$

10. B.

$$\text{If } (3x + 4)(3x - 4) = 20,$$

$$9x^2 - 16 = 20$$

$$9x^2 - 16 + 16 = 20 + 16$$

$$9x^2 = 36$$

$$x^2 = 4$$

$$3x^2 = 12$$

11. D. Let $x =$ the number of 10-person tables. Let $y =$ the number of 8-person tables. Then $x + y = 25$ and $10x + 8y = 220$.

Multiply the first equation through by -8 and then add the two resulting equations.

$$-8(x + y) = -8(25) \;\rightarrow\; -8x - 8y = -200$$
$$10x + 8y = 220 \quad\;\;\rightarrow\; \underline{10x + 8y = 220}$$
$$2x = 20$$
$$x = 10$$

Since $\;x + y = 25$,

$$10 + y = 25$$

$$10 + y - 10 = 25 - 10$$

$$y = 15 \text{ tables seat 8 people.}$$

12. C, D, and E. The triangle inequality theorem states that the sum of any two sides of a triangle must be greater than the third side. Since the given triangle has two sides with lengths of 7 and 15, the length of the third side x must be

$$15 - 7 < x < 15 + 7$$

$$8 < x < 22$$

Hence, 15, 16, and 21 are possible values of x.

13. **E.** The sum in degrees of the interior angles of a polygon with n sides is $(n-2) \cdot 180$.

For a 20-sided polygon, the sum is $(20-2) \cdot 180 = 18 \cdot 180 = 3240°$.

Since a regular polygon has equal angles, each angle of a regular polygon with 20 sides will have a measure of: $3240° \div 20 = 162°$.

14. **B.** The first seven terms of the sequence are

1st term $= -1$ 5th term $= (27)(-3) = -81$

2nd term $= (-1)(-3) = 3$ 6th term $= (-81)(-3) = 243$

3rd term $= (3)(-3) = -9$ 7th term $= (243)(-3) = -729$

4th term $= (-9)(-3) = 27$

15. $\dfrac{55}{81}$

The ratio of $\dfrac{5}{9}$ to $\dfrac{9}{11} = \dfrac{\frac{5}{9}}{\frac{9}{11}}$

$$= \frac{5}{9} \div \frac{9}{11}$$

$$= \frac{5}{9} \cdot \frac{11}{9}$$

$$= \frac{55}{81}$$

16. **A, C, D, and F.**

$$\begin{array}{ll}
\text{If } x^2 - 8 = 8 & \text{and} \quad y^2 - 25 = 0 \\
x^2 - 8 + 8 = 8 + 8 & \quad y^2 - 25 + 25 = 0 + 25 \\
x^2 = 16 & \quad y^2 = 25 \\
x = \pm\sqrt{16} & \quad y = \pm\sqrt{25} \\
x = \pm 4 & \quad y = \pm 5
\end{array}$$

Therefore, the possible values of $x + y$ are

$$4 + 5 = 9$$
$$4 + -5 = -1$$
$$-4 + 5 = 1$$
$$-4 + -5 = -9$$

17. D. There are 5 different combinations of a total of 8 with a single throw of a pair of dice: 2 and 6, 6 and 2, 3 and 5, 5 and 3, and 4 and 4. Since there are $6 \cdot 6 = 36$ possible outcomes for a single throw, the probability of throwing a total of 8 is $\dfrac{5}{36}$.

18. B.

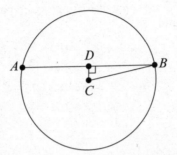

Since C is the center of the circle, $\overline{CD} \perp \overline{AB}$ because a segment drawn from the center of a circle to any chord of the circle will always be perpendicular to the chord and will always bisect the chord. $\triangle BCD$ is a right triangle with legs whose lengths are $CD = 5$ and $BD = 12$. Using the Pythagorean theorem

$$(BC)^2 = (CD)^2 + (BD)^2$$
$$(BC)^2 = (5)^2 + (12)^2$$
$$(BC)^2 = 25 + 144$$
$$(BC)^2 = 169$$
$$BC = \sqrt{169} = 13$$

The radius of the circle is 13.

19. C.

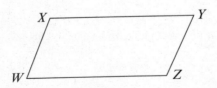

In any parallelogram, consecutive angles are supplementary. Since $\angle X$ and $\angle Y$ are consecutive angles, $\angle X + \angle Y = 180°$, with $\angle X = \angle Y + 28$.

$$(\angle Y + 28) + \angle Y = 180$$
$$2 \cdot \angle Y + 28 = 180$$
$$\text{Hence,} \quad 2 \cdot \angle Y + 28 - 28 = 180 - 28$$
$$2 \cdot \angle Y = 152$$
$$\angle Y = 76°$$

Since $\angle Y$ and $\angle Z$ are consecutive angles of a parallelogram, they are supplementary and

$$\angle Y + \angle Z = 180°$$
$$76 + \angle Z = 180$$
$$76 + \angle Z - 76 = 180 - 76$$
$$\angle Z = 104°$$

20. $\dfrac{-4}{3}$

Since $5x(5x - 4)(3x + 4)(x + 1)(x - 3) = 0$, then

$$5x = 0 \quad \underline{\text{or}} \quad 5x - 4 = 0 \quad \underline{\text{or}} \quad 3x + 4 = 0$$
$$\frac{5x}{5} = \frac{0}{5} \qquad 5x - 4 + 4 = 0 + 4 \qquad 3x + 4 - 4 = 0 - 4$$
$$x = 0 \qquad\qquad 5x = 4 \qquad\qquad 3x = -4$$
$$\frac{5x}{5} = \frac{4}{5} \qquad\qquad \frac{3x}{3} = \frac{-4}{3}$$
$$x = \frac{4}{5} \qquad\qquad x = \frac{-4}{3}$$

$$\underline{\text{or}} \quad x + 1 = 0 \quad \underline{\text{or}} \quad x - 3 = 0$$
$$x + 1 - 1 = 0 - 1 \qquad x - 3 + 3 = 0 + 3$$
$$x = -1 \qquad\qquad x = 3$$

Hence, the smallest value of x is $\dfrac{-4}{3}$.

Section 2

1. B. The area A of a triangle with base b and height h is

$$A = \frac{1}{2}bh$$
$$81 = \frac{1}{2}(18)h$$
$$81 = 9h$$
$$9 = h$$

The area A of a trapezoid with bases B and b and height h is

$$A = \frac{1}{2}h(B+b)$$

$$80 = \frac{1}{2}h(10+6)$$

$$80 = \frac{1}{2}h(16)$$

$$80 = 8h$$

$$10 = h$$

Hence, Quantity B has the greater value.

2. D. Since x could be positive or negative and y could be positive or negative, the relationship between x and y cannot be determined from the information given.

As an example, $x = 7$ and $y = 3$ will yield $x^2 - y^2 = 40$ with $x > y$. But $x = -7$ and $y = 3$ will yield $x^2 - y^2 = 40$ with $x < y$.

3. B. There are $2^3 = 8$ possible outcomes for 3 flips of a coin. There are 3 possible outcomes for 2 heads and 1 tail: HHT, HTH, and THH, with a probability of $\frac{3}{8}$.

There are 4 possible outcomes for at least 2 tails: TTT, TTH, THT, and HTT, with a probability of $\frac{4}{8} = \frac{1}{2}$.

Hence, Quantity B has the greater value.

4. A.

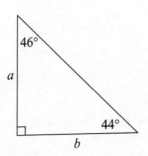

Since the triangle is a right triangle, its two acute angles must be complementary and total 90°. $90 - 46 = 44°$. Since the larger of two sides of a triangle is opposite the larger of two angles of a triangle, $b > a$ and $\dfrac{a}{b} < 1$.

Hence, Quantity A has the greater value.

5. C. Since there are 3 feet in a yard, the number of feet in 48 yards is $3 \cdot 48 = 144$.

Since there are 8 pints in a gallon, the number of pints in 18 gallons is $8 \cdot 18 = 144$.

Hence, the two quantities are equal.

6. A. While there are many numbers that are factors of 210, there are only four prime factors: 2, 3, 5, and 7.

There are three perfect cubes between 1 and 100: 8, 27, and 64.

Therefore, Quantity A has the greater value.

7. D. If $x = 1$, $2^{x+2} = 2^3 = 8$ and $3^x = 3^1 = 3 \rightarrow 2^{x+2} > 3^x$

If $x = 2$, $2^{x+2} = 2^4 = 16$ and $3^x = 3^2 = 9 \rightarrow 2^{x+2} > 3^x$

If $x = 3$, $2^{x+2} = 2^5 = 32$ and $3^x = 3^3 = 27 \rightarrow 2^{x+2} > 3^x$

If $x = 4$, $2^{x+2} = 2^6 = 64$ and $3^x = 3^4 = 81 \rightarrow 2^{x+2} < 3^x$

Hence, the relationship between 2^{x+2} and 3^x cannot be determined from the information given.

8. D. Let $z = $ the third number.

If the average of three numbers x, y, and z is 15, then

$$\frac{x+y+z}{3} = 15$$

$$\frac{x+y+z}{3} \cdot 3 = 15 \cdot 3$$

$$x + y + z = 45$$

$$x + y + z - (x + y) = 45 - (x + y)$$

$$z = 45 - x - y$$

9. E. Since $n = 9m$ and the value of m is increased by 5, then $9(m + 5) = 9m + 45 = n + 45$.

Hence, the value of n is increased by 45.

10. **C and E.**

For choice A, the line $x = 5$ is a vertical line whose slope is undefined.

For choice B, the line $y = 3$ is a horizontal line with slope $= 0$.

Choices C, D, E, and F should be expressed in slope-intercept form, $y = mx + b$, as follows:

Choice C:
$$2x - y = 9$$
$$2x - y - 2x = 9 - 2x$$
$$-y = 9 - 2x$$
$$\frac{-y}{-1} = \frac{9 - 2x}{-1}$$
$$y = -9 + 2x, \text{ or } y = 2x - 9, \text{ and the slope } m = 2$$

Choice D:
$$3x + 4y = 12$$
$$3x + 4y - 3x = 12 - 3x$$
$$4y = 12 - 3x$$
$$\frac{4y}{4} = \frac{12 - 3x}{4}$$
$$y = 3 - \frac{3}{4}x, \text{ or } y = -\frac{3}{4}x + 3, \text{ and the slope } m = -\frac{3}{4}$$

Choice E:
$$5x - 3y = 15$$
$$5x - 3y - 5x = 15 - 5x$$
$$-3y = 15 - 5x$$
$$\frac{-3y}{-3} = \frac{15 - 5x}{-3}$$
$$y = -5 + \frac{5}{3}x, \text{ or } y = \frac{5}{3}x - 5, \text{ and the slope } m = \frac{5}{3}$$

Choice F:
$$2x - 7y = 20$$
$$2x - 7y - 2x = 20 - 2x$$
$$-7y = 20 - 2x$$
$$\frac{-7y}{-7} = \frac{20 - 2x}{-7}$$
$$y = -\frac{20}{7} + \frac{2}{7}x, \text{ or } y = \frac{2}{7}x - \frac{20}{7}, \text{ and the slope } m = \frac{2}{7}$$

11. $\dfrac{17}{72}$

$$\text{Since } x\Delta y = x^{-y} + y^{-x},$$
$$2\Delta 3 = 2^{-3} + 3^{-2}$$
$$= \frac{1}{2^3} + \frac{1}{3^2}$$
$$= \frac{1}{8} + \frac{1}{9}$$
$$2\Delta 3 = \frac{9}{72} + \frac{8}{72} = \frac{17}{72}$$

12. A, C, and E. Since a and b are positive integers such that $a + b = 7$, the possible ordered pairs (a, b) are $(1, 6)$, $(6, 1)$, $(2, 5)$, $(5, 2)$, $(3, 4)$, and $(4, 3)$.

If $a = 3$ and $b = 4$, $3a + 5b = 3(3) + 5(4) = 29$.

If $a = 4$ and $b = 3$, $3a + 5b = 3(4) + 5(3) = 27$.

If $a = 5$ and $b = 2$, $3a + 5b = 3(5) + 5(2) = 25$.

Note that $3a + 5b \neq 28$, $3a + 5b \neq 26$, and $3a + 5b \neq 24$ since $3a + 5b$ will be odd for all possible values of a and b.

13. B. The lowest half (lowest 50%) make up the bottom 7 bars of the graph. Note that the percentages corresponding to these income brackets are approximately 14%, 7%, 6%, 6%, 6%, 6%, and 6%, which total approximately 50%. The people at the top of these income brackets earn approximately $40,000 per year.

14. $\dfrac{1}{3}$

The population that earns between $45,000 and $100,000 per year makes up approximately 33% of the total population, which is approximately $\dfrac{1}{3}$ of the total population. Note that the percentages corresponding to these income brackets are approximately 5%, 9%, 10%, and 9%, whose sum is approximately 33%.

15. C and D. The area A of any triangle with base b and height h is $A = \dfrac{1}{2}bh$. If the two sides 16 and 20 are legs of the right triangle, then its area A is $A = \dfrac{1}{2}bh = \dfrac{1}{2}(16)(20) = 160$.

If the hypotenuse is 20 and one leg is 16, then the Pythagorean theorem can be used to find the length of the other leg of the right triangle.

$$c^2 = a^2 + b^2$$
$$20^2 = 16^2 + b^2$$
$$400 = 256 + b^2$$
$$b^2 = 400 - 256$$
$$b^2 = 144$$
$$b = \sqrt{144} = 12$$

The area A of the triangle is $A = \frac{1}{2}bh = \frac{1}{2}(12)(16) = 96$.

16. **D.** The number of 2-men committees that can be formed from a group of 5 men is a combination of 5 objects taken 2 at a time:

$$C(5, 2) = \frac{5!}{2!(5-2)!} = \frac{5!}{2! \cdot 3!} = \frac{5 \cdot 4 \cdot 3!}{2! \cdot 3!} = \frac{5 \cdot 4}{2 \cdot 1} = 10$$

The number of 2-women committees that can be formed from a group of 6 women is a combination of 6 objects taken 2 at a time:

$$C(6, 2) = \frac{6!}{2! \cdot (6-2)!} = \frac{6!}{2! \cdot 4!} = \frac{6 \cdot 5 \cdot 4!}{2! \cdot 4!} = \frac{6 \cdot 5}{2 \cdot 1} = 15$$

The total number of 2-men and 2-women committees that can be formed is the product of their two totals: $10 \cdot 15 = 150$.

17. **65**

Let x = 1st integer	$x + 3$ = 4th integer
$x + 1$ = 2nd integer	$x + 4$ = 5th integer
$x + 2$ = 3rd integer	$x + 5$ = 6th integer

Since the sum of the integers is 375,

$$x + x + 1 + x + 2 + x + 3 + x + 4 + x + 5 = 375$$
$$6x + 15 = 375$$
$$6x + 15 - 15 = 375 - 15$$
$$6x = 360$$
$$x = 60$$

Hence, the largest of the 6 consecutive integers is $x + 5 = 60 + 5 = 65$.

18. **C.** The area A of a rectangle with base b and height h is

$$A = bh$$
$$= (100 \text{ feet})(180 \text{ feet})$$
$$= 18,000 \text{ square feet}$$

Since there are 9 square feet in 1 square yard (3 feet × 3 feet), the number of square yards of carpet needed is $18,000 \div 9 = 2,000$.

19. **B.** The median of a set of 15 different numbers is the middle number (8th) when the numbers have been written in order from smallest to largest or from largest to smallest. Decreasing the smallest number only would have no effect on the middle number of the set and the median would be unchanged. Each of the other answer choices would change the median.

20. **B.**

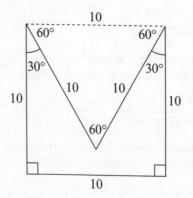

The segment connecting the vertices of the given 30° angles results in a square with sides whose length is 10. The triangle formed is a equiangular triangle since each of its angles will measure 60°. Since any equiangular triangle is also an equilateral triangle, the three sides of the triangle have the same length of 10.

Hence, the perimeter P of the figure is $P = 5 \cdot 10 = 50$.

Chapter 9

Practice Test 2

This chapter contains one full-length Quantitative Reasoning test designed to give you extra practice and insight. Although this practice test does not adapt by section (as the computer adaptive test does) based upon your previous sections' correct or incorrect answers, you will gain valuable test-taking skills and insight into your strengths and weaknesses. The practice test is followed by answers, analysis, and answer explanations.

The format, level of difficulty, question structure, and number of questions are similar to those on the actual Quantitative Reasoning section of the GRE General Test. The actual GRE is copyrighted and may not be duplicated; these questions are not taken directly from actual tests.

When taking this practice test, try to simulate the test conditions. Remember the total testing time when you take the computer-based GRE is about 3 hours and 45 minutes, but only 70 minutes are allowed for the Quantitative Reasoning questions. Budget your time effectively. If you need a break, stop the clock and take a 10-minute break after the first 20 questions. Try to spend no more than 1½ minutes on each question.

    Section 1: Quantitative Reasoning (20 questions)

    Section 2: Quantitative Reasoning (20 questions)

General Directions: For each question, indicate the best answer, using the directions given.

- All numbers used are real numbers.

- All figures are assumed to lie in a plane unless otherwise indicated.

- Geometric figures, such as lines, circles, triangles, and quadrilaterals, are not necessarily drawn to scale. That is, you should **not** assume that quantities, such as lengths and angle measurements, are as they appear in the figure. You should assume, however, that lines shown as straight are actually straight, points on a line are in the order shown, and more generally, all geometric objects are in the relative position shown. For questions with geometric figures, you should base your answer on geometric reasoning, not on estimating or comparing quantities by sight or by measurement.

- Coordinate systems, such as xy-planes and number lines, are drawn to scale; therefore, you can read, estimate, or compare quantities in such figures by sight or by measurement.

- Graphical data presentations, such as bar graphs, pie graphs, and line graphs, are drawn to scale; therefore, you can read, estimate, or compare data values by sight or by measurement.

Answer choices in this study guide have lettered choices A, B, C, D, E, etc., for clarity, but letters will not appear on the actual exam. On the actual computer version of the exam, you will be required to click on ovals or squares to select your answer.

HELPFUL HINT

○ oval—answer will be a single choice.

□ square box—answer will be one or more choices.

Section 1: Quantitative Reasoning

Time: 35 minutes

20 questions

Directions: For questions 1 to 7, compare Quantity A and Quantity B, using additional information centered above the two quantities if such information is given. Select one of the following four answer choices for each question:

Ⓐ Quantity A is greater.

Ⓑ Quantity B is greater.

Ⓒ The two quantities are equal.

Ⓓ The relationship cannot be determined from the information given.

	Quantity A	**Quantity B**
1.	the percent increase from 70 to 100	the percent decrease from 80 to 50

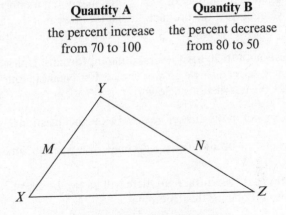

In the figure, $MN = 12, XZ = 20,$
$MY = 8, NZ = 4, MX = a,$
$NY = b,$ and $\overline{MN} \parallel \overline{XZ}.$

	Quantity A	**Quantity B**
2.	MX	NY

	Quantity A	**Quantity B**
3.	$1^2 + 2^2 + 3^2 + 4^2 + 5^2 + 6^2$	$1^3 + (-2)^3 + 3^3 + (-4)^3 + 5^3$

Quantity A	Quantity B
4.	the ratio of the circumference to the diameter of a circle with a radius of 8	the ratio of the circumference to the diameter of a circle with a diameter of 20

Quantity A	Quantity B
5.	the speed when traveling 140 miles in 105 minutes	the speed when traveling 117 miles in 90 minutes

Quantity A	Quantity B
6.	the mean of 5 consecutive odd integers whose sum is 345	the median of 5 consecutive odd integers whose sum is 345

Quantity A	Quantity B
7.	the maximum number of negative integers if the product of 8 integers is negative	the maximum number of negative integers if the product of 9 integers is positive

Directions: Questions 8 to 20 have several different formats. Unless otherwise directed, select a single answer choice. For **Numeric Entry** questions, follow the instructions below.

Write out your answer in the answer box(es) below the question.

- Your answer may be an integer, a decimal, or a fraction, and it may be negative.
- If a question asks for a fraction, there will be two boxes, one for the numerator and one for the denominator.
- Equivalent forms of the correct answer, such as 2.5 and 2.50, are all correct. Fractions do not need to be reduced (simplified) to lowest terms.
- Write out the exact answer unless the question asks you to round your answer.

8. If the average (arithmetic mean) of x, y, z, 8, and 15 is 12, what is the value of $x + y + z$?

   Ⓐ 8

   Ⓑ 20

   Ⓒ 23

   Ⓓ 37

   Ⓔ 60

9. If all possible diagonals are drawn from one vertex of a 10-sided polygon, how many triangles are formed?

   Ⓐ 6

   Ⓑ 7

   Ⓒ 8

   Ⓓ 9

   Ⓔ 10

10. If $5^{mn} = 625$, where m and n are positive integers, which of the following could be a value of n? Indicate *all* that apply.

   Ⓐ 1

   Ⓑ 2

   Ⓒ 3

   Ⓓ 4

   Ⓔ 5

11. If the line $5x - 3y = c$ passes through the point $(-2, 2)$, what is the value of c?

12. How much greater than $x^2 - 5x - 11$ is $x^2 - 5x + 6$?

   Ⓐ -17

   Ⓑ -5

   Ⓒ 5

   Ⓓ 11

   Ⓔ 17

Questions 13 and 14 refer to the following information.

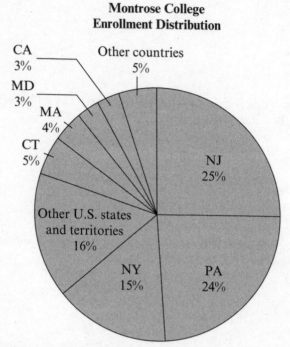

**Montrose College
Enrollment Distribution**

CA
3%

Other countries
5%

MD
3%

MA
4%

CT
5%

NJ
25%

Other U.S. states
and territories
16%

NY
15%

PA
24%

Breakdown of Montrose College Students by Place of Residence

13. What is the approximate ratio of Montrose College students from Connecticut (CT) and Massachusetts (MA) to students from New Jersey (NJ), New York (NY), and Pennsylvania (PA)?

Ⓐ $\dfrac{1}{6}$

Ⓑ $\dfrac{1}{7}$

Ⓒ $\dfrac{1}{8}$

Ⓓ $\dfrac{1}{9}$

Ⓔ $\dfrac{1}{10}$

14. If the number of Montrose College students from other countries is 140, then what is the number of students from Pennsylvania (PA)?

15. If $24\sqrt{24} = x\sqrt{z}$, where x and z are positive integers and $x > z$, which of the following could be the value of xz if $24\sqrt{24}$ is expressed in its simplified radical form?

Ⓐ 24
Ⓑ 48
Ⓒ 96
Ⓓ 288
Ⓔ 576

16. If $a^2 - 3a < 10$, which of the following CANNOT be a value of a? Indicate *all* that apply.

Ⓐ −3
Ⓑ −2
Ⓒ −1
Ⓓ 3
Ⓔ 4
Ⓕ 5

17. If $x^2 - y^2 = -72$ and $x + y = 12$, what is the value of y?

18. The lengths of two sides of a triangle are 15 and 25. Which of the following CANNOT be the perimeter of the triangle?

Ⓐ 75
Ⓑ 65
Ⓒ 55
Ⓓ 45
Ⓔ All of the above are possible values of the perimeter.

Question 19 refers to the following information.

x	−1	2	3	0
y	4	1	−4	5

19. The table above represents a relationship between x and y. Which of the following equations describes the relationship?

Ⓐ $y = 1 - 3x$

Ⓑ $y = x + 5$

Ⓒ $y = x^2 - 5$

Ⓓ $y = x^2 + 5$

Ⓔ $y = -x^2 + 5$

20. If the legs of a right triangle have lengths $x + 2$ and $x - 3$, which of the following represents the length of the hypotenuse of the triangle?

Ⓐ $\sqrt{x - 1}$

Ⓑ $\sqrt{2x^2 + 13}$

Ⓒ $\sqrt{2x^2 - 2x + 13}$

Ⓓ $\sqrt{2x^2 - 10x + 13}$

Ⓔ $\sqrt{2x^2 + 2x + 13}$

Section 2: Quantitative Reasoning

Time: 35 minutes

20 questions

Directions: For questions 1 to 7, compare Quantity A and Quantity B, using additional information centered above the two quantities if such information is given. Select one of the following four answer choices for each question:

   Ⓐ   Quantity A is greater.

   Ⓑ   Quantity B is greater.

   Ⓒ   The two quantities are equal.

   Ⓓ   The relationship cannot be determined from the information given.

	Quantity A	**Quantity B**
1.	the x-intercept of the line $5x + 6y + 30 = 0$	the y-intercept of the line $5x + 6y + 30 = 0$

	Quantity A	**Quantity B**
2.	the number of prime numbers between 80 and 90	the number of prime numbers between 90 and 100

$$81^6 = 27^{x-4}$$

	Quantity A	**Quantity B**
3.	x	12

	Quantity A	**Quantity B**
4.	the slope of the line $5x + 3y = 15$	the slope of the line $3x + 5y = 15$

$$m \otimes n = \frac{m+n}{3m+4n} \text{ for all}$$

non-zero numbers m and n

	Quantity A	**Quantity B**
5.	$10 \otimes 15$	$15 \otimes 10$

425

	Quantity A	**Quantity B**
6.	a combination of 20 items taken 12 at a time	a combination of 20 items taken 8 at a time

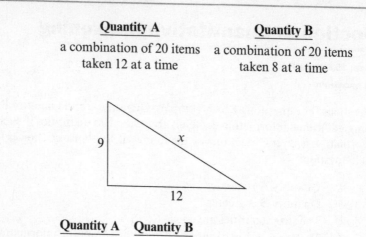

	Quantity A	**Quantity B**
7.	x	15

Directions: Questions 8 to 20 have several different formats. Unless otherwise directed, select a single answer choice. For **Numeric Entry** questions, follow the instructions below.

Write out your answer in the answer box(es) below the question.

- Your answer may be an integer, a decimal, or a fraction, and it may be negative.

- If a question asks for a fraction, there will be two boxes, one for the numerator and one for the denominator.

- Equivalent forms of the correct answer, such as 2.5 and 2.50, are all correct. Fractions do not need to be reduced (simplified) to lowest terms.

- Write out the exact answer unless the question asks you to round your answer.

8. What is the degree measure of the largest angle of a triangle if its angles are in the ratio 4:5:6?

Ⓐ   12

Ⓑ   48

Ⓒ   60

Ⓓ   72

Ⓔ   144

9. If the leg of a right triangle has a length of 12 and its hypotenuse has a length of 20, what is the area of the triangle?

Ⓐ   96

Ⓑ   120

Ⓒ   160

Ⓓ   192

Ⓔ   240

10. How many different 3-digit numbers can be formed from the digits 4 through 9 if no digit is repeated in any number?

Ⓐ   512

Ⓑ   216

Ⓒ   125

Ⓓ   120

Ⓔ   60

11. What is the decimal value of 0.07^3?

12. Which of the following are equal to 3^{100}? Indicate *all* that apply.

Ⓐ 9^{25}

Ⓑ 9^{50}

Ⓒ 27^{25}

Ⓓ 81^{20}

Ⓔ 81^{25}

Ⓕ 243^{20}

13. If y varies inversely to x and $y = 2.4$ when $x = 3.5$, what is the value of x when $y = 16$?

Ⓐ   0.0525

Ⓑ   0.525

Ⓒ   5.25

Ⓓ   52.5

Ⓔ   525

14. What is the value of y at the vertex of the graph of $y = 2x^2 - 4x + 9$?

$$\boxed{}$$

15. What is the area of an equilateral triangle whose sides have a length of 16?

Ⓐ $32\sqrt{3}$

Ⓑ 64

Ⓒ $64\sqrt{3}$

Ⓓ 128

Ⓔ $128\sqrt{3}$

16. What is the sum in degrees of the interior angles of a polygon with 18 sides?

$$\boxed{}$$

17. Which of the following is the closest approximation of $\sqrt{119}$?

Ⓐ 10.5

Ⓑ 10.7

Ⓒ 10.9

Ⓓ 11.1

Ⓔ 11.2

18. Which of the following additional scores would NOT change the median of the set of scores 7, 2, 8, 5, 10, 7, and 9? Indicate *all* that apply.

Ⓐ 2

Ⓑ 4

Ⓒ 6

Ⓓ 7

Ⓔ 8

Ⓕ 9

19. Simplify: $5\sqrt{18} + 3\sqrt{32} - 4\sqrt{50} + 3\sqrt{8}$

Ⓐ $7\sqrt{8}$

Ⓑ $11\sqrt{2}$

Ⓒ $13\sqrt{2}$

Ⓓ $7\sqrt{108}$

Ⓔ $53\sqrt{2}$

20. How many different committees of 3 men and 2 women can be formed from 5 men and 4 women?

Ⓐ 20

Ⓑ 30

Ⓒ 40

Ⓓ 50

Ⓔ 60

Answer Key

Section 1

1. A
2. B
3. A
4. C
5. A
6. C
7. B
8. D
9. C
10. A, B, D
11. −16
12. E
13. B
14. 672
15. D
16. A, B, F
17. 9
18. D
19. E
20. C

Section 2

1. B
2. A
3. C
4. B
5. B
6. C
7. D
8. D
9. A
10. D
11. .000343, or 0.000343
12. B, E, F
13. B
14. 7
15. C
16. 2880
17. C
18. A, B, C, D
19. C
20. E

Charting and Analyzing Your Test Results

The first step in analyzing your results is to chart your answers. Use the answer key and chart to identify your strengths and areas of improvement. The answers and explanations following this chart will help you solve the practice problems, but you should re-evaluate your results as you look for the following:

- Trends
- Types of errors (frequently repeated errors)
- Low scores in results of *specific* topic areas

This re-examination and analysis is a tremendous asset to help you maximize your best possible score. The answers and explanations following this chart will provide you with clarification to help you solve these types of questions in the future.

Analysis/Tally Sheet

			Number Incorrect		
Content Style Topic	**Total Possible**	**Number Correct**	**(A) Simple Mistake**	**(B) Misread Problem**	**(C) Lack of Knowledge**
Arithmetic Section 1 – Questions 1, 3, 7 Section 2 – Questions 2, 11, 17, 19	7				
Algebra Section 1 – Questions 10, 11, 12, 15, 16, 17, 19 Section 2 – Questions 1, 3, 4, 5, 12, 13, 14	14				
Geometry Section 1 – Questions 2, 4, 9, 18, 20 Section 2 – Questions 7, 8, 9, 15, 16	10				

(continued)

Analysis/Tally Sheet (*continued*)

Content Style Topic	Total Possible	Number Correct	Number Incorrect (A) Simple Mistake	(B) Misread Problem	(C) Lack of Knowledge
Data Analysis Section 1 – Questions 6, 8 Section 2 – Questions 6, 10, 18, 20	6				
Word Problems Section 1 – Question 5	1				
Data Interpretation Section 1 – Questions 13, 14	2				
Total Possible Explanations for Incorrect Answers: Columns A, B, and C					
Total Number of Answers Correct and Incorrect	40	Add the total number of correct answers here: _____	Add columns A, B, and C: _____ Total number of incorrect answers		

Answers and Explanations

Section 1

1. A. The percent increase from 70 to 100 is

$$\frac{\text{increase amount}}{\text{original amount}} = \frac{100 - 70}{70} = \frac{30}{70} = 0.428 = 42.8\%$$

The percent decrease from 80 to 50 is

$$\frac{\text{decrease amount}}{\text{original amount}} = \frac{80 - 50}{80} = \frac{30}{80} = 0.375 = 37.5\%$$

Hence, Quantity A has the greater value.

2. B.

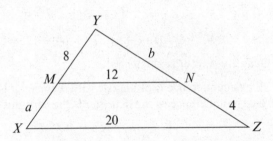

Since $\overline{MN} \parallel \overline{XZ}$, $\triangle MYN \sim \triangle XYZ$ and $\dfrac{MY}{XY} = \dfrac{NY}{ZY} = \dfrac{MN}{XZ}$.

Find MX:

$$\frac{MY}{XY} = \frac{MN}{XZ}$$

$$\frac{8}{a+8} = \frac{12}{20} = \frac{3}{5}$$

$$3(a+8) = 8 \cdot 5$$

$$3a + 24 = 40$$

$$3a + 24 - 24 = 40 - 24$$

$$3a = 16$$

$$a = \frac{16}{3} = 5\frac{1}{3} = MX$$

Find NY:

$$\frac{NY}{ZY} = \frac{MN}{XZ}$$
$$\frac{b}{b+4} = \frac{12}{20} = \frac{3}{5}$$
$$5b = 3(b+4)$$
$$5b = 3b+12$$
$$5b - 3b = 3b+12 - 3b$$
$$2b = 12$$
$$b = 6 = NY$$

Hence, Quantity B has the greater value.

3. A.

$$1^2 + 2^2 + 3^2 + 4^2 + 5^2 + 6^2 = 1 + 4 + 9 + 16 + 25 + 36 = 91$$
$$1^3 + (-2)^3 + 3^3 + (-4)^3 + 5^3 = 1 + (-8) + 27 + (-64) + 125 = 81$$

Hence, Quantity A has the greater value.

4. C. Since the circumference C of a circle with diameter d is $C = \pi d$, the ratio of the circumference to the diameter is the constant π.

$$\frac{C}{d} = \frac{\pi d}{d}$$
$$\frac{C}{d} = \pi$$

Hence, the two quantities are equal.

5. A. The distance d traveled at a rate r over a period of time t is $d = rt$.

The speed (rate) to travel 140 miles in 105 minutes is

$$d = rt$$
$$140 \text{ miles} = r \cdot 105 \text{ minutes}$$
$$\frac{140}{105} = \frac{105r}{105}$$
$$r = \frac{4}{3} = 1\frac{1}{3} \text{ miles per minute}$$

The speed (rate) to travel 117 miles in 90 minutes is

$$d = rt$$
$$117 \text{ miles} = r \cdot 90 \text{ minutes}$$
$$\frac{117}{90} = \frac{90r}{90}$$
$$r = \frac{13}{10} = 1\frac{3}{10} \text{ miles per minute}$$

Hence, Quantity A has the greater value.

6. **C.** The mean of 5 consecutive integers whose sum is 345 is $345 \div 5 = 69$.

To find the median of 5 consecutive odd integers whose sum is 345, let $x = $ the first odd integer.

Then $x + 2 = $ the second odd integer.

Then $x + 4 = $ the third odd integer.

Then $x + 6 = $ the fourth odd integer.

Then $x + 8 = $ the fifth odd integer.

$$x + x + 2 + x + 4 + x + 6 + x + 8 = 345$$
$$5x + 20 = 345$$
$$5x + 20 - 20 = 345 - 20$$
$$5x = 325$$
$$x = 65$$
$$x + 2 = 67$$
$$x + 4 = 69$$
$$x + 6 = 71$$
$$x + 8 = 73$$

The median is also 69, so the two quantities are equal.

7. **B.** If the product of 8 integers is negative, there must be an odd number of negative integers as factors. Therefore the maximum number of negative integers is 7. If the product of 9 integers is positive, there must be an even number of negative integers as factors. Therefore the maximum number of negative integers is 8.

Hence, Quantity B has the greater value.

8. **D.** The average of x, y, z, 8, and 15 is

$$\frac{x+y+z+8+15}{5} = 12$$

$$\frac{x+y+z+23}{5} = 12$$

$$\frac{x+y+z+23}{5} \cdot 5 = 12 \cdot 5$$

$$x+y+z+23 = 60$$

$$x+y+z+23-23 = 60-23$$

$$x+y+z = 37$$

9. **C.** The number of diagonals possible from any one vertex of a polygon with 10 sides is $n - 2$.

Not coincidentally, $(n - 2)(180°)$ is the total number of degrees in a polygon with n sides.

For a 10-sided polygon, $n - 2 = 10 - 2 = 8$ possible triangles.

10. **A, B, and D.** Since $5^{mn} = 625$ and $5^4 = 625$, $mn = 4$.

The possible positive integer values for m or n are 1, 2, and 4.

11. **−16**

Since the line $5x - 3y = c$ passes through the point $(-2, 2)$,

$$5x - 3y = 5(-2) - 3(2) = c$$

$$= -10 - 6 = c$$

$$= -16 = c$$

12. **E.** The difference between $x^2 - 5x - 11$ and $x^2 - 5x + 6$ is

$$\left(x^2 - 5x + 6\right) - \left(x^2 - 5x - 11\right)$$

$$= x^2 - 5x + 6 - x^2 + 5x + 11$$

$$= 17$$

13. **B.** The percentage of students at Montrose College from MA and CT is $4 + 5 = 9$.

The percentage of students at Montrose College from NJ, PA, and NY is $25 + 24 + 15 = 64$.

Therefore, the approximate ratio of students from MA and CT to students from NJ, PA, and NY is $\dfrac{9}{64} \approx \dfrac{1}{7}$ because $\dfrac{9}{64} = .140625$ and $\dfrac{1}{7} = .142857$.

14. 672

Let $x = $ total student population.

Since 5% of the students at Montrose College come from other countries,

$$5\% \text{ of } x = 140$$
$$0.05 \cdot x = 140$$
$$\frac{0.05x}{0.05} = \frac{140}{0.05}$$
$$x = 2800$$

Since 24% of the students at Montrose College come from PA,

$$\text{students from PA} = 24\% \text{ of } 2800$$
$$= (0.24)(2800)$$
$$= 672$$

15. D.

$$24\sqrt{24} = 24\sqrt{4 \cdot 6}$$
$$= 24 \cdot 2\sqrt{6}$$
$$= 48\sqrt{6}$$

Since $48\sqrt{6} = x\sqrt{z}$ where $x > z$, then $xz = 48 \cdot 6 = 288$.

16. A, B, and F.

If $a = -3$, $a^2 - 3a = (-3)^2 - 3(-3) = 9 + 9 = 18 > 10$.

If $a = -2$, $a^2 - 3a = (-2)^2 - 3(-2) = 4 + 6 = 10$.

If $a = -1$, $a^2 - 3a = (-1)^2 - 3(-1) = 1 + 3 = 4 < 10$.

If $a = 3$, $a^2 - 3a = (3)^2 - 3(3) = 9 - 9 = 0 < 10$.

If $a = 4$, $a^2 - 3a = (4)^2 - 3(4) = 16 - 12 = 4 < 10$.

If $a = 5$, $a^2 - 3a = (5)^2 - 3(5) = 25 - 15 = 10$.

17. 9

$$x^2 - y^2 = (x + y)(x - y) = -72$$

Since $x + y = 12$,

$$(x + y)(x - y) = -72$$
$$12(x - y) = -72$$
$$x - y = \frac{-72}{12} = -6$$

Solving the system of equations,

$$x + y = 12$$
$$\underline{x - y = -6}$$
$$2x = 6$$
$$x = \frac{6}{2} = 3$$

Since $x + y = 12$
$$3 + y = 12$$
$$y = 12 - 3 = 9$$

18. **D.** The triangle inequality theorem states that the sum of any two sides of a triangle must be greater than the third side. Since two of the triangle's sides are 15 and 25, the length of the third side x must be

$$25 - 15 < x < 25 + 15$$
$$10 < x < 40$$

The perimeter of the triangle is $x + 15 + 25$ or $x + 40$.

Since $10 < x < 40$,
$$10 + 40 < x + 40 < 40 + 40$$
$$50 < x + 40 < 80$$

Hence, the perimeter of the triangle cannot be 45.

19. **E.** The equation $y = -x^2 + 5$ satisfies all four pairs of values for x and y.

$x = -1, -x^2 + 5 = -(-1)^2 + 5 = -1 + 5 = 4.$

$= 2, -x^2 + 5 = -(2)^2 + 5 = -4 + 5 = 1.$

If $x = 3$, $-x^2 + 5 = -(3)^2 + 5 = -9 + 5 = -4$.

If $x = 0$, $-x^2 + 5 = -(0)^2 + 5 = 0 + 5 = 5$.

20. **C.** The Pythagorean theorem states that for any right triangle with legs a and b and hypotenuse c,

$$
\begin{aligned}
c^2 = a^2 + b^2 &= (x+2)^2 + (x-3)^2 \\
&= x^2 + 4x + 4 + x^2 - 6x + 9 \\
c^2 &= 2x^2 - 2x + 13 \\
c &= \sqrt{2x^2 - 2x + 13}
\end{aligned}
$$

Section 2

1. **B.** The x-intercept of a line is the point $(x, 0)$ where the graph crosses the x-axis. For the line $5x + 6y + 30 = 0$,

$$
\begin{aligned}
5x + 6(0) + 30 &= 0 \\
5x + 30 &= 0 \\
5x + 30 - 30 &= 0 - 30 \\
5x &= -30 \\
x &= -6
\end{aligned}
$$

The y-intercept of a line is the point $(0, y)$ where the graph crosses the y-axis. For the line $5x + 6y + 30 = 0$,

$$
\begin{aligned}
5(0) + 6y + 30 &= 0 \\
6y + 30 &= 0 \\
6y + 30 - 30 &= 0 - 30 \\
6y &= -30 \\
y &= -5
\end{aligned}
$$

Hence, Quantity B has the greater value.

2. **A.** There are two prime numbers between 80 and 90: 83 and 89. There is only one prime number between 90 and 100: 97. Hence, Quantity A has the greater value.

3. C. Since $81 = 3^4$ and $27 = 3^3$,

$$81^6 = 27^{x-4}$$
$$\left(3^4\right)^6 = \left(3^3\right)^{x-4}$$
$$3^{24} = 3^{3(x-4)}$$
$$3^{24} = 3^{3x-12}$$

Therefore, $3x - 12 = 24$
$$3x - 12 + 12 = 24 + 12$$
$$3x = 36$$
$$x = 12$$

Hence, the two quantities are equal.

4. B. A linear equation in the form $y = mx + b$ has a slope of m.

If $5x + 3y = 15$,
$$5x + 3y - 5x = 15 - 5x$$
$$3y = -5x + 15$$
$$y = -\frac{5}{3}x + 5$$

the line has a slope $m = -\dfrac{5}{3}$.

If $3x + 5y = 15$,
$$3x + 5y - 3x = 15 - 3x$$
$$5y = -3x + 15$$
$$y = -\frac{3}{5}x + 3$$

the line has a slope $m = -\dfrac{3}{5}$.

Hence, Quantity B has the greater value.

5. B.

Since $m \otimes n = \dfrac{m+n}{3m+4n}$,

$$10 \otimes 15 = \frac{10+15}{3(10)+4(15)} = \frac{25}{30+60} = \frac{25}{90} = \frac{5}{18}$$

and $15 \otimes 10 = \dfrac{15+10}{3(15)+4(10)} = \dfrac{25}{45+40} = \dfrac{25}{85} = \dfrac{5}{17}$.

Hence, Quantity B has the greater value.

6. C. A combination of 20 items taken 12 at a time is

$$C(20, 12) = \frac{20!}{12!(20-12)!} = \frac{20!}{12! \cdot 8!}$$

A combination of 20 items taken 8 at a time is

$$C(20, 8) = \frac{20!}{8!(20-8)!} = \frac{20!}{8! \cdot 12!}$$

Hence, the two quantities are equal. Note that it is not necessary to evaluate the expressions.

7. D.

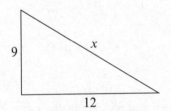

If the triangle was a right triangle, the Pythagorean theorem would yield a value for the hypotenuse $x = 15$. However, there is no information given that would allow you to conclude that the triangle is a right triangle.

Hence, the relationship cannot be determined from the given information.

8. D. Since the sum of the angles of a triangle is 180°,

$$4x + 5x + 6x = 180°$$
$$15x = 180$$
$$\frac{15x}{15} = \frac{180}{15}$$
$$x = 12°$$

Therefore, the angles would measure $4x = 4(12) = 48°$, $5x = 5(12) = 60°$, and $6x = 6(12) = 72°$.

9. A. The Pythagorean theorem states that for any right triangle with legs a and b and hypotenuse c,

$$c^2 = a^2 + b^2$$
$$20^2 = 12^2 + b^2$$
$$400 = 144 + b^2$$
$$400 - 144 = 144 + b^2 - 144$$
$$256 = b^2$$
$$b = \sqrt{256} = 16$$

The area A of a triangle with base b and height h is

$$A = \frac{1}{2}bh$$
$$= \frac{1}{2}(16)(12)$$
$$A = 96$$

10. D. Since there are 6 numbers in the digits 4 through 9 and the order of the digits is important, this is a permutation of 6 objects taken 3 at a time. The total number of outcomes possible is

$$P(6, 3) = \frac{6!}{(6-3)!} = \frac{6!}{3!} = \frac{6 \cdot 5 \cdot 4 \cdot 3\!\!\!/\,!}{3\!\!\!/\,!} = 6 \cdot 5 \cdot 4 = 120$$

11. .000343, or 0.000343

$$0.07^3 = (.07)(.07)(.07)$$
$$= (.0049)(.07)$$
$$= .000343, \text{ or } 0.000343$$

12. **B, E, and F.**

$$9^{50} = \left(3^2\right)^{50} = 3^{2 \cdot 50} = 3^{100}$$
$$81^{25} = \left(3^4\right)^{25} = 3^{4 \cdot 25} = 3^{100}$$
$$243^{20} = \left(3^5\right)^{20} = 3^{5 \cdot 20} = 3^{100}$$

13. **B.** Since y varies inversely to x, $y = \dfrac{k}{x}$, where k is the constant of the variation.

If $y = 2.4$ when $x = 3.5$,

$$2.4 = \frac{k}{3.5}$$
$$(2.4)(3.5) = \frac{k}{3.5} \cdot 3.5$$
$$k = 8.4 \text{ and } y = \frac{8.4}{x}$$

If $y = 16$,

$$16 = \frac{8.4}{x}$$
$$16 \cdot x = \frac{8.4}{x} \cdot x$$
$$16x = 8.4$$
$$\frac{16x}{16} = \frac{8.4}{16}$$
$$x = 0.525$$

14. 7

The value of x at the vertex of a parabola of the form
$y = ax^2 + bx + c$ is $x = \dfrac{-b}{2a}$.

For the parabola $y = 2x^2 - 4x + 9$, $x = \dfrac{-b}{2a} = \dfrac{-(-4)}{2(2)} = \dfrac{4}{4} = 1$.

Substitute $x = 1$ in the equation.

$$y = 2x^2 - 4x + 9$$
$$= 2(1)^2 - 4(1) + 9$$
$$= 2 - 4 + 9$$
$$y = 7$$

15. C.

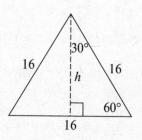

The area A of a triangle with base b and height h is $A = \dfrac{1}{2}bh$.

The altitude of an equilateral triangle forms a 30°–60°–90° triangle with a hypotenuse equal to the side of the equilateral triangle. The height h is opposite the 60° angle in the 30°–60°–90° triangle and is equal to $\dfrac{\sqrt{3}}{2}$ times the length of the hypotenuse, or $h = \dfrac{\sqrt{3}}{2} \cdot 16 = 8\sqrt{3}$.

The area A of a triangle with base b and height h is

$$A = \frac{1}{2}bh$$
$$= \frac{1}{2}(16)(8\sqrt{3})$$
$$A = 64\sqrt{3}$$

16. **2880**

The sum in degrees of the interior angles of a polygon with n sides is $(n-2) \cdot 180°$. For a polygon with 18 sides,

$$\begin{aligned}(n-2) \cdot 180° &= (18-2) \cdot 180° \\ &= (16)(180°) \\ &= 2880°\end{aligned}$$

17. **C.** Since $10^2 = 100$ and $11^2 = 121$, $\sqrt{119}$ is between 10 and 11. Since 119 is very close to 121, but slightly less than 121, $\sqrt{119}$ is very close to and slightly less than $\sqrt{121} = 11$.

Hence, a reasonable approximation would be $\sqrt{119} \approx 10.9$. Note that $(10.9)^2 = 118.81$.

18. **A, B, C, and D.** The median of a set of data is the middle number of the set if there is an odd number of items in the set. The median of a set of data is the mean of the two middle numbers of the set if there is an even number of items in the set. The data should first be arranged in order from smallest to largest or from largest to smallest for the given set of scores: 2, 5, 7, 7, 8, 9, 10.

The median is 7, which is the middle score.

For the set of scores 2, 2, 5, 7, 7, 8, 9, 10, the median is $(7+7) \div 2 = 14 \div 2 = 7$.

For the set of scores 2, 4, 5, 7, 7, 8, 9, 10, the median is $(7+7) \div 2 = 14 \div 2 = 7$.

For the set of scores 2, 5, 6, 7, 7, 8, 9, 10, the median is $(7+7) \div 2 = 14 \div 2 = 7$.

For the set of scores 2, 5, 7, 7, 7, 8, 9, 10, the median is $(7+7) \div 2 = 14 \div 2 = 7$.

For the set of scores 2, 5, 7, 7, 8, 8, 9, 10, the median is $(7+8) \div 2 = 15 \div 2 = 7\frac{1}{2}$.

For the set of scores 2, 5, 7, 7, 8, 9, 9, 10, the median is: $(7+8) \div 2 = 15 \div 2 = 7\frac{1}{2}$.

19. C.

$$5\sqrt{18} = 5\sqrt{9 \cdot 2} = 5 \cdot 3\sqrt{2} = 15\sqrt{2}$$
$$3\sqrt{32} = 3\sqrt{16 \cdot 2} = 3 \cdot 4\sqrt{2} = 12\sqrt{2}$$
$$4\sqrt{50} = 4\sqrt{25 \cdot 2} = 4 \cdot 5\sqrt{2} = 20\sqrt{2}$$
$$3\sqrt{8} = 3\sqrt{4 \cdot 2} = 3 \cdot 2\sqrt{2} = 6\sqrt{2}$$

Hence, $5\sqrt{18} + 3\sqrt{32} - 4\sqrt{50} + 3\sqrt{8}$
$$= 15\sqrt{2} + 12\sqrt{2} - 20\sqrt{2} + 6\sqrt{2}$$
$$= 13\sqrt{2}$$

20. E. The number of 3-men committees that can be formed from a group of 5 men is a combination of 5 objects taken 3 at a time, or

$$C(5, 3) = \frac{5!}{3!(5-3)!} = \frac{5!}{3! \cdot 2!} = \frac{5 \cdot 4 \cdot \cancel{3!}}{\cancel{3!} \cdot 2!} = \frac{5 \cdot 4}{2 \cdot 1} = \frac{20}{2} = 10$$

The number of 2-women committees that can be formed from a group of 4 women is a combination of 4 objects taken 2 at a time, or

$$C(4, 2) = \frac{4!}{2!(4-2)!} = \frac{4 \cdot 3 \cdot \cancel{2!}}{2! \cdot \cancel{2!}} = \frac{4 \cdot 3}{2 \cdot 1} = \frac{12}{2} = 6$$

The total number of 3-men and 2-women committees that can be formed is the product of the preceding two answers: $10 \cdot 6 = 60$.

Final Preparation

One Week before the Exam

1. **Clear your schedule.** Try to avoid scheduling appointments or events during this week so that you can focus on your preparation.

2. **GRE website.** Check the GRE website at www.ets.org/gre for updated exam information.

3. **Review your notes** from this study guide and make sure that you know the question types, basic skills, strategies, and directions for each section of the test.

4. **Practice tests.** Allow yourself enough time to review the practice problems you have already completed from this study guide. If you haven't yet taken the practice tests, take the practice tests during this week. Be sure to time yourself as you practice.

5. **Computer skills development.** Computer-based simulated practice is critical at this time so that the necessary computer skills are fresh in your mind. If you haven't yet taken the online practice test, go to the GRE website at www.ets.org/gre and take the GRE POWERPREP II practice test. Even if you have already worked the online problems, rework the problems so that you are at ease with skipping questions, marking questions, moving forward and backward, and using the on-screen calculator.

6. **Testing center.** Make sure that you are familiar with the driving directions to the test center and the parking facilities.

7. **Relax the night before the exam.** Your mental preparation is as important as your study preparation. The evening before the exam, try to get a good night's sleep. Trying to cram a year's worth of reading and studying into one night can cause you to feel emotionally and physically exhausted. Save your energy for exam day.

Exam Day

1. **Arrive early.** Arrive at the exam location in plenty of time (at least 30 minutes early).

2. **Dress appropriately** to adapt to any room temperature. If you dress in layers, you can always take off clothing to adjust to warmer temperatures.

3. **Identification.** Remember to bring the required identification documents: valid photo-bearing ID and your authorization voucher (if you requested one from ETS).

4. **Electronic devices.** Leave all electronic devices at home or in your car (cell phone, smartphone, PDA, calculator, etc.). You may also be asked to remove your watch during the exam.

5. **Answer easy questions first.** Start off crisply, working the questions you know first (within each section of 20 questions), then going back and trying to answer the others. Use the elimination strategy to determine if a problem is possibly solvable or too difficult to solve.

6. **Don't get stuck on any one question.** Never spend more than 1½ minutes on a multiple-choice question.

7. **Guess** if a problem is too difficult or takes too much time. Remember, there is no penalty for guessing.

8. **Use the notepad provided** as a test-taking advantage. Perform calculations, redraw diagrams, note eliminated choices, or simply make helpful notes to jog your memory.